THE
OPEN HAND
Celebration
COOKBOOK

THE
OPEN HAND

Celebration

COOKBOOK

Great Chefs Cook for
Festive Occasions

Compiled and edited by
Stanley Eichelbaum

Illustrations by Deborah Zemke

POCKET BOOKS
New York   London   Toronto   Sydney   Tokyo   Singapore

POCKET BOOKS, a division of Simon & Schuster Inc.
1230 Avenue of the Americas, New York, NY 10020

Library of Congress Cataloging-in-Publication Data

The Open Hand celebration cookbook : great chefs cook for festive
    occasions / compiled and edited by Stanley Eichelbaum;
    illustrations by Deborah Zemke.
        p.   cm.
    Includes index.
    ISBN: 0-671-73740-6 : $22.00
    1. Cookery. 2. Menus. I. Eichelbaum, Stanley.
TX714.063 1991   91-17982
641.5—dc20   CIP

First Pocket Books hardcover printing October 1991

10 9 8 7 6 5 4 3 2 1

POCKET and colophon are registered trademarks of Simon & Schuster Inc.

Printed in the U.S.A.

Design and illustrations by Deborah Zemke. The drawings are dedicated
to Steven Miller.
Calligraphy by Brenda Walton.
Typography in Bembo by ATG/Ad Type Graphics, Sacramento, California.

To William R. Grose
with appreciation
and thanks

CONTENTS

W I N T E R

FOREWORD

If there's anything we've learned since Project
Open Hand was founded in 1985, it's that the
long-term survivors of AIDS are characterized
by one significant trait: they're able to live life
to the fullest and make every day count.

We have provided meals to those afflicted
with AIDS for all these years and have
observed that it takes a special appreciation
of life to fight the dreaded disease and be
among the survivors. It means that they have
the tenacity to begin each day with courage,
verve, and a sufficiently full agenda to keep
them going year after year in defiance of all
medical knowledge.

This book is dedicated to people everywhere
who celebrate life and make every day count.

Ruth Brinker
Founder, Project Open Hand
2720 17th Street
San Francisco, CA 94110

PREFACE

All important events in life — christenings, bar mitzvahs, birthdays, weddings — are celebrated with food. And in many civilizations, food is an important part even of burial rites. Food is the universal language, the common denominator that brings people together in all parts of the world. What would Christmas and Thanksgiving be like without food? Food permits you to give of yourself to friends, family, loved ones.

For me, the best cooking is done with family and chef friends, whether here at home or at any one of a series of outdoor events that brings us together: a hunting trip, a ski weekend, a summer picnic, a sailboat outing, or even a wild-mushroom hunt.

Contrary to the popular image of the professional chef as jealous, secretive, and egocentric, there is rarely any competition at these cookouts. Everyone has fun, and together we prepare and enjoy good, simple food. There is a sharing of ideas and recipes, a togetherness, and a friendship that cooking together always produces among chefs.

My own wedding was such an affair. I got married at Craig Claiborne's home on Long Island twenty-five years ago. The dinner was prepared by a group of my chef friends. Helping to cook — in addition to Craig and Henry Creel (his dear friend and chief dishwasher) — were René Verdon, Pierre Franey, Roger Fessaguet, Jean Vergnes, Jean-Claude Szurdak, Ed Giobbi, and, of course, me. I was cooking happily in the kitchen with all my friends until an hour before the wedding, when they threw me out, insisting that I shower and change before the ceremony.

It was a great day, we had a great meal, and, not surprisingly, I remember the food in great detail, because it was lovingly prepared for me by my friends. Cooking with friends is what this book represents. I think I know most of the chefs whose recipes are included here, and I've enjoyed their food and hospitality many times. I hope this collection of their recipes — contributed in the spirit of friendship and sharing — brings many happy moments to you, your family, and your friends. Happy times!

Jacques Pépin
Madison, Connecticut

EDITOR'S INTRODUCTION

The thought of doing a new cookbook for
the benefit of Project Open Hand led us
to a theme of fun and festivity: food as
a celebration of life, food as a pleasurable
accompaniment to a joyous occasion.

We asked the prominent chefs of the San
Francisco Bay area to consider the kind of
meal they would prepare for a happy event,
such as a birthday, wedding, reunion, or
holiday. We wanted them to think of a meal
they'd fixed, or always wanted to fix, in their
leisure time. And since chefs have so little
free time, our theme presented something
of a challenge to the chefs we invited to
participate.

But they responded with gratifying élan and
generosity. And our request brought in some
fascinating menus and recipes, some of them
nostalgic recollections of meals traditionally
enjoyed with family, or meals vividly remem-
bered because they were shared with close
friends.

The recipes that our chefs came up with are,
for the most part, unusual and exotic. They
would make wonderful additions to your
culinary repertoire, and are perfect as party
food. A good many of the recipes represent
the multiethnic nature of Bay area cuisine.
But the ingredients should not be too
difficult to find, since even our basic supermarkets have installed sections for ethnic
foods. And if you enjoy exploring the ethnic
markets, you should have no problem.

The cheerful mood of this new cookbook is
meant to bring you closer to Project Open

Hand and its important work distributing meals to AIDS victims. The organization founded by Ruth Brinker is, at this writing, feeding 1,100 men, women, and children every day. The first Open Hand cookbook, published in 1989, was a best-seller. We'd be grateful to have another best-seller on our hands, since the funding needs of Open Hand continue unabated.

Stanley Eichelbaum
San Francisco, California

s p r i n g

SPECIALTIES OF THE BASQUE COUNTRY

Stuffed Squid in Their Ink

Poulet Basquaise

Piperade

Basque Fisherman's Sandwich

Merveilles (Pastry Fritters)

serves eight

Gérald Hirigoyen is a native Basque who was raised in Biarritz, France. He started working at age thirteen in a small pastry shop. At eighteen, he went to Paris to apprentice with the well-known pastry chef and caterer Jean Millet. A San Francisco resident since 1980, he has cooked in French restaurants such as *Le Castel* and *Lafayette* and is presently the chef at *Le St. Tropez*.

I always remember the fights that took place in the kitchen between my mother and father, both excellent, strongly opinionated home cooks. It always started the day before with one or the other worrying about what we would have to eat the next day and who would be cooking. For my part, I always got a kick out of it and ended up helping.

Recently, my sister reminded me that at the age of eight, I was making chocolate mousse on my own. By the time I was twelve, I wanted to be a cook. I started at thirteen, and here I am, enjoying every bit of it.

I have gathered here a few specialties from my native Basque country. I hope you enjoy them. Apetitu-on ("bon appétit" in Basque).

STUFFED SQUID IN THEIR INK *serves eight*

2 pounds squid
1 onion, chopped
3 tablespoons olive oil
3 cloves garlic, crushed
1/2 cup bread crumbs
Salt and pepper
1½ cups dry white wine
2 tomatoes, peeled,
  seeded, and chopped
Chili powder
2 tablespoons cornstarch
Dash of Armagnac or
  cognac

Clean the squid. Cut off the head and tentacles, and set aside the tentacles. Remove the bone from the tail. Open the body and throw away the entrails. Make sure to keep the ink sacs.

Start making the stuffing by cutting the squid tentacles into little strips. In a sauté pan, cook half the chopped onion in 1 tablespoon olive oil until golden brown. Add a crushed garlic clove and the squid strips. Cook slowly for 30 minutes. Add the bread crumbs, salt, and pepper, and then fill the squid bodies with the stuffing. Fasten the ends with toothpicks.

Heat the remaining 2 tablespoons olive oil in a sauté pan and lightly brown the squid together with the remaining onion and garlic. Add the white wine, tomatoes, and chili powder, and simmer for about 30 minutes.

Squeeze the ink from the sacs into a cup. Mix in a little cornstarch, and stir into the sauce. Add a dash of Armagnac (or cognac), season with salt and pepper, and simmer, covered, for 1 hour. Taste for seasoning before serving.

POULET BASQUAISE *serves eight*

About 1 hour before serving time, remove chickens from refrigerator and bring to room temperature. Dry chickens well. Cut up each chicken into 2 breast pieces, 2 legs, and 2 thighs. Set aside. With a cleaver, chop back-bones, wings, and necks into l-inch pieces. In a deep skillet, brown chopped chicken pieces in 3 tablespoons olive oil.

Add the onions and brown lightly around the edges. Add the peppers, garlic, ham, tomatoes, tomato paste, and sugar. Cover and cook over low heat for 15 minutes.

Meanwhile, season the whole chicken pieces with salt and pepper, and in another skillet, over high heat, brown the pieces on all sides in remaining 3 tablespoons oil. Lower heat, cover, and cook 5 minutes. Pour off all the fat. Add the wine, cover, and cook 10 minutes.

Remove bones from the tomato sauce and skim off all the fat. Remove garlic cloves. Peel and crush them, and return to the sauce.

Add the sauce to the chicken pieces and cook slowly, uncovered, until breasts are tender. Remove breasts, and cook legs and thighs for 10 more minutes. Return breasts to sauce and reheat. Add cayenne, or fold in hot pepper rings. Serve garnished with chopped parsley.

2 chickens, 3½ to
   4 pounds each
6 tablespoons aromatic
   olive oil
1½ cups coarsely chopped
   onions
2 cups coarsely chopped
   mixed green and
   red peppers
6 small, or 4 medium,
   cloves garlic, unpeeled
3 ounces Bayonne ham,
   diced
2 pounds red-ripe
   tomatoes, peeled,
   seeded, and cut into
   large chunks
2 teaspoons tomato paste
2 good pinches of sugar
Salt and freshly ground
   pepper
1/2 cup dry white wine
1/4 teaspoon cayenne
   pepper, or 1 small fresh
   hot pepper, seeded and
   cut into extra-thin rings
Chopped fresh parsley

PIPERADE *yields three cups*

2 large red peppers
2 large green peppers
1/4 cup olive oil
1 large onion, sliced
6 large tomatoes, peeled,
    seeded, and cut into
    chunks
2 cloves garlic, sliced
1/2 small chili pepper,
    seeded and chopped,
    or 1/2 teaspoon chili
    powder
1 sprig thyme
Salt

Roast the peppers over a flame until the skin puffs up. Peel and core the peppers, removing the seeds, and cut them into strips. Heat the olive oil in a sauté pan, add the onion, and sauté until golden brown. Add the pepper strips, tomatoes, garlic, chili, and thyme. Cook slowly, covered, for about 30 minutes. Season with salt to taste.

The piperade can be served in an omelette, or with a slice of Bayonne ham that's been quickly sautéed for 15 seconds on each side.

BASQUE FISHERMAN'S SANDWICH *serves four*

2 tomatoes
2 roasted pimentos
2 bunches scallions
2 hard-boiled eggs
5 ounces pitted black
    Niçoise olives
8 ounces sautéed tuna
    (or use canned)
8 ounces anchovies
4 round individual French
    rolls, or 1 baguette
Olive oil
Salt and pepper

Slice the tomatoes. Cut the pimentos lengthwise.

Chop the scallions, eggs, and olives. Cut the tuna and anchovies into small pieces and mix together with the chopped ingredients.

Cut the bread. Put the sliced tomato on the bottom slice of bread. Sprinkle with a little olive oil, and salt and pepper. Add the tuna mixture, and put the pimento on top. Sprinkle with olive oil and top with another slice of bread.

MERVEILLES (Pastry Fritters) *serves eight*

Sift the flour and baking powder into a bowl and mix in 4 eggs, the butter, salt, and lemon zest. Work into a smooth dough, adding the remaining egg if the dough is too dry. Cover with plastic wrap and let rest for 1 hour.

Roll out dough on a floured table to about 1/4 inch thick, and cut out circles with a 2-inch cookie cutter.

Heat the oil in a deep fryer or deep, heavy pan. When oil is hot, drop the merveilles in. Turn them once, cooking 45 seconds on each side, until puffed up and light golden brown. Remove with a slotted spoon. Drain on paper towels. Sprinkle with powdered sugar. May be served hot or cold.

3½ cups flour
1 teaspoon baking powder
4 or 5 eggs
8 tablespoons butter
1/4 teaspoon salt
Zest of 1 lemon
Vegetable oil for
    deep-frying
Powdered sugar

Amey B. Shaw

ANY EXCUSE FOR A PARTY

Apple Consommé

*Monkfish with Flageolets,
Tomatoes, and Charred Garlic Aïoli*

*Lamb Tenderloin with Smoked
Ancho Chili Sauce*

Potatoes Gratin

Vanilla Crisps with Raspberries

serves eight

Amey B. Shaw has been cooking in the Bay area for fifteen years and was the chef at Berkeley's *Fourth Street Grill* and San Francisco's *Maltese Grill* before assuming her present post as chef of *Bentley's Seafood Grill & Oyster Bar* in San Francisco.

Cooking professionally is fun, but is especially satisfying when it's done for close friends. When my kitchen at home was remodeled (a job that took more than five months), I felt like celebrating, and invited a few people over for dinner. I served this meal as the "Hooray, It's Finally Finished Party," and they all loved the food. Ironically, the most popular dish was the simplest — the potatoes gratin.

APPLE CONSOMMÉ *serves eight*

To make the brown stock, preheat oven to 400° F. Place in a baking pan the beef and veal bones, carrots, onions, leeks, and garlic, and roast for about 1 hour, or until very brown. Transfer to a stock pot. Deglaze the roasting pan with the wine, scraping up any bits of browned meat, and add to stock pot. Cover with cold water. Bring to a boil and skim. Add remaining ingredients, and cover with more cold water. Return to a boil and skim, if necessary. Let simmer for 10 hours. Strain and refrigerate. The next day, skim off all the fat.

To make the consommé, mix together the ground beef, vegetables, parsley, pepper-corns, egg whites, and egg shells in a large pot. Cover with the cold, defatted brown stock. Bring to a boil, stirring constantly. Simmer for 1 hour. Strain through cheese-cloth. Add salt to taste. Keep hot.

(continued next page)

For brown stock:
10 pounds beef shin bones
10 pounds veal shanks
6 carrots, peeled and
   coarsely chopped
3 large onions, quartered
4 leeks, washed and cut up
2 heads garlic, cut in half
2 cups good quality red
   wine
10 black peppercorns
6 bay leaves
3 or 4 sprigs thyme
8 tart apples, cored

For consommé:
2 cups lean ground beef
2 carrots, peeled and
   minced
2 leeks, white part only,
   minced
1 onion, peeled and
   minced
4 parsley stems
3 peppercorns
3 egg whites, slightly
   beaten
3 egg shells
Brown stock, made
   previously
Kosher salt

For consommé garnish:
2 carrots, peeled and
chopped
1 small onion, peeled and
chopped
1 rib celery, washed and
chopped
3 bay leaves
6 peppercorns
1 tablespoon kosher salt
4 cups water
2 whole chicken breasts,
bone in
3 tart apples
1 lemon

To prepare the garnish, put all the ingredients, except the chicken, apples, and lemon in a pot. Bring to a boil, cover, and simmer for 20 minutes. Add the chicken and poach for about 12 minutes, until barely cooked. Let cool in poaching liquid. Remove, bone, and skin chicken. Julienne the chicken and set aside.

Peel and core the apples. Dice into 1/2-inch cubes. Squeeze lemon juice over them, toss, and set aside.

To assemble, carefully ladle the hot consommé into warmed soup bowls. Garnish with the julienned chicken and diced apples. Serve immediately.

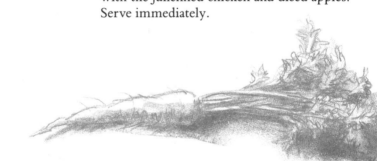

MONKFISH WITH FLAGEOLETS, TOMATOES, AND CHARRED GARLIC AÏOLI *serves eight*

For flageolets:
5 ounces fresh flageolet
beans, or 2/3 cup dried
1 carrot, peeled and cut
in half
1 onion, peeled and stuck
with 2 cloves
Bouquet garni of thyme,
bay leaf, celery rib,
parsley stems, and
peppercorns

For the dried flageolets, soak overnight in cold water. Drain and rinse. Place fresh or dried beans in a large saucepan and cover with water. Add carrot, onion, and bouquet garni, and cook over medium-high heat until tender, about 40 minutes for fresh and 1 hour for dried. Remove carrot, onion, and bouquet garni, and drain the beans. Keep warm.

To prepare the aïoli, char the garlic by placing the unpeeled cloves in a heavy pan over high heat. Turn frequently. Or you can place them on a rack and char them directly over a gas flame or charcoal fire. When the garlic skin is blackened and the cloves are soft, remove from the heat and let cool. Squeeze the garlic into a mortar. Add salt and pound to a paste.

Place the egg yolks in a bowl. Whisk until lemon colored. Add the oil, drop by drop, whisking continuously until the mixture thickens. Continue adding the oil in a steady stream until the oil is incorporated. Whisk in the garlic paste, pepper, lemon juice, and hot water. Set aside.

To prepare the monkfish, place fillets in a shallow bowl. Pour olive oil over them to coat and add thyme. Let stand at room temperature for about 1 hour.

Heat a large sauté pan over medium-high heat. Remove fish from marinade and wipe dry. Add fresh olive oil to coat sauté pan. Add fish, sprinkle with salt, and brown gently on both sides. When cooked to desired doneness, remove fish from pan and keep warm. Turn heat to high and deglaze the pan with wine. Reduce liquid until syrupy and add the fish stock. Reduce to a glaze and add the diced tomatoes. Turn off heat.

Assemble by spreading a spoonful of aïoli on each plate. Spoon flageolets on top. Place the monkfish on the beans and pour the tomatoes over the fish. Drizzle more aïoli over the fish and serve.

For aïoli:
10 cloves garlic, unpeeled
1/3 teaspoon kosher salt
3 egg yolks
1 cup fruity olive oil
1/8 teaspoon freshly
  ground black pepper
1 tablespoon lemon juice
1½ tablespoons hot water

For monkfish:
1½ pounds monkfish
  fillets
Olive oil
1 tablespoon chopped
  fresh thyme
Kosher salt
1 cup white wine
1 cup fish stock
9 medium tomatoes,
  preferably red and
  yellow, peeled, seeded,
  and diced

LAMB TENDERLOIN WITH SMOKED ANCHO CHILI SAUCE *serves eight*

8 lamb tenderloins,
   5 ounces each

For marinade:
1 cup freshly ground
   black pepper
1/2 cup kosher salt
3 sprigs fresh thyme
2 cups olive oil

For ancho chili sauce:
10 ancho chilies, stemmed
   and seeded
10 cloves garlic, peeled
2 large onions, peeled
6 tomatoes
2 carrots, peeled and
   chopped
2 ribs celery, washed and
   chopped
2 tablespoons cumin seed,
   toasted and ground
4 cups lamb stock

Marinate the lamb by rubbing pepper and salt generously into fillets. Place in a nonreactive bowl and add thyme and olive oil. Cover and refrigerate overnight. The next day, remove the lamb from marinade and wipe dry.

Make the sauce by placing the chilies and garlic in a smoker (or under a broiler). When browned, remove and put in a 2-quart saucepan. Add remaining ingredients. Bring to a boil, then simmer until vegetables are soft. Strain and keep warm.

Sauté the lamb fillets in a very hot pan. When brown, remove to a cutting board. Slice and arrange on a plate. Ladle sauce over lamb and serve.

POTATOES GRATIN *serves eight*

Preheat oven to 375° F. Butter a 1½–quart baking dish. Slice the potatoes as thinly as possible and immediately put in cold water to prevent discoloring.

Drain water and pat potato slices dry. Arrange them in a single layer on the bottom of the buttered dish. Sprinkle with salt and pepper. Arrange a second layer of potatoes, and continue until all the slices are layered. Pour cream over potatoes. Cover and bake 45 minutes.

Uncover and bake for another 15 minutes, or until top is golden and bubbling. Let cool 10 minutes and serve on a bed of arugula.

4 russet potatoes, peeled
1 cup cream
Kosher salt
Freshly ground black
  pepper

4 cups loosely packed
  arugula

VANILLA CRISPS WITH RASPBERRIES
makes eight crisps

4 cups raspberries

For crisps:
2/3 cup butter, softened
1¼ cups powdered sugar
1½ cups all-purpose flour
4 egg whites
Cannoli mold

For pastry cream:
1 cup milk
1 vanilla bean, split
   lengthwise
3 egg yolks
1/4 cup sugar
2 teaspoons all-purpose
   flour
Pinch of salt
1/2 cup heavy cream,
   whipped

Puree 2 cups raspberries (reserve rest) in a food processsor, strain, and set aside.

To make the crisps, blend the butter and powdered sugar in a large mixing bowl. Slowly add the flour. Add egg whites, a little at a time until a smooth batter forms. Whisk and chill in refrigerator overnight.

Preheat oven to 350° F. Butter a large baking sheet. Spread thin layer of batter in four-inch rounds on the sheet. Bake about 3 minutes, until golden. Remove and wrap crisp around cannoli mold. When set, remove from mold and set aside in an airtight container.

To make pastry cream, heat milk and vanilla bean in a saucepan until scalding. In a bowl, stir egg yolks, sugar, flour, and salt until smooth. Slowly add hot milk. Return to saucepan and bring to a boil for 1 minute, stirring constantly. Remove vanilla bean and pour mixture into a buttered dish. Let cool completely. Fold in whipped cream and refrigerate.

To assemble, pipe cream into the crisps. Place small mound of raspberries in center of the plate, arranging crisps like spokes in a wheel. Spoon raspberry puree around each cookie and serve.

Joyce Goldstein

A PASSOVER SEDER WITH LARGESSE

Matzoh Ball Soup

Pickled Salmon

Gefilte Fish for Passover

Chopped Chicken Liver

Cornish Hens with Apricots, Tomatoes, Onions, and Spices

Susan's Passover Sponge Cake

serves ten

J oyce Goldstein is the chef-owner of San Francisco's *Square One* restaurant and the author of *The Mediterranean Kitchen* (Morrow, 1989). She writes a monthly column for the *San Francisco Chronicle* and travels nationwide as a teacher and lecturer.

When I was a child, Passover was not celebrated with any regularity in my family. Sometimes we would go to my aunt's house, and I remember waiting for the seemingly endless ritual meal to be over so I could play. The food was overcooked and not very tasty to my already jaded palate.

Over the past few years a group of us from San Francisco restaurants have begun to celebrate Passover together. Barbara Tropp from China Moon, Patty Unterman from Hayes Street Grill, Larry Bain, Catherine Pantsios, and Rachel Gardner from Zola's, and assorted friends and family have come together at our houses and restaurants to share both the traditional Passover ceremony and some really wonderful food. No one is in a rush to leave the table. We are usually too sated to move.

MATZOH BALL SOUP *serves twelve*

6 eggs
3/4 cup cold water
1/3 cup rendered
   chicken fat
1 teaspoon salt
1/2 teaspoon white pepper
3 cups plus 3 tablespoons
   matzoh meal
20 cups chicken stock,
   reduced to 10 cups
1/2 cup chopped parsley

In a large bowl, lightly whisk together the eggs with cold water. Add the chicken fat and stir until it dissolves. Add salt and pepper. Gradually but quickly stir in the matzoh meal with a spoon. Do not overbeat. Chill the mixture for an hour.

Line two large pans with parchment paper. With a large soupspoon dipped in cold water, form the chilled matzoh-ball mixture into medium-sized balls, about 1½ inches in diameter. Place these on the pans and refrigerate while you bring two large pots of salted water to a boil.

Drop in the matzoh balls, cover the pots, and reduce the heat after the water comes back to a boil. Simmer the matzoh balls 30 to 40 minutes, or until one tests cooked all the way through when cut in half. They should have doubled in size. Drain the balls and set aside. They can hold for a few hours at room temperature.

Just before serving, bring chicken broth to a boil. Season with salt and pepper to taste. Add the matzoh balls and heat through. Ladle into bowls and sprinkle generously with chopped parsley.

PICKLED SALMON *serves twelve*

This is a reworking of an old family recipe. My mother-in-law used to take lox, also known as smoked salmon, soak it in water for days to remove the salt, and then put the fish in pickling brine. I thought, since we get great local salmon, why not use fresh fish for this dish? I tried it, and it has become a much-requested favorite at my restaurant during the salmon season. At Passover, we serve it paired with gefilte fish as a special holiday fish plate. The onions are not just a visual garnish. They pick up the flavor of the marinade and are a delicious counterpoint to the salmon.

2½ cups white vinegar
2 cups water
1/2 cup sugar
4 tablespoons kosher salt
4 pounds salmon fillet, skin and small bones removed
4 tablespoons mixed pickling spices
12 bay leaves
4 white or yellow onions, sliced 1/4 inch thick

Bring the vinegar, water, sugar, and salt to a boil. Let the mixture cool completely.

Cut the salmon into pieces approximately 1 inch by 2 inches.

In a ceramic crock, glass bowl, or plastic container, place a layer of salmon pieces, then a sprinkling of pickling spices and bay leaves, then a layer of sliced onions. Repeat with layers of salmon, spices, and onions until you've used them all. Pour the cooled marinade over the fish. If the fish tends to float, weight it down with a ceramic plate. Cover the container and refrigerate for 3 to 5 days.

Serve the salmon, along with the marinated onions, with matzoh, or, after Passover, with rye bread. A small cucumber salad with a sour-cream dressing is also a nice accompaniment, if this is a meatless meal.

GEFILTE FISH FOR PASSOVER
serves fifteen to twenty

For fish stock:
Bones, heads, and skins of
    12 pounds of whole pike
    and whitefish
4 onions, chopped
2 carrots, chopped
1 piece celery root,
    chopped, about 1 cup
Pinch of sugar
1/8 cup peppercorns
1 cinnamon stick
4 quarts water

For fish balls:
6 pounds of combined
    whitefish and pike
    fillets, in equal
    amounts
4 medium onions, pureed
    in a food processor
6 eggs
4 tablespoons matzoh
    meal
1/2 cup ice water
2 tablespoons kosher salt
1½ tablespoons sugar
1 teaspoon white pepper
Pinch of ground
    cinnamon (optional)
3 tablespoons almonds,
    very finely ground

For horseradish:
1 pound horseradish root
1/2 cup white vinegar
Sugar and salt to taste

A Sephardic-inspired recipe, it makes about 45 small pieces of gefilte fish. This is a lot of work to make just a little, so why not make a lot? The fish keeps well for about four days.

To prepare the fish stock, combine the ingredients in a large pot, bring to a boil, skim, and simmer for 30 minutes. Strain and chill.

To prepare the fish balls, grind the fish twice in a meat grinder for a very fine texture. Turn out onto a plastic chopping board. Combine the fish, onions, and eggs with a chopper. Mix well. Keep chopping and add the matzoh meal and ice water, a bit at a time. Add the seasonings and ground almonds. Place in a bowl and chill the mixture over ice for a few hours.

Make a tiny sample fish ball from the chilled mixture and poach it in some fish stock. Adjust seasoning. Then, with wet hands, form the fish mixture into ovals, 2½ inches long. Place these on sheet pans lined with parchment paper. Refrigerate until ready to poach.

Bring the stock to a boil. Add the fish balls, reduce the heat, and cover the pan. Simmer for 30 minutes, turning and basting occasionally with the broth. Remove the cooked fish with a slotted spoon and set aside in containers. Add sliced carrots to the simmering stock and cook for about 7 minutes. Remove carrots and set aside. Reduce the fish stock by half. Adjust seasoning with salt and pepper. Pour stock over the gefilte fish. Pour the rest over carrot slices. Refrigerate until required.

Peel horseradish root and cut into small pieces. Puree in food processor with white vinegar. Add sugar and salt to taste. Cover until ready to serve. Garnish each piece of fish with one or two carrot slices. Pass around the horseradish in a serving bowl.

For garnish:
Carrot slices, 1/4 inch thick, from 12 peeled carrots

CHOPPED CHICKEN LIVER *serves ten to twelve*

Not exactly the healthiest thing to eat, but the best.

Melt the chicken fat in two pans. In one, sauté the onions until they are a dark golden brown. Set aside. In the other, sauté the livers until they are medium rare. They should still be pink, but not quivery.

Chop the livers. Chop the hard-boiled eggs. If you choose to do this in a food processor, just pulse them very quickly, and in very small batches. You don't want to lose the chunky texture.

Combine with the browned onions and add the pan juices. Do this while ingredients are still warm. Season to taste with salt and pepper. if the mixture seems a little dry, add more chicken fat. Serve with matzoh.

8 tablespoons chicken fat
2 to 3 yellow onions, chopped fine
1 pound chicken livers, well trimmed
6 to 8 hard-boiled eggs
Salt and pepper

CORNISH HENS WITH APRICOTS, TOMATOES, ONIONS, AND SPICES *serves ten*

4 tablespoons chicken fat
  or olive oil
5 cups chopped yellow
  onions
1½ tablespoons plus
  1 teaspoon ground
  cinnamon
1 teaspoon ground cloves
4 cups canned Italian
  plum tomatoes, diced
  and juices reserved
4 cups dried apricots,
  soaked in warm water,
  to expand to 6 cups
  after soaking
3 cups chicken stock or
  water (apricot soaking
  liquid, some tomato
  juices, and water
  combined will do
  nicely)
1/2 cup brown sugar
10 Cornish hens, or
  poussins, each about
  1 pound
Salt and pepper to taste

Melt the fat or heat the oil in a large sauce-pan. Add the onions and sauté over low heat for about 3 minutes. Add the ground spices minus 1 teaspoon cinnamon and cook 3 more minutes. Add about 1/2 cup of the reserved tomato liquid, stir, and simmer. Puree half the soaked apricots in a food processor. Coarsely chop the remainder. Add the pureed apricots, along with the diced tomatoes and 1 cup chicken stock, to the onions, and simmer 5 minutes.

Puree half the onion mixture in the processor. Return the pureed mixture to the pan. Add the chopped apricots, brown sugar, and another cup of stock. Simmer 5 minutes. Add remaining stock to make a medium-thick sauce. Adjust seasoning. Set aside. Sauce can be made well ahead of time.

Preheat oven to 450° F. Place Cornish hens in a roasting pan on a rack and sprinkle with salt, pepper, and remaining cinnamon. Roast about 30 minutes. When birds are cool enough to handle, cut them in quarters and warm them in the apricot sauce.

This sauce may be used with sautéed chicken (boneless breasts, or breasts and thighs). Brown the chicken, deglaze the pan with stock, and then add the sauce. Warm chicken in the sauce and cook until done.

SUSAN'S PASSOVER SPONGE CAKE
serves ten to twelve

This is a light, delicious cake with a delicate flavor and wonderful, moist texture, unlike all those dry, heavy Passover sponge cakes we've had. It was developed by Susan Lynn of *Square One*'s pastry department.

Beat the egg yolks with 1/2 cup sugar and the juice and zest until mixture is pale and holds a ribbon. Beat the egg whites with 1/2 cup sugar and pinch of salt until stiff. Fold the yolks into the whites. Then fold in the sifted cake meal, potato starch, and vanilla.

Pour the batter into an ungreased 10-inch tube pan and put in a cold oven. Turn on oven to 325° F and bake for about 45 minutes. It's done when a toothpick inserted in the cake comes out clean. Invert to cool. Serve with fresh berries or fruit compote.

10 eggs, separated
1 cup sugar
Zest and juice of one
    orange and one lemon
Pinch of salt
1/2 cup plus 2 tablespoons
    Passover cake meal,
    sifted
1 tablespoon plus 2
    teaspoons potato starch,
    sifted
1 teaspoon vanilla

Margaret Fox

A PERFECT BREAKFAST FOR A LONG WEEKEND

Five-Spice Applesauce

Crunchy Huckleberry Muffins

Scrambled Eggs with Smoked Salmon and Fresh Herbs

serves six

Margaret Fox has been a resident of Mendocino, California, since 1975, and opened her highly esteemed restaurant, *Café Beaujolais,* in that town fifteen years ago. Her cookbooks, *Café Beaujolais* and *Morning Food* (Ten Speed Press, 1984 and 1990), describe her experiences in the always chaotic, entertaining restaurant business. She lives with her husband, chef Christopher Kump, and their three black dogs in a wood bordered by an antique fruit orchard.

My idea of a perfect breakfast is a leisurely sampling of different flavors and textures. Mendocino's north coast contains such appealing indigenous ingredients that combining them in this menu ensures satisfaction and delight. Enjoy yourself on any holiday or long weekend you may want to try these recipes.

FIVE-SPICE APPLESAUCE *serves six*

Peel, seed, and core the apples. Cut them into small chunks. Place all the ingredients except the lemon juice in a large saucepan that has a tight-fitting lid. Cover, turn heat to medium, and cook apples until tender. Mash with a potato masher, or put through a food mill. Season with lemon juice to taste.

8 apples (pippins are a good choice)
1¾ cups apple juice
1 tablespoon minced fresh ginger
1½ teaspoons ground cinnamon
1/2 teaspoon each allspice, ground cloves, and crushed anise seed
Lemon juice to taste

CRUNCHY HUCKLEBERRY MUFFINS
makes about two dozen

Preheat oven to 400° F. In a large bowl, mix together the eggs, sugar, oil, cream, and vanilla. Set aside.

In another bowl, sift together the nutmeg, flours, and baking powder. Add egg mixture to the flour bowl and stir quickly, just enough to blend ingredients, for about 15 seconds. Fold in nuts and frozen berries and pour into muffin tins prepared with either paper cups or nonstick spray. Bake for 18 to 20 minutes, until golden.

2 eggs
1/2 cup brown sugar, packed
1/2 cup vegetable oil
1 cup heavy cream
1½ teaspoons vanilla extract
1/4 teaspoon ground nutmeg
1 cup each white and whole wheat flour
1 tablespoon baking powder
1 cup chopped and lightly toasted walnuts or pecans
1 cup huckleberries, frozen (otherwise they'll disintegrate and bleed into the muffins)

SCRAMBLED EGGS WITH SMOKED SALMON AND FRESH HERBS *serves six*

12 eggs
1/4 teaspoon Tabasco
  sauce
1/2 teaspoon kosher salt
Freshly ground pepper
  to taste
3 tablespoons cold water
2 tablespoons butter
1/2 cup minced red onion
6 ounces smoked salmon,
  cut into small pieces,
  about 3/4 inch square
1 tablespoon each minced
  tarragon, chives, and
  parsley

In a bowl, whisk together eggs, Tabasco, salt, pepper, and water until combined. In a 10-inch nonstick sauté pan, melt the butter and add onion, cooking over medium heat for about 5 minutes, until onion is soft but not browned. Add salmon, eggs, and herbs, stirring with a wooden spatula until eggs become creamy. Serve immediately.

David Lebovitz

CALIFORNIA DESSERTS WITH ASIAN FLAVORS

Ginger-Butterscotch Custard

Red Banana Cake

Sesame Spreadouts

Coconut-Chocolate Macaroons

Plum Wine and Mixed Berry Ice

serves six

David Lebovitz learned to cook in a small restaurant in Ithaca, New York, prior to moving to California, where he spent seven years in the pastry department of *Chez Panisse* in Berkeley. He currently works in San Francisco as pastry chef at Bruce Cost's *Monsoon*, a pan-Asian restaurant known for its adventurous cuisine. Lebovitz produces Western desserts with Asian flavors.

These desserts were inspired by the flavors and textures of Asian cooking, and you may find them interesting enough to try at your next party, particularly if it's a tea party.

They're meant to be inviting, refreshing, eclectic, and unusual. I like to present guests with a variety of pastries and ices — nothing too heavy, especially after hearty Shanghai cuisine or spicy Thai dishes.

I'm intrigued by the smoky teas, sweet and pungent wines, assertive spices and herbs, and the tropical fruits of Southeast Asia. Through numerous trips to Chinese markets, herbalists, tea shops, and produce stalls, I have been inspired and challenged to create desserts that reflect the cross-cultural diversity of the food available in the Bay Area.

Sometimes when I cook, I try to use the principles of harmony with nature that I practice in aikido. It is then that I feel that my guests are being treated to desserts which reflect my personal respect for the ingredients that I'm using.

GINGER-BUTTERSCOTCH CUSTARD *serves six*

1/4 pound fresh ginger
2 cups heavy cream
1/8 teaspoon salt
1 teaspoon brown sugar
6 egg yolks, lightly beaten
1/2 teaspoon vanilla
    extract

Slice ginger and place in a pan. Cover with water and bring to a boil. Cook for 1/2 to 1 minute. Drain.

Put cream in a saucepan. Add the ginger and salt. Let steep for 1 to 2 hours, until the ginger taste has reached your satisfaction.

With a slotted spoon, remove the ginger, and add the brown sugar to cream. Reheat the mixture, stirring to dissolve the sugar. Slowly add the mixture to the egg yolks, stirring constantly. Strain through a fine-mesh strainer. Add vanilla.

Pour mixture into custard cups and place them in a pan of hot water. Cover with foil and bake in a 350° F oven for about 40 minutes, until the custards are just set. They should jiggle slightly in the center when shaken. Serve warm or at room temperature.

RED BANANA CAKE *serves twelve*

Cream butter and sugar. Add vanilla and brandy. Mix in eggs one at a time until fully incorporated. Add banana puree. Activate the baking soda by adding 1 tablespoon boiling water, and add to mixture.

Mix dry ingredients, and add half to wet mixture. Add the buttermilk. Add remaining dry mixutre. Stir in the pecans.

Pour into a buttered and floured 9-inch cake pan. Bake in a 350° F oven for 30 to 35 minutes, until a toothpick inserted in the center of cake comes out clean.

This cake goes well with rum buttercream and coffee-flavored praline.

1/2 cup plus one tablespoon unsalted butter
1½ cups sugar
1 teaspoon vanilla extract
1 teaspoon brandy
2 eggs, at room temperature
2 cups red banana puree, made from ripe bananas and 2 tablespoons strong coffee
3/4 teaspoon baking soda
2½ cups flour
1½ teaspoons baking powder
1/8 teaspoon salt
1/2 teaspoon cinnamon
6 tablespoons buttermilk
1¼ cups pecans, toasted and finely chopped

SESAME SPREADOUTS *makes about thirty cookies*

Cream the butter and sugar. Add lemon zest and egg white and mix well. Mix in flour, salt, vanilla, and sesame seeds.

Form dough into 1-inch balls. Place on a baking sheet lined with parchment paper. Make sure to leave about 3 inches between each ball to allow room for spreading out. Press each ball flat and bake in a 350° F oven for 10 to 12 minutes, until golden brown. Cool cookies on baking sheet.

1/2 cup unsalted butter
3/4 cup sugar
Zest of 1 lemon, finely chopped
1 egg white
3 tablespoons flour
1/8 teaspoon salt
1/2 teaspoon vanilla extract
1½ cups sesame seeds

COCONUT-CHOCOLATE MACAROONS
makes about 25

6 egg whites
1¾ cup sugar
6 ounces unsweetened
   shredded or flaked
   coconut
3 tablespoons flour
2 teaspoons vanilla extract
1/8 teaspoon salt
2 ounces bittersweet
   chocolate

Place all ingredients except chocolate in a heavy saucepan and cook over medium heat until the mixture begins to look dry and starts scorching the sides of pan. Remove from heat and let cool.

Form into 1-inch balls and place on a baking sheet lined with parchment paper. Bake in a 350° F oven for 20 to 25 minutes, until lightly browned. Chop the chocolate and melt over hot water. Dip bottoms of the macaroons in the melted chocolate and let cool upside down.

PLUM WINE AND MIXED BERRY ICE
makes one and a half quarts

1-liter bottle plum wine
   (my choice is Kinsen)
2½ cups water
1¾ cups sugar
1 pound berries (raspberries,
   boysenberries, or any
   other)

In a saucepan, bring wine, water, and sugar to a boil, and cook for at least 10 minutes to burn off alcohol, since it prevents the ice from freezing. Add berries and steep for 1 hour.

Strain or pass through a food mill.

Chill the mixture and freeze in an ice-cream maker according to manufacturer's instructions. If you don't have an ice-cream maker, put the mixture in a metal tray, place in your freezer, and stir with a fork every few hours until it is icy and frozen.

Yahya Salih

A FEAST FOR RAMADAN

Fresh Pomegranate Juice

Tabouleh

Nineveh Kibbee

Lamb and Rice Dolmas

Baklava

serves six

Yahya Salih came to California from Mosul, Iraq, in 1975, at the age of twenty-two. He was initiated into California cuisine while working under Jeremiah Tower at the *Balboa Cafe* in San Francisco. He has since opened his own restaurant, *YaYa,* offering a California version of Middle Eastern food. He is currently writing a cookbook dedicated to his mother and consisting of her recipes from Nineveh.

For those of the Moslem faith, Ramadan is a month-long celebration which commemorates the revelations of the holy Koran. Everyone fasts from sunrise to sunset. No one eats, drinks, or smokes during daylight hours. When the sun goes down, one may eat and drink until dawn of the following day.

The fast is traditionally broken with fresh fruit juice, and then everyone sits down to a feast. In Mosul, where I was born and raised in a district adjoining the ruins of ancient Nineveh, this is a popular menu during Ramadan and my favorite as a child.

Because of the differences in the Moslem and Christian calendars, Ramadan occurs at different times in the Christian year. Currently, it falls in the spring.

TABOULEH *serves six*

1/2 cup bulgur (very fine grade)
2 bunches parsley
1 tomato, seeded and diced
2 scallions, chopped
3 to 4 fresh mint leaves, chopped
2 tablespoons fresh lemon juice
3 tablespoons olive oil
Salt and pepper to taste

Place bulgur in 1/2 cup cold water and let stand for 1/2 hour.

Remove heavy stems of parsley and finely chop by hand. Squeeze dry the chopped parsley in a dish towel.

Combine parsley, tomato, scallions, and mint. Squeeze bulgur in palm of hand to remove excess moisture. Add to tomato mixture.

Pour lemon juice and oil on mixture. Let stand for 15 minutes. Mix together with both hands. Season with salt and pepper to taste. Serve at room temperature as an appetizer.

NINEVEH KIBBEE (Dumplings) *serves six*

For dough:
2 cups bulgur
2 cups organic cracked wheat
2 cups boiling water
Salt and pepper to taste

For stuffing:
2 tablespoons olive oil
1 pound diced lean lamb or beef
1 onion, chopped
1 tablespoon allspice
Salt and pepper to taste
1/2 cup yellow raisins
1/2 cup pine nuts

To prepare dough, place ingredients in a pan and cover with 2 cups boiling water. Let stand 30 minutes. Process the mixture in a food processor until smooth. Treat it the same way you would cookie or pie dough. Form it into 12 balls, 1 to 2 inches in diameter. Slowly form a hole in each ball with your forefinger. Start from the center and work outward, and enlarge it as much as possible to achieve a cuplike shape.

To make the stuffing, heat the olive oil in a sauté pan and cook the meat and onion, stirring constantly, until it almost turns brown. Add the allspice, salt, and pepper. Finish cooking. Mix in the yellow raisins and pine nuts. Remove from heat and cool for 10 minutes.

Stuff hollowed-out balls with meat mixture. Pinch the ends together to seal top, and close securely so that the stuffing does not leak out.

Fill large pot halfway with water and bring to a boil, adding salt. While water is at a rolling boil, drop in kibbees one at a time. They will sink to the bottom. Cook 5 minutes, or until they float to the surface, which means they are cooked and ready to eat. Serve warm by themselves, or with a sauce of yogurt (or crème fraîche), mint, and cucumber.

LAMB AND RICE DOLMAS *serves six*

Place 5 cups salted water in a saucepan and bring to a boil. Add 2 cups rice. Cook over medium heat for 20 minutes, until water is absorbed and rice is done. Combine rice with other ingredients. Season with salt and pepper to taste.

Clean and separate Swiss chard leaves and cut off tough ends. Place 2 tablespoons stuffing in center of each leaf. Fold from ends to center, then roll leaves over and arrange dolmas seam side down in a 5-quart saucepan the bottom of which has been covered with 2 tablespoons vegetable oil. (The stuffing may also be used for scooped-out zucchini, baby eggplant, or onion.)

Place dolmas side by side in pan, leaving 1/2 inch between them, as they will expand. Arrange them in layers until you have used up leaves and stuffing. Place pan over high heat

For dolma stuffing:
2 cups rice, preferably basmati
1½ cups cooked chopped lean lamb
2 tomatoes, seeded and diced
2 tablespoons allspice
1 tablespoon chopped garlic
Salt and pepper
(Note: omit the meat for vegetarian dolmas)

2 bunches Swiss chard
2 tablespoons vegetable oil

(continued next page)

For sauce:
2 tablespoons tomato
   paste
2 tablespoons tomato
   sauce
Juice of 1/2 lemon
4 cups water

for no more than 2 minutes, until the oil
starts to sizzle. Remove from heat.

To prepare the sauce, mix together the tomato
paste, tomato sauce, lemon juice, and water.
Slowly add the mixture to the pan of dolmas
until the liquid peeks out at you when you
push dolmas with your hand. Season with
salt and pepper to taste.

Place a heavy plate or the lid of a stone crock
over top layer of dolmas to hold them in
place. Otherwise, the leaves will loosen up
and the stuffing will fall out. Cover the pan.

Cook over high heat for 10 to 15 minutes,
until the liquid begins to boil. Lower heat and
cook for 15 more minutes. Remove heavy
plate from inside pan. Replace cover on pan
and simmer for 30 more minutes.

Uncover pan and allow dolmas to cool. To
serve, place a large serving platter over top of
pan and invert quickly. Slam contents firmly
onto serving dish to remove dolmas all at once.

BAKLAVA *makes fifty pieces*

Brush the pan with melted butter.

Prepare the filling by mixing together the walnuts (or pistachios), sugar, and cardamom. Set aside.

Place a sheet of phyllo on the greased sheet pan. Brush the entire surface with melted butter. Repeat the process until you have a stack of 25 phyllo sheets. Spread the nut filling over the top layer of phyllo. Cover with another sheet of phyllo and brush with butter. Repeat until you have used up all the phyllo sheets.

Slice the unbaked baklava with a sharp knife into diamond-shaped portions. First cut it lengthwise on the diagonal at approximately 1-inch intervals. Then slice it in the other direction straight up and down, also 1 inch apart.

Bake in a 350° F oven for 45 minutes to 1 hour, or until the phyllo is crisp and golden brown.

In the meantime, prepare the syrup by combining the sugar, water, and lemon juice in a heavy saucepan and cooking over moderate heat until the sugar is dissolved and turns a light amber color. (If you prefer a sweeter syrup, use half the amount of sugar and 1 cup honey.)

Immediately after removing the sheet pan from the oven, pour the syrup over the baklava. Let cool and serve.

For filling:
3 cups walnuts or
   pistachios, chopped
1/2 cup sugar
2 tablespoons cardamom

2 pounds phyllo-dough
   sheets (available in
   1-pound packages)
1½ pounds butter, melted
12-by-17-inch cake pan

For syrup:
4 cups sugar
1½ cups water
1 tablespoon lemon juice
(or, if you wish, use 2 cups
   sugar and 1 cup honey)

Marlene Levinson

A BRUNCH FOR A SAILING PARTY IN MAY

Chilled Champagne

*Beer-Poached Prawns in Spicy
Lemon Marinade*

Curried Liver Pâté

Chopped Herring

*Salmon Steaks with
Cucumber-Yogurt Sauce*

Spinach-Filled Scallion Soufflé Roll

*Chiffonade of Radicchio and Arugula
with Garlic Vinaigrette*

Praline Mousse with Fresh Berries

serves six

M arlene Levinson has been teaching cooking and developing menus for restaurants in
the San Francisco area for fifteen years. She
trained with and was assistant to the legend-
ary French chef and teacher Josephine Araldo.

*I prepared this meal for some friends who invited my husband and me out on
their boat for the opening day of the San Francisco yachting season. It was the first
Sunday in May, and a sunny day was forecast. We expected a pleasant, relaxing
sail on the bay without having to stand around cooking in the galley.*

*I opted to bring the brunch. The evening before, I was able to prepare the
menu, except for the salmon, which I grilled just before I left home that morning.
All the food, other than the praline mousse, which was kept refrigerated, was
served at room temperature with, of course, the chilled champagne.*

BEER-POACHED PRAWNS IN SPICY LEMON MARINADE *serves six*

Shell and devein the prawns. If time permits, soak in cold salted water overnight in refrigerator to draw out impurities.

Prepare marinade by whisking together the ingredients; use a generous amount of chili flakes. Place in a container with sliced onion, garlic, and lemon.

Drain and rinse the prawns. Place in a non-aluminum saucepan. Cover with the beer, adding water to cover prawns completely. Season with salt and pepper.

Cook on high heat, stirring continuously, until prawns are about three-fourths done, about 5 minutes. They should be undercooked, since acidic marinade will finish cooking them. Drain and rinse with cold water. Place in marinade and keep chilled for at least 24 hours. To serve, drain marinade of liquid. Serve prawns on a bed of sliced onion.

1 pound medium prawns (about 25)
12 ounces beer
1/4 teaspoon salt
1/4 teaspoon pepper

For marinade:
3/4 cup olive oil
1/2 cup lemon juice
1 teaspoon Dijon-style mustard
Salt, pepper, and chili flakes to taste

1 medium onion, thinly sliced
3 to 4 cloves garlic, sliced or mashed slightly
1 lemon, quartered and thinly sliced

CURRIED LIVER PÂTÉ *yields one pound*

1/2 cup unsalted butter
1 medium onion, chopped
1 clove garlic, crushed
1 teaspoon curry powder
1½ tablespoons flour
1/2 pound chicken livers,
   chopped
1/4 cup sherry, Marsala,
   or white wine
1/4 teaspoon allspice
1/4 teaspoon freshly
   ground pepper
1/4 teaspoon salt
1 large egg

Melt butter in a skillet and sauté onions for a few minutes. Add garlic and curry powder. Stir in the flour, and add remaining ingredients, except egg. Cover and cook over low heat for 15 minutes, or until livers are cooked and no longer pink. Puree mixture with the egg in a food processor or blender.

Place in a 16-ounce ovenproof crock with a tight-fitting lid, or use a double thickness of aluminum foil. Bake in a pan of hot water in a 350° F oven for 30 minutes, or until top is set. Cool at room temperature before refrigerating. Best if made a day ahead to let flavor develop. Serve with sourdough-baguette rounds.

CHOPPED HERRING *yields one and a half cups*

1 jar, 8 to 10 ounces, wine
   herring snacks, drained,
   and finely chopped
1 hard-boiled egg, finely
   chopped
1 small tart apple, peeled,
   cored, and finely
   chopped
1/2 small red onion (or to
   taste), finely chopped
1/2 teaspoon sugar

Combine the ingredients and set aside for at least an hour to let flavors mix. Serve with rye rounds.

SALMON STEAKS WITH CUCUMBER-YOGURT SAUCE *serves six*

Prepare cucumber sauce by combining the ingredients and allowing flavors to marry by refrigerating several hours, or overnight.

Barely coat the salmon with olive oil. Season to taste with salt, pepper, and herbs. Marinate a few hours before cooking. Sauté, poach, steam, or grill, as desired. Serve with a dollop of sauce on the side.

6 salmon steaks,
  6 ounces each
Olive oil
Salt, pepper, and any
  desired herbs, such
  as dill, tarragon, and
  basil

For cucumber sauce:
1½ cups unpeeled, grated
  English cucumber
1/2 cup plain yogurt
  (crème fraîche or sour
  cream may be
  substituted)
1/2 cup mayonnaise
1 tablespoon chopped
  parsley
1 tablespoon grated
  yellow onion, or to taste
1 tablespoon red or white
  wine vinegar
Salt, pepper, and chopped
  dill to taste

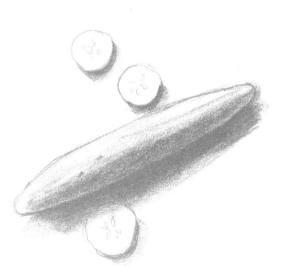

SPINACH-FILLED SCALLION SOUFFLÉ ROLL
serves six

For soufflé roll:
4 tablespoons butter
1/3 cup flour
1 cup milk, heated
Salt, pepper, nutmeg, and
    cayenne to taste
4 egg yolks
2/3 cup grated cheese:
    Swiss, cheddar, or other
3 to 4 scallions, sliced fine
6 egg whites
Pinch of salt

For filling:
2 bunches spinach,
    washed and stemmed
8 ounces cream cheese
1 to 2 cloves garlic,
    minced
2 to 3 scallions, sliced fine
Salt and pepper

In a double boiler over medium heat, melt the butter and stir in the flour. Cook together for a minute or two, then add the milk. Season to taste with salt, pepper, nutmeg, and cayenne. Whisk until smooth, cover, and let cook for 10 to 15 minutes. Remove from the heat and stir in yolks, cheese, and sliced scallions.

Beat the whites stiff with a pinch of salt. Stir one-third of the whites into the base mixture to lighten. Gently fold in remaining two-thirds. Spread mixture evenly in generously greased and floured jelly-roll pan and place in preheated 375° F oven for 20 to 25 minutes, until top is golden brown.

To prepare the filling, bring a pan of water to a boil and add spinach. Remove when the leaves have wilted. Drain and squeeze out excess water. Heat the cream cheese with the garlic in a saucepan. Purée the spinach in a food processor with the scallions and warmed cream cheese. Season to taste with salt and pepper.

When soufflé has finished baking, place first a towel and then a cookie sheet over the pan. Invert. If the soufflé sticks to the pan, gently loosen with a spatula. Spread the filling evenly over the soufflé, leaving 1/2 inch uncovered at one end, on the longer side. Using the towel to guide the soufflé, roll up. At this point, the soufflé roll can be refrigerated or frozen.

Before serving, bring soufflé roll to room temperature, then heat in a 325° F oven for

25 minutes. It's best to keep the roll wrapped in aluminum foil until the last 10 minutes, to keep it moist. Serve sliced, warm or at room temperature. You can serve it with a hollandaise sauce or crème fraîche seasoned with herbs and/or caviar.

CHIFFONADE OF RADICCHIO AND ARUGULA WITH GARLIC VINAIGRETTE *serves six*

Combine the garlic and olive oil and set aside. Stack the arugula leaves and cut into a chiffonade of thin, ribbonlike strips. Do the same with the basil. Halve the radicchio, remove tough stems, and slice into thin strips. Remove garlic from olive oil by straining oil over salad mix. Toss and add the vinegar. Season with salt and pepper.

2 to 3 cloves garlic, crushed
1/4 cup olive oil
2 cups arugula, leaves only
About 15 fresh basil leaves
1 head radicchio
Optional: Belgian endive, sliced thin, chicory frisée, or watercress leaves
2 to 3 tablespoons red or white wine vinegar
Salt and freshly ground pepper to taste

PRALINE MOUSSE WITH FRESH BERRIES
serves six

6 egg yolks
3/4 cup sugar
1½ cups milk, heated
1 tablespoon gelatin
1/3 cup praline powder
 (see below)
1/2 cup heavy cream,
 whipped
1/4 cup kirsch
1 teaspoon vanilla
2 egg whites, beaten stiff
 with a pinch of salt
Buttered 6-cup decorative
 mold
2 cups fresh seasonal
 berries

For praline powder:
1/2 cup sugar
1 tablespoon water
1/2 cup whole almonds
 (with skins)
Oiled jelly-roll pan and
 oiled metal spatula

To prepare praline powder, combine sugar and water in a heavy saucepan. Cook over medium heat, stirring constantly, until mixture is golden brown. Add almonds and keep stirring until almonds pop. Pour onto oiled pan. To cool quickly, push mixture around with the spatula. When cool and hard, place pieces in a blender and pulverize to a powder. Keep leftover praline powder in the freezer, as it tends to get syrupy at room temperature or in refrigerator.

To make mousse, stir together the yolks and sugar. Slowly, while stirring, add the hot milk. Place mixture in a double boiler over medium heat. Soften the gelatin in a little cold water and stir it in. Keep stirring until the mixture thickens. Remove from the heat and whisk in the praline powder. Cool. Season the whipped cream with kirsch and vanilla, and fold into cooled mixture. Fold in the stiff egg whites. Pour into the mold and hit several times against the counter to remove air bubbles. Chill until set.

When ready to serve, unmold onto platter and decorate with berries, plus additional whipped cream, if you wish.

Maggie Waldron

CELEBRATING CINCO DE MAYO

Grilled Duck with Green Pumpkin Seed Sauce

Little Loins of Pork Grilled for Sandwiches

Charcoal-Grilled Steak with Poblano Chilies

Grilled Tamales in Husks★

Grilled Parmesan Cheese

Mexican Fruit Popsicles★

serves four

★Recipes not included

Maggie Waldron is senior vice president and executive creative director of the Ketchum Food Center in San Francisco, a unit of Ketchum Communications specializing in the marketing of fresh fruits and vegetables. A former magazine editor, television director, and author of several cookbooks, she is currently working on a book, *Healing Foods,* to be published by William Morrow.

On Cinco de Mayo wherever in the world there is a Mexican community, you can find food vendors with the most astonishing cooking contraptions turning out some of the best food you or I have ever eaten. The best of it is grilled over hot coals and crammed into smoky tortillas with drifts of green and red salsas, roasted chilies and onions, fresh cheese, and sour cream.

We celebrate the day on our houseboat in Sausalito, across the bay from San Francisco, with two or three barbecues set up on the deck. Since most of our friends are, like Mexicans, persistent noshers, the whole menu is made up of antojitos, which means "little whims." Here are a few that I like to serve.

GRILLED DUCK WITH GREEN PUMPKIN SEED SAUCE *serves four*

5- to 6-pound duck, cut
    into serving pieces
3/4 cup hulled unsalted
    pumpkin seeds, toasted
6 peppercorns
Pinch of cumin seeds
1 cup tomatillos, husks
    removed (if using
    canned, drain)
4 fresh serrano chilies,
    cut up
1 medium onion, cut up
2 cloves garlic, crushed
3 sprigs epazote (strongly
    flavored herb found in
    Latin markets)
3 sprigs cilantro
Handful of greens (radish
    tops, lettuce, parsley, etc.)

Prick the skin of the duck with fork tines held upright to render out the fat without piercing the flesh. Grill duck over mesquite, 9 to 10 minutes to a side.

While the duck is cooking, make the sauce. Grind the pumpkin seeds, peppercorns, and cumin seeds in a blender and set aside. Puree the rest of the ingredients and pour into a saucepan. Bring to a boil and stir in pumpkin-seed mixture. Taste for seasoning and remove from fire, or sauce will curdle. Serve duck with sauce, which should be very *picante,* and warm grilled tortillas.

LITTLE LOINS OF PORK GRILLED FOR SANDWICHES *serves six to eight*

2-pound pork loin, sliced
    into 1-inch steaks
1/2 cup white vinegar
1 to 2 teaspoons red
    pepper flakes
1 onion, chopped
2 cloves garlic, crushed
Salt, cayenne pepper, and
    freshly ground black
    pepper
Lard
Crusty round rolls, split

Marinate the pork in a mixture of the vinegar, red pepper, onion, garlic, and seasonings for 1 hour at room temperature. Pat dry. Rub with a little lard and grill over coals, about 1 minute to a side. Serve in little round rolls with red or green salsa and finely shredded lettuce.

CHARCOAL-GRILLED STEAK WITH
POBLANO CHILIES *serves six to eight*

Trim fat from steaks with a sharp knife, slit the steaks open horizontally, and pound lightly with the side of a cleaver. Season with salt and pepper and a little lime juice. Grill fast over coals. At the same time, grill the chilies until nicely charred. Wrap a chunk of steak and a chili in a warm corn tortilla with a spoonful of guacamole.

4 skirt steaks, 1 pound each
Salt and freshly ground pepper
1/3 cup fresh lime juice
6 to 8 fresh poblano chilies
Warm corn tortillas

GRILLED PARMESAN CHEESE *serves eight*

With a sturdy knife, slice the cheese into 1-inch-thick squares. Brush lightly with oil. Set in a hinged grill about 6 inches from coals and cook, turning, until cheese is slightly brown and soft but still holds its shape. Serve immediately, sprinkled with oregano.

1 pound not-too-dry Parmesan cheese
Olive oil
Crushed fresh oregano leaves

Mary Etta Moose

THE SEASON'S FIRST: THE BOUNTIFUL MONTH OF MAY

*Roasted King Salmon with
Dungeness Crab Crust and Yellow
Pepper Coulis*

*Ragoût of Spring Lamb, Fennel, and
Mint with Drunken Prune Triangles*

*Fresh Pineapple Ice Cream with
Ginger and Lime Tuiles*

serves four

M ary Etta Moose was co-owner and executive chef of San Francisco's *Washington Square
Bar & Grill* from 1973 to 1989 and is presently consulting chef for low-fat specialties.
She is coauthor with Brian St. Pierre of *The
Flavor of North Beach* (Chronicle Books,
1981). Her recipes and articles have appeared
in numerous cookbooks, magazines, and
newspapers.

*More than any holiday, the occasion most inspirational to cooks is the market
at a change of seasons. For this reason, my menu celebrates the bounty of the
month of May, when fruits and vegetables are at their peak, and spring lamb and
salmon reappear. All the wonderful things that have been missing for a while are
available again, and spur the cook to create.*
The recipes I've chosen meet healthful limits of fat and cholesterol.

ROASTED KING SALMON WITH DUNGENESS CRAB CRUST AND YELLOW PEPPER COULIS
serves four

Preheat oven to 475° F. Moisten salmon fillet with lemon juice. Lay it in a flameproof baking dish brushed with 1/2 teaspoon olive oil. Mix the crabmeat, bread crumbs, egg white, and tarragon with salt and pepper to taste, and spread mixture atop the salmon. Dot with remaining olive oil and bake, uncovered, for 15 minutes.

Transfer fillet to a broiling pan and slip under broiler for 5 minutes to brown the crust while you quickly prepare the coulis.

Deglaze baking pan with vinegar. Purée yellow pepper and onion in a food processor and add to pan with chopped tarragon and salt and pepper to taste. Heat through. Divide fillet into four portions. Spoon coulis beside each portion.

12-ounce fillet of salmon
Juice and grated zest of
   1 lemon
1½ teaspoons olive oil
4 ounces crabmeat
1/2 cup fresh bread
   crumbs
1 egg white
1 tablespoon chopped
   fresh tarragon, plus
   1 teaspoon for coulis
Kosher salt
Freshly ground pepper
1/2 tablespoon tarragon
   vinegar
1 yellow pepper, seeded
   and chopped
1/2 sweet onion, such as
   Vidalia or Maui,
   chopped

RAGOÛT OF SPRING LAMB, FENNEL, AND MINT *serves four*

1 pound lean lamb, leg or
    loin, cut into 1/2-inch
    cubes
2 cloves garlic, chopped
White of 2 leeks, chopped
1 teaspoon fennel seeds,
    crushed
Salt and pepper
1/4 cup wine reserved
    from soaked prunes (see
    prune triangle recipe)
2 cups unsalted chicken
    stock
1 tablespoon cornstarch
1/4 cup dry red wine
1/2 pound fresh fennel,
    cut into 1/4-inch dice
1/3 cup fresh mint leaves,
    chopped

Sear meat on all sides over high heat in a non-stick skillet. Transfer meat to a flameproof casserole. Combine next five ingredients in the skillet. Press a sheet of waxed paper over surface. Cover pan. Bring to a simmer and cook at low heat for 5 minutes.

Transfer contents of skillet to casserole. In a saucepan, bring chicken stock to a simmer, then pour into casserole. Dissolve cornstarch in red wine and stir into casserole, bringing liquid to a boil while stirring. Cover, reduce heat, and simmer 30 minutes, until meat is tender. After 15 minutes, add the fennel. Add the chopped mint in the last 5 minutes.

Pan juices should have thickened into a sauce. If not, pour the liquid into a saucepan and boil down. Taste and adjust seasoning. Spoon ragoût over the drunken prune triangles.

DRUNKEN PRUNE TRIANGLES *serves four*

Soak prunes overnight, or longer, in wine. Halve garlic head horizontally, sprinkle with fennel seeds, and re-form. Wrap in foil and bake 40 minutes in 350° F oven.

Drain soaked prunes, reserving the wine for ragoût. Chop prunes and combine with cheese, crumbs, mint, lemon zest, salt, and pepper in bowl of food processor. Squeeze in the baked, caramelized garlic and process until smooth.

Place a heaping teaspoon of filling in center of each wonton skin. Moisten edges with water and fold into triangles, pressing edges closed. May be made ahead to this point and stored in a container dusted with rice flour to prevent sticking. Will hold in refrigerator overnight, in freezer up to a week.

About 25 minutes before serving time, bring 6 quarts of salted water to a boil. Add triangles. When water returns to the boil, add 1 cup cold water. When water boils again, the triangles should be done (if cooking from a frozen state, introduce another cup of cold water to the process). Drain, divide into four bowls, and top with ragoût. Garnish with mint sprigs.

6 prunes
6 ounces dry red wine
1 head garlic
1/4 teaspoon fennel seeds
1/2 cup part-skim ricotta
  cheese
1/4 cup bread crumbs
2 tablespoons fresh mint,
  chopped
Minced zest of 1 lemon
Salt and pepper to taste
20 wonton skins
Extra mint sprigs for
  garnish

FRESH PINEAPPLE ICE CREAM *yields 2 cups*

1 small pineapple
1/2 pint vanilla frozen
   yogurt

Cut pineapple into chunks. Freeze a cupful of chunks. Process frozen chunks into a slush. Add frozen yogurt and process until smooth. Refreeze in a covered plastic container until serving time.

GINGER AND LIME TUILES *makes eight tuiles*

1 egg white
3 tablespoons sugar
1 tablespoon butter,
   melted
1½ tablespoons flour
Freshly ground pepper
3 tablespoons slivered
   almonds
Grated zest of 2 limes
1 teaspoon grated fresh
   ginger

Preheat oven to 375° F. Mix egg white and sugar. Add butter. Beat in flour and a couple of grindings of pepper. Add almonds, lime zest, and ginger. Lightly dust a nonstick cookie sheet with flour.

Make two batches of four tuiles each, spaced well apart on the pan. Using a circular motion with the back of a spoon, spread a scant tablespoon of batter for each tuile into a very thin 5-inch circle. Bake about 6 minutes, or until slightly brown at edges.

Working fast, carefully slide cookies off sheet with a metal spatula and drape them over a horizontal broomstick handle to give them a curved shape. Slide cookies off broomstick after they crisp. Should they firm up before the shaping, return them to the oven to soften. Serve with ice cream. Store leftovers in an airtight container.

Carlo Middione

AN ITALIAN
ANNIVERSARY DINNER

Brodetto di Carciofini e Pastina
(Little Soup of Baby Artichokes and
Tiny Pasta)

Vitello alla Birbante
(Veal Thief's Style)

Pere della Contessa
(The Countess's Pears)

serves six

Carlo Middione is the chef and co-owner
with his wife, Lisa, of *Vivande*, a high-style
Italian deli and restaurant in San Francisco.
He is the author of *Pasta! Cooking It, Loving
It* (Irena Chalmers, 1982) and *The Food of
Southern Italy* (Morrow, 1987).

*Anniversaries are usually thought of as momentous occasions, whereas, in
reality, they are simply moments of note to revive memories of certain events. In
my case, they are invariably pleasant memories. Weddings come to mind first, but
let us not forget birthdays, graduations, the first solo drive on the freeway without
hitting anything, and so forth.*

*Anniversaries should be shared with others, and that surely means food in one
form or another. Why have a gathering if you can't eat? John Ray, the English
naturalist, said, "Feasting makes no friends." But who could agree with that? I
prefer what Montaigne said in one of his essays: "A feast not profuse but elegant;
more of salt than of expense," salt, in this case, meaning wit and conviviality.*

*The menu that follows is one that is festive but not opulent, ambitious but not
too much, and, above all, delicious. It's the kind of menu that can be used over and
over again, perhaps with a little variation from time to time, if you feel the need.*

BRODETTO DI CARCIOFINI E PASTINA (Little Soup of Baby Artichokes and Tiny Pasta) *serves six*

1 medium yellow onion,
  peeled and diced
  very fine
2 tablespoons extra virgin
  olive oil
8 baby artichokes (or use
  bottoms of larger ones)
2 tablespoons lemon juice
Salt and freshly ground
  pepper to taste
6 cups good quality
  chicken stock,
  preferably homemade
4 ounces pastina (acini
  pepe, riso, orzo, or a
  combination)
1/2 cup small fresh peas
  (or use frozen)
2 large eggs
1/3 cup grated
  Parmigiano-Reggiano
  cheese

Sauté the onion in the olive oil over medium heat until translucent, about 5 minutes, stirring often. Meanwhile, trim the baby artichokes of any tough outer leaves until you see some yellow ones. Dip the artichokes in 2 cups cold water with lemon juice added to keep them from turning black. Cut about 1 inch off the top of each artichoke and trim the bottom and stem. If using only hearts of larger artichokes, clean them of all leaves and the beard and proceed as directed.

Drain the artichokes, pat them dry, and cut them in half the long way. Lay the halves flat and cut across to make slices about 1/8 inch thick. Add them to the onion and stir well. Cook for about 5 minutes, or until tender but not soft. Season with some salt and pepper.

Meanwhile, heat the chicken stock to a simmer. Remove the onion-and-artichoke mixture from the heat and keep warm. Add the pastina to the simmering stock and cook for about 6 minutes, or until the pastina is al dente.

Heat a soup tureen and keep it handy. Add the onion-and-artichoke mixture to the simmering stock and stir well. Add the peas and let cook for about 3 minutes. Break the eggs into a medium dish and whip them with a fork. Add the cheese and continue to whip for a moment more. Pour the hot stock into the tureen and then drizzle the egg-and-cheese mixture over the top to form little "rags." Serve piping hot at once. The soup is delicious served with toasted slices of Italian bread rubbed with raw garlic and drizzled with a bit of extra virgin olive oil.

VITELLO ALLA BIRBANTE (Veal Thief's Style)
serves six

The whimsical name of this dish stems from the wry humor of the Italians, who jokingly say anything this good is even better if you have stolen all the ingredients.

Dredge the veal scallops in the flour and set them aside. Heat the butter and olive oil in a large skillet over medium heat until the butter begins to froth a bit. Sauté the veal scallops 3 or 4 at a time, replenishing the butter and olive oil as needed. Put aside the veal in a warm place, and add all other ingredients except the wine to the pan. Gently sauté the mixture until the pine nuts are just golden. Add the wine and cook 1 to 2 minutes more.

Serve the scallops on hot plates and spoon on some of the sauce. Serve immediately with freshly toasted Italian bread.

18 medium veal scallops, about 2 pounds, pounded to less than 1/4 inch thick
Flour for dredging veal
6 tablespoons unsalted butter
2 tablespoons extra virgin olive oil
2 bay leaves
2 large cloves garlic, peeled and chopped medium coarse
3 heaping tablespoons pine nuts
6 anchovy fillets, minced fine
Salt and freshly ground black pepper to taste
1/2 cup dry white wine

PERE DELLA CONTESSA (The Countess's Pears)
serves six

3 cups dry white wine,
    such as Orvieto or
    Alcamo Blanco
3 cups water
5 ounces granulated sugar
2 bay leaves
2 branches fresh mint, or
    about 10 leaves, plus
    6 more leaves for
    garnish
7 ripe but very firm pears,
    such as Bosc or Comice
1 cup whipping cream
2 tablespoons powdered
    sugar
2 tablespoons dry Marsala
2 tablespoons brandy
3 ladyfingers

Combine the white wine, water, granulated sugar, and herbs in a deep pan that is just big enough to hold the pears, and bring to a simmer. Meanwhile, leave the stems on the pears but peel and core them, scooping out the seed pod from underneath and leaving as much of the fruit as possible intact.

Put the pears upright in the simmering liquid so it reaches their tops. Or you can lay them down if you wish and turn them over from time to time. Simmer for about 15 to 20 minutes, or until the pears are tender but not overcooked and falling apart. Remove them carefully from the liquid and put them on a cooling rack to drain. Refrigerate the pears, covered in plastic wrap, until needed (may be done a day ahead).

Remove the herbs from the liquid and reduce until only 1/2 cup remains. When ready to serve, baste the pears well with the reduced cooking liquid until they glisten.

Whip the cream with the powdered sugar, Marsala, and brandy until it is slightly thick but runny. Finely chop one of the pears, discarding the stem, and fold it into the cream. Finely chop the ladyfingers and fold them in as well.

Nap each plate with some of this sauce and place a pear on it in the center. Garnish the top of each pear with a fresh mint leaf. Serve immediately with a glass of Marsala or some Poire Williams liqueur and additional ladyfingers or plain cookies.

Bradley M. Ogden

A MAY DAY FESTIVAL

Grilled Leeks with Caper Beurre Blanc

Grilled Pacific Salmon with Asparagus and Smoked Bacon–Black Olive Vinaigrette

Herb and Nasturtium Salad

Rhubarb-Strawberry Crisp

serves four

Bradley M. Ogden is a graduate of the Culinary Institute of America in Hyde Park, New York. He was the chef at the *American Restaurant* in Kansas City, Missouri, until 1983, when he came to California to launch the restaurant in San Francisco's *Campton Place Hotel.* He gained a reputation for his inventive treatment of traditional American food and in 1989 became the owner and executive chef of the *Lark Creek Inn,* situated in a redwood grove in Larkspur, California. He is the author of *Breakfast, Lunch and Dinner with Bradley Ogden* (Random House, 1991).

May Day is an age-old custom that has been celebrated in many countries as a spring festival or a time of renewal. The custom of gathering flowers and leaving them on doorknobs can be traced to the Romans, who gathered flowers to honor the goddess of spring.

Each spring, I eagerly look forward to the abundance that the markets will soon be offering. The menu I've suggested is a combination of some of the items that make an early appearance and are a harbinger of the bounty that is to come.

GRILLED LEEKS WITH CAPER
BEURRE BLANC *serves four*

20 small leeks, about
   1/2 inch in diameter
1/4 cup olive oil
Kosher salt and freshly
   ground black pepper

For caper beurre blanc:
1 cup dry white wine
2 shallots, thinly sliced
6 whole black
   peppercorns
1 cup cold unsalted
   butter, cut into
   1/2-inch pieces
2 tablespoons capers,
   coarsely chopped

1 hard-cooked egg
   (optional)
2 tablespoons chopped
   Italian parsley

Remove all wilted or brown outer layers from the leeks. Trim off the roots close to the end of the stalk. Do not trim too closely or the leeks will fall apart when cooked. Cut the leeks to a uniform length, 5 to 6 inches, and split the tops to within 2 inches of the base. Soak in cold water for 5 minutes and then rinse carefully to remove all sand and dirt. Drain.

Blanch the leeks in a large pot of boiling, salted water until the white parts are just tender when squeezed, about 5 minutes. As soon as they are done, submerge the leeks in an ice-water bath until cool; then drain and set aside. The leeks can be covered and refrigerated overnight if necessary.

To prepare the caper beurre blanc, place the wine, shallots, and peppercorns in a small saucepan over medium heat. When the liquid has reduced to about 2 tablespoons, lower the heat and begin whisking in the butter. Add only one piece at a time at first, allowing it to melt before adding the next. After about 1/4 of the butter has gone in and the sauce has started to thicken, the butter can be added more rapidly.

After all the butter has been added, remove from heat and strain through a fine strainer. The sauce can be kept over warm, not hot, water for a few minutes while you are grilling the leeks. Stir in the capers, taste, and add a pinch of salt if needed, just before serving.

To finish the leeks, brush them with olive oil and season with salt and pepper. Grill them

over a hot charcoal fire until browned on
both sides. Serve on a warm platter or individual serving plates. Spoon over them the
warm caper beurre blanc and top with a little
sieved hard-cooked egg and a sprinkling of
chopped parsley.

GRILLED PACIFIC SALMON WITH ASPARAGUS AND SMOKED BACON–BLACK OLIVE VINAIGRETTE *serves four*

Bring a large pot of salted water to a boil.
Drop in the asparagus and cook for approximately 60 seconds, or until barely tender.
Remove and place immediately in an ice-water
bath. When cool, remove from water and
drain.

Coat the asparagus and salmon lightly with
olive oil, and add salt and pepper. Set aside.

In a skillet, cook the bacon until crisp,
retaining the rendered fat. When the bacon
is cooked, reduce heat to low, add the garlic,
shallots, and olives, and sauté until the garlic
is a light golden brown. Remove from heat
and add the vinegar and olive oil. Set aside.

Place the salmon steaks on a hot grill. Cook
for 5 minutes on each side. At the same time,
grill the asparagus, turning the spears until
they are warmed through. Spoon some vinaigrette onto the asparagus.

Arrange the salmon and asparagus on warm
serving plates with the herb and nasturtium
salad. Spoon the vinaigrette over the salmon
and serve immediately.

1 pound medium
asparagus, cut into
5-inch lengths
4 salmon steaks, 1 inch
thick and about
6 ounces each
1/4 cup olive oil
Kosher salt and freshly
ground black pepper

For the vinaigrette:
2 ounces diced smoked
bacon
1/2 teaspoon chopped
garlic
1 tablespoon chopped
shallots
1 tablespoon pitted and
chopped dry-cured
black olives
1/4 cup white wine
vinegar
1/4 cup olive oil

HERB AND NASTURTIUM SALAD *serves four*

1 bunch watercress,
  stems removed
1/4 cup chervil leaves
1/2 cup Italian-parsley
  leaves
1 small bunch chives, cut
  into 3-inch pieces
1/2 cup cilantro leaves
Olive oil, enough to coat
  the leaves lightly
Kosher salt and freshly
  ground black pepper
1/2 cup nasturtium flowers

Toss the leaves and herbs together with a light coating of olive oil. Season with salt and pepper. Arrange on serving plates and sprinkle with nasturtium petals.

RHUBARB-STRAWBERRY CRISP *serves six*

For the topping:
3/4 cup flour
1/3 cup firmly packed
  light brown sugar
1/3 cup granulated sugar
1/4 teaspoon salt
1/4 teaspoon ground
  cinnamon
1/8 teaspoon ground
  ginger
6 tablespoons cold
  unsalted butter

1½ pounds firm, fresh
  rhubarb
1 pint strawberries,
  stemmed and hulled
1/2 cup sugar
2 tablespoons flour

Preheat oven to 400° F.

Prepare the topping by mixing the flour, sugars, salt, and spices together in a medium mixing bowl. Cut in the butter until the mixture resembles coarse meal.

Trim the rhubarb and cut into thick slices, 1/3 to 1/2 inch. If the strawberries are small, leave them whole. Otherwise, cut in half. Toss the fruit in a bowl with the sugar and flour. Pour the fruit into a 9- or 10-inch square baking dish. Sprinkle the topping evenly over the fruit.

Bake in the preheated oven for 25 to 30 minutes, or until the top is browned and the juices are bubbling up around the edge. Remove from the oven and cool for at least 15 minutes before serving.

Serve with vanilla ice cream or whipped cream.

Judith Ets-Hokin

A MOTHER'S DAY BRUNCH

Minted Grapefruit Juice

*Orange Yogurt Pancakes
with Strawberries*

Coiled Bacon

Chocolate Almond Macaroons

serves four

Judith Ets-Hokin is the author of *The San
Francisco Dinner Party Cookbook* (Houghton
Mifflin, 1975) and *The Home Chef: Fine
Cooking Made Simple* (Celestial Arts, 1988).
She is the director and primary instructor of
the *Judith Ets-Hokin Culinary School*, founded
in 1973 with a curriculum for the home chef.

    *Perhaps the best gift for Mother — after the handmade "I love you, Mother"
card — is a home-cooked meal prepared by the kids, with a little help from Dad.*
    *Our menu is traditional with some new additions, like fresh mint in the grape-
fruit juice and yogurt in the pancakes. I've proposed making the pancakes small
because they're easier to turn, and indicated how to twist the bacon into a spiral
because it looks nicer.*
    *Moreover, the recipes are the kind that can be prepared ahead and finished
quickly and easily. The night before, you may wish to set the table, make the
juice, prepare the strawberries and batter for the pancakes, twist and refrigerate the
bacon, and bake the cookies. Be sure, though, to hide the cookies, because you may
have none left for Mother if someone finds them.*
    *Before brunch, pour the juice and cook the bacon while you're making the
pancakes. Then, wake up Mother.*

MINTED GRAPEFRUIT JUICE *serves four*

1/2 cup water
8 fresh mint leaves,
    chopped
1/4 cup sugar
4 cups grapefruit juice
4 mint sprigs for garnish

Combine the water, mint leaves, and sugar in a small saucepan and bring to a boil. Simmer 5 minutes. Allow the syrup to cool, and strain.

Combine the mint syrup and grapefruit juice and chill overnight. To serve, pour the juice into chilled glasses and garnish each with a sprig of mint.

ORANGE YOGURT PANCAKES WITH STRAWBERRIES *serves four*

1 pint basket of
    strawberries, rinsed,
    hulled, and sliced
2 tablespoons sugar
Chopped zest of 1 orange
1/2 cup orange juice
3 tablespoons sugar
3/4 cup plain yogurt
1 large egg
2 tablespoons melted
    unsalted butter
1 cup flour
1 teaspoon baking soda
1/2 teaspoon baking
    powder
1/4 teaspoon salt
4 tablespoons melted
    unsalted butter (for the
    griddle)
4 tablespoons plain yogurt
    for garnish
Warm maple syrup

In a serving bowl, toss the sliced strawberries and sugar.

In a large mixing bowl, combine the orange zest, juice, sugar, yogurt, egg, and butter. Beat until well combined. If you want to do the batter ahead of time, stop here, and combine the dry ingredients just before making the pancakes.

Add the flour, baking soda, baking powder, and salt. Stir until combined. The batter will be thick.

Heat a griddle or large skillet until hot and brush with some melted butter. Spoon the batter onto the griddle, spreading each pancake to form a 3-inch round. Cook the pancakes 1 to 2 minutes each side. Transfer to an ovenproof platter. (This may be done an hour in advance.) Warm the pancakes for 5 minutes in a 350° F oven before serving.

Garnish each serving with yogurt, and pass the strawberries and maple syrup at the table.

COILED BACON *serves four*

Twist the bacon slices into spirals, and arrange them in rows on the rack of a broiler pan. Stick skewers across the ends of the bacon rows, top and bottom, so that the spirals will not untwist while cooking.

Bake in a preheated 375° F oven for 15 minutes, or until crisp. Drain on paper towels. Serve with the pancakes.

12 slices thick-sliced bacon
Wooden or metal skewers

CHOCOLATE ALMOND MACAROONS
makes about three dozen

Whisk the egg whites until foamy. Add the salt, and whisk until soft peaks form. Gradually whisk in the sugar and beat until glossy. Fold in the ground nuts, chocolate, and vanilla.

Drop by rounded teaspoonfuls onto lightly greased baking sheets. Bake in a 300° F oven for 20 minutes, or until lightly browned but still moist in the center. Remove to wire racks to cool.

3 egg whites, at room temperature
Dash of salt
3/4 cup sugar
3/4 cup ground almonds
3 ounces semisweet chocolate, ground
1 teaspoon vanilla

Nathan Peterson

REMEMBERING CATALONIA

*Pan-Seared Calamari with
Lemon, Garlic, and Parsley*

*Green Beans, Oranges, and Mint
with Olive Toasts*

*Mar i Muntana: Prawns and
Chicken with Hazelnuts and
Chocolate*

Plum Sorbet

serves four

Born and raised in food-rich and culturally
abundant Berkeley, Nathan Peterson started
eating, learning, and cooking at an early age
and hasn't stopped. He's traveled extensively
in Europe and is currently the chef at the
Bay Wolf restaurant in Oakland, California.

*This is a perfect meal for anyone who has visited Catalonia and longs to
remember. Or for anyone who wants to be culinarily encouraged to visit for the
first time.*

PAN-SEARED CALAMARI WITH LEMON, GARLIC, AND PARSLEY *serves four*

Have all ingredients ready before beginning. Dry the calamari well on towels. In a large cast-iron pan, heat 2 tablespoons olive oil until almost smoking. Add the calamari and let them brown as much as possible, but don't shake the pan. Stir them around a little until well browned and glazed all over, about 3 minutes in all. Remove from the pan and drain in a colander.

Rinse the pan. Add 1 tablespoon olive oil, and over low heat, sauté the garlic. Add the lemon juice and sherry vinegar. Continue to cook over medium heat until reduced by half. Stir in the extra virgin olive oil.

Return the drained calamari to the pan and toss gently, with the chopped parsley, to reheat. Divide the calamari among 4 plates and garnish with Italian-parsley sprigs and lemon zest.

2 pounds fresh calamari, cleaned, split, and cut on the diagonal
3 tablespoons olive oil
1 tablespoon chopped garlic
2 tablespoons fresh lemon juice
1 tablespoon sherry vinegar
2 tablespoons extra virgin olive oil
2 tablespoons chopped fresh Italian parsley
Italian-parsley sprigs and lemon zest for garnish

GREEN BEANS, ORANGES, AND MINT WITH OLIVE TOASTS *serves four*

1/2 pound green beans
2 oranges, peeled, white
   part removed, and sliced
   into thin rounds
4 fresh mint leaves,
   julienned

For the olive spread:
1 cup black olives
1 teaspoon chopped garlic
1 teaspoon chopped fresh
   oregano
Pinch of red pepper flakes
1 tablespoon olive oil

For the dressing:
2 shallots, finely diced
1/4 cup red wine vinegar
1/4 cup fresh orange juice
1/2 cup olive oil
Salt and pepper to taste

1 baguette of French
   bread for 12 toasts

French the green beans using the end of a potato peeler, or cut lengthwise by hand to achieve a long, thin bean. Blanch the beans in boiling salted water for 2 minutes. Drain and set aside.

To prepare the olive spread, rinse the black olives and chop finely. Add the garlic, oregano, pepper flakes, and olive oil. Toss together and set aside.

Cut the bread diagonally into 1/4-inch slices. Brush the slices with some olive oil. Bake on a sheet pan in a preheated 375° F oven for 8 to 10 minutes, or until lightly toasted.

To make the dressing, combine in a small saucepan the shallots, red wine vinegar, and orange juice. Bring to a boil and reduce by half. Cool the mixture and stir in the olive oil. Season with salt and pepper.

To assemble, divide the olive spread evenly on 12 toasts. Place 3 toasts on each of 4 salad plates. Toss the green beans in the dressing and mound in the center of each plate. Place the orange rounds on each plate, and garnish with the mint.

MAR I MUNTANA: PRAWNS AND CHICKEN WITH HAZELNUTS AND CHOCOLATE
serves four

To make the broth, heat the olive oil in a large saucepan, add the tomatoes and garlic, and simmer until soft and mushy. Add the white wine and cook 2 minutes, then add the chicken stock and simmer slowly for 1/2 hour. Pass the broth through a food mill or strainer and return to the pot. Add the saffron and set aside.

To prepare the picada, grind the toasted hazelnuts fine in a food processor fitted with a chopping blade. Remove the nuts to a bowl. Grind the chocolate and garlic in the processor, and combine with the nuts. Add the chopped herbs and orange zest to the nut mixture and set aside.

In a large casserole, brown the onion lightly in olive oil. Add the prawns and chicken cubes and season with salt and pepper. Add the saffron broth and simmer 2 minutes. Stir in the picada a little at a time. The sauce will begin to thicken. Continue adding the picada until the chicken and prawns are done, about 4 minutes.

Serve the dish with saffron rice and greens.

1 pound prawns, shelled and deveined
1 whole boneless and skinless chicken breast, cut into 1-inch cubes
1/2 white onion, sliced

For the broth:
1 tablespoon olive oil
4 tomatoes, peeled, seeded, and chopped
2 cloves garlic
1/2 cup dry white wine
3 cups chicken stock
Pinch of saffron

For the picada (sauce base):
1/2 cup hazelnuts, toasted, with as much skin removed as possible
2 ounces Ibarra chocolate (available in Latin markets), chopped
3 cloves garlic
1/2 cup finely chopped Italian parsley
1/2 cup finely chopped basil leaves
1/2 teaspoon finely chopped orange zest

PLUM SORBET *serves four*

2/3 cup sugar
2/3 cup water
1¼ pounds ripe plums,
   enough to yield 2 cups
   of plum puree
1 tablespoon lemon juice
1½ teaspoons vodka
   (optional)

Make a simple syrup by combining the sugar and water in a saucepan. Stir over medium heat until the sugar dissolves, then allow to come just to a boil. Remove from the heat and chill thoroughly before adding to plums.

Rinse and dry the plums. Cut in half, discard the pits, and cut the halves into quarters. Place the plums into the work bowl of a food processor and pulse until broken up.

Add the chilled simple syrup to the work bowl and process with the plums until light and smooth. Strain the mixture through a medium sieve and taste before adding the lemon juice. Depending on the variety and ripeness of the plums, you may choose to add more or less lemon juice. The vodka is optional, as it prevents the sorbet from freez-ing completely. Process in an ice-cream maker according to the manufacturer's directions.

Garnish the sorbet with fresh seasonal fruit.

Fred Wertheim

A WEDDING FEAST FOR FIFTY

Passed Hors d'Oeuvres:

Crisped New Potato Skins with
Sour Cream and Golden Caviar

Steak Tartare on Toast Rounds

Belgian Endive Leaves with
Dungeness Crab Legs

Dinner:

Norwegian Smoked Salmon
Tart with Crème Fraîche and
Tobiko Caviar

Roasted Veal Medallions with
Morel Mushroom Sauce

Wild Rice with Currants and
Pine Nuts

Fresh Asparagus in a
Light Butter Sauce

Composed Salad of Limestone
Lettuce and Radicchio with
Citronnade Dressing

St. André and Brie Cheeses
with Melba Toasts and Grapes

Almond Tuile Cups with Bavarian
Cream, Fresh Berries, and
Chocolate Sauce

Wedding Cake of Your Choice

Fred Wertheim has been cooking since he
was fifteen, forty-six years ago. He studied in
the kitchens of the best San Francisco hotels,
including the *Palace, St. Francis, Fairmont,*
and *Mark Hopkins,* at a time when they
engaged some of the world's leading French-
trained chefs. A top San Francisco caterer,
he's run his own company, the *Fred Wertheim
Experience,* since 1975.

*I am happy that I developed my culinary skills using the wonderful fresh
products available in California. Although some parts of chefing are seemingly
mystical, it succeeds when chefs begin with the finest ingredients. Perfection, which
I strive for, can then become one's passion. I am happiest when I create a new dish
and design the presentation artistically. Clearly, people eat with their eyes as well
as their mouths.*

*The menu I devised represents a variety of tastes reflecting the cuisines of the
United States and France, with a touch of Japan, as in the use of Tobiko caviar.
The ingredients can be found in large cities around the country. However, the
recipes may present somewhat of a challenge for the inexperienced cook. Nonethe-
less, they are worth a try, for the end product is truly delicious. Even if a wedding
is not on the horizon, the menu will make an outstanding dinner party.*

CRISPED NEW POTATO SKINS WITH SOUR CREAM AND GOLDEN CAVIAR *makes 100 pieces*

Wash potatoes. Place on a baking pan in a single layer and sprinkle with oil and salt. Bake in a 350° F oven for 45 minutes, until a toothpick inserted in potato meets little resistance. Let cool. Cut potatoes in half and scoop out, using a melon baller. Be sure to leave 1/8 inch of potato next to skin for a potato cup. Fry cups in hot oil until golden brown. Drain on absorbent paper. Season with salt and pepper to taste. Pipe a small amount of sour cream into cup. Spoon a small amount of caviar on top. Serve immediately. These should be eaten hot.

50 small red boiling
  potatoes
Vegetable oil
Salt and pepper
1 pint sour cream
12 ounces golden caviar

STEAK TARTARE ON TOAST ROUNDS
makes 100 pieces

Combine meat, yolks, Worcestershire sauce, oil, and salt and pepper to taste. Form into balls, place on toasted bread rounds, then shape the balls into domes, covering edges of bread rounds. Dent top of each dome with a chopstick, making a small hole, and place in it a caper or chopped onion. They can be refrigerated for several hours before serving.

4 pounds top round steak,
  trimmed of all sinew
  and fat, cut into cubes,
  and finely ground twice
  in a meat grinder.
8 egg yolks
2 ounces Worcestershire
  sauce
1/2 cup extra virgin
  olive oil
Salt and pepper to taste
100 bread rounds, cut 1½
  inches round from a
  quality white bread,
  lightly buttered, then
  baked until crisp in
  275° F oven
Capers and finely
  chopped yellow onions
  for garnish

BELGIAN ENDIVE LEAVES WITH DUNGENESS CRAB LEGS *makes 100 pieces*

12 heads Belgian endive
100 cooked shelled crab
  legs (good luck!)
100 small basil leaves
  for garnish

For basil mayonnaise:
2 egg yolks plus 1 whole
  egg
1 tablespoon lemon juice
2 teaspoons Dijon
  mustard
Pinch of cayenne
Salt and pepper
2 cups light olive oil
1/4 cup packed chopped
  basil

Cut bottom stemlike core off endives. Separate leaves and trim into 3½-inch lengths. Each endive head should yield about 10 useful leaves. Soak in cold water (not iced) overnight in the refrigerator.

To prepare basil mayonnaise, place egg yolks, whole egg, lemon juice, mustard, cayenne, salt, and pepper in bowl of food processor and combine. Drizzle in oil. Fold in chopped basil. Chill overnight.

To assemble, dry the endive leaves. Pipe 1/2 teaspoon basil mayonnaise on bottom half of each leaf. Place a crab leg on the mayonnaise. Garnish with small basil leaves. Serve immediately, as the endive leaves tend to wilt if left out of refrigerator for an hour or so.

NORWEGIAN SMOKED SALMON TART WITH CRÈME FRAÎCHE AND TOBIKO CAVIAR
makes fifty

Form 50 tart shells by pressing circles of puff pastry into 50 4½-inch shallow tart pans. Keep well chilled until ready to bake. Bake until golden, according to pastry manufacturer's instructions. Cool, and carefully remove from pans.

Spoon one scant tablespoon crème fraîche over bottom of each tart shell and spread evenly. Top with red-onion slices and black pepper. Layer salmon slices on top to cover.

Pipe small ring of crème fraîche in center of tart and fill with 1/4 teaspoon Tobiko caviar. For garnish, artistically arrange chives and borage flowers on plate alongside tart. Serve as first course of dinner.

8 pounds puff pastry (available commercially)
2 sides Norwegian smoked salmon (about 2 pounds each), thinly sliced and trimmed of gray fat
1 quart crème fraîche
6 ounces Tobiko caviar
2 medium onions, sliced paper thin
150 fresh chives
100 borage flowers
Black pepper

ROASTED VEAL MEDALLIONS WITH MOREL MUSHROOM SAUCE *serves fifty*

12 ounces dried morels
7 boneless white veal
  rib eyes, about
  2½ pounds each, to
  serve 7-plus
4 large onions, thickly
  sliced
14 long branches whole
  rosemary
1 cup butter
Salt and pepper
3 quarts veal demiglace
  (reduced veal stock)
3 cups Madeira

Soak morels in hot water to cover until tender and clean. Drain and rinse under cold water. Pat dry with paper towels. Cut into bite-sized pieces. Sauté morel pieces lightly in butter.

Place well-trimmed veal rib eyes on sheet pans with scattered sliced onions and rosemary sprigs. Dot veal with butter. Salt and pepper to taste just before roasting.

Roast in 350° F oven for 25 to 30 minutes, until medium rare. Allow veal to rest for 5 minutes prior to carving.

To make sauce, combine demiglace with Madeira over high heat and reduce by half, or until sauce coats back of spoon. Add morels and simmer for 10 minutes.

Cut veal into 1/4- to 1/2-inch slices. Give 2 per serving. Spoon sauce over veal, and be sure that each serving gets some morels. Serve as dinner entrée with wild rice and asparagus.

WILD RICE WITH CURRANTS AND PINE NUTS *serves fifty*

Soak wild rice overnight in water. Toast pine nuts in 300° F oven until golden. Heat Madeira in saucepan and flame off alcohol, then pour over the currants and soak overnight.

Peel shallots, then dice into 1/8-inch pieces and sauté slowly in 1 cup butter until browned and sweet.

About 1½ hours before party, drain rice, then bring to a boil in fresh water for 5 minutes. Drain and repeat. After rice comes to a second boil, cover with chicken stock and return to a boil, then cook slowly in covered pot until grains open, about 45 minutes. Drain thoroughly.

Combine rice with shallots, pine nuts, currants, remaining cup of butter, and salt and pepper to taste. Serve with veal.

This dish can be prepared a day ahead and reheated in a double boiler at serving time.

8 cups long-grain
   wild rice
2 cups pine nuts
1 cup Madeira
1½ cups dried currants
2 pounds shallots
2 cups butter
3 quarts chicken stock
Salt and pepper

ASPARAGUS IN A LIGHT BUTTER SAUCE
serves fifty

150-plus jumbo asparagus
2 cups butter, melted
Salt and pepper

Peel asparagus and tie in bunches of 20. Cook in simmering water until crisp-tender, about 5 minutes. Dress with melted butter, salt, and pepper. Serve 3 per person with veal.

COMPOSED SALAD OF LIMESTONE LETTUCE AND RADICCHIO WITH CITRONNADE DRESSING *serves fifty*

24 heads limestone lettuce
8 heads radicchio

Wash salad greens and dry in a salad spinner. Tear into bite-size pieces.

For citronnade dressing:
2 egg yolks
3 tablespoons Dijon
   mustard
3 tablespoons lemon juice
3 tablespoons white wine
   vinegar
3 cloves garlic, passed
   through a press
2¼ cups light olive oil
Salt and pepper
Pinch of cayenne

To prepare citronnade dressing, place all ingredients, except oil and seasonings, in bowl of electric mixer and combine. Drizzle in oil gradually, beating constantly. Season with salt, pepper, and cayenne to taste.

Add dressing very lightly to greens, and toss. Carefully arrange on salad plates.

ST. ANDRÉ AND BRIE CHEESES WITH MELBA TOASTS AND GRAPES *serves fifty*

Cut baguettes into 1/4-inch slices (yielding approximately 70 slices per loaf). Lightly butter. Toast in 275° F oven until crisp.

Cut cheeses into wedges. Arrange cheese wedges, Melba toasts, and grapes (cut into small bunches) on trays lined with ti leaves (available at florists). The cheese trays should be passed.

3 baguettes of
  French bread
2 cups butter
2 pounds ripened
  St. André cheese
1 kilo (2.2 pounds) wheel
  of perfectly ripened
  Brie cheese
2 pounds red grapes
2 pounds green grapes

ALMOND TUILE CUPS WITH BAVARIAN CREAM, FRESH BERRIES, AND CHOCOLATE SAUCE *makes fifty*

To make almond tuiles, preheat oven to 350° F. Combine all tuile ingredients by hand. Form a smooth paste. Cut parchment paper into 6-inch squares. Place 4 squares on each baking sheet, and place 1 heaping tablespoon of batter in center of each square. Flatten rounds to 3-inch diameter. Bake for 12 minutes, or until cookies are a nice golden

(continued next page)

For almond tuile cups:
4 cups finely ground
  almonds
13 cups sugar
1½ cups unsalted butter,
  softened
1/4 cup plus 1 tablespoon
  flour
1/2 cup milk

Parchment paper

For Bavarian cream:
10½ cups milk
3 cups sugar
36 egg yolks
2 tablespoons vanilla
    extract
1/4 cup Grand Marnier
24 strips of leaf gelatin
1½ cups cold water
7½ cups heavy cream

For chocolate sauce:
8 cups heavy cream
3½ pounds semisweet
    chocolate (preferably
    Belgian), finely
    chopped
Myers's dark rum to taste

4 pints raspberries
4 pints blueberries,
    cleaned
4 pints strawberries,
    cleaned, trimmed, and
    quartered
Mint sprigs for garnish

brown. Let cookies sit for 1 minute. Lift each cookie on its parchment-paper square and mold around an overturned Pyrex custard cup. Remove paper. Remove from mold, as tuile will soon become brittle.

To make Bavarian cream, heat the milk and sugar to a simmer in a saucepan. Whisk egg yolks in a bowl and stir in a little hot-milk mixture. Pour yolks into the saucepan with remaining hot-milk mixture and stir constantly over low heat until custard coats a spoon. Strain custard into a bowl. When cool, add the vanilla and Grand Marnier.

Soften gelatin leaves in a bowl of cold water. When leaves are pliable, squeeze off excess water and place in top of double boiler with 1½ cups water. Heat gelatin and water over simmering water until gelatin is completely dissolved. Stir into custard.

Whip the cream until it holds very soft peaks. Set the bowl of custard over ice and stir constantly. When custard is cool, and of a similar consistency to the whipped cream, quickly whisk it into the cream. Refrigerate overnight.

To make chocolate sauce, heat cream to a simmer. Remove from heat and add chocolate. Stir until smooth. When cool, stir in rum.

To assemble dessert, use 10-inch plates, and ladle 4 tablespoons chocolate sauce onto the center of each plate. Spread sauce to make a larger circle. Place tuile cup in the middle of the sauce. Using a pastry bag fitted with a large star tip, pipe 1/4 cup Bavarian cream into each tuile. Top with a mixture of raspberries, blueberries, and quartered strawberries. Garnish plates with sprig of mint.

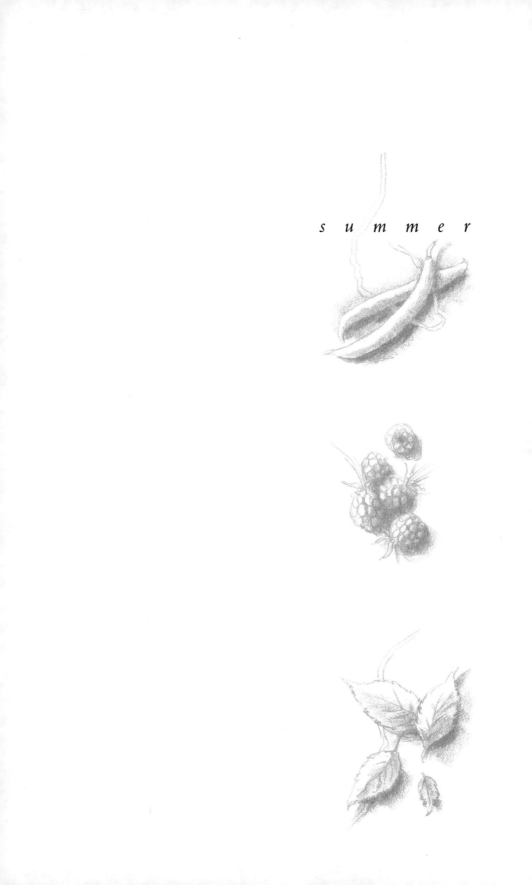

s u m m e r

Cindy Pawlcyn

A JUNE BIRTHDAY BRUNCH

Fraises des Bois with
Crème Fraîche

Buckwheat Crêpes with Ham
Hock and Tomato Ragoût

Arugula and Mâche Salad with
Lemon Balsamic Vinaigrette

Chocolate Pecan Cake with
Chocolate Sauce and
Bourbon Cream

serves eight

Cindy Pawlcyn has worked in restaurant
kitchens since she was thirteen. She resides in
Saint Helena, California, and is executive
chef and part owner of the immensely successful Real Restaurant group, which operates
Mustards Grill and *Tra Vigne* in the Napa
Valley and *Fog City Diner, Rôti,* and *Bix*
in San Francisco.

I chose to do a June birthday brunch party because my birthday is in June,
and we started doing brunch not long ago at Rôti. June is also a perfect month to
take advantage of great seasonal produce. I therefore start my menu with fresh
fraises des bois, the first berries of the season in this area. The wild-strawberry
course should include champagne, and I would recommend Deutz, if possible.

FRAISES DES BOIS WITH CRÈME FRAÎCHE
serves eight

4 cups cleaned fraises
    des bois (wild
    strawberries)
1 cup crème fraîche
8 lime wedges

For crème fraîche:
2 tablespoons buttermilk
1 cup whipping cream

To make crème fraîche, stir buttermilk into cream. Mix well, but do not incorporate air. Cover and let sit in a warm place for 12 hours. Chill. It will thicken as it cools.

Serve the wild strawberries in individual bowls with a dollop or two of crème fraîche and a wedge of lime.

BUCKWHEAT CRÊPES WITH HAM HOCK AND TOMATO RAGOÛT *serves eight*

For crêpes:
2/3 cup all-purpose flour
1/3 cup buckwheat flour
1/4 teaspoon salt
3 eggs
1/4 cup soda water
3/4 cup whipping cream
4 tablespoons melted
    butter
1 tablespoon chopped
    thyme
2 tablespoons finely
    sliced chives
Salt and white pepper

To make crêpe batter, mix together the flours and salt, and work eggs into the mixture. Add alternately the soda water, cream, and melted butter. Mix well. Strain. Add thyme and chives to mixture, and salt and pepper to taste. Let stand overnight. If too thick, correct consistency with more soda water.

Over medium heat, melt some butter in a small sauté pan (nonstick kind works best) or crêpe pan. Coat bottom thinly with crêpe batter. Cook until golden brown. Flip to other side and let it dry out. Store crêpes on a plate between sheets of waxed paper.

To braise ham hocks, sauté vegetables in butter in medium-sized pot, add ham hocks and remaining ingredients, and cover with cold water. Bring to a boil, reduce heat, and let simmer for 1½ to 2 hours, until the meat easily falls from the bone. Remove from heat. When cool enough to handle, remove ham hocks. Strain the braising liquid, degrease, and set aside. Pull meat from ham hocks, discarding bones, fat, and gristle. Shred the meat.

To make the ragoût, melt some butter in a heavy-bottomed pan, and sauté leek and garlic. Add the tomatoes and deglaze. Add the ham, braising liquid, and thyme. Over medium heat, reduce by half. Add remaining butter, pinch of pepper, chives, and parsley. Swirl to incorporate.

Combine cheeses, and place 2 or 3 tablespoons on half of each crêpe. Fold over twice into fourths. Place in lightly buttered skillet and bake in moderately hot oven for three minutes. Use one or two filled crêpes per portion. Place atop ham ragoût on large plate. Garnish with chives.

For braising ham hocks:
1 tablespoon butter
1 onion, quartered
1 tomato, quartered
1 carrot, sliced
1 rib celery, sliced
2 ham hocks
1 clove garlic, crushed
1 sprig thyme
1 bay leaf
2 sprigs parsley
4 peppercorns

For ragoût:
2 tablespoons butter
1 leek, thinly sliced
1 clove garlic, minced
1/2 cup tomato concassé
  (2 tomatoes, skinned,
  seeded, and chopped)
3 to 4 ounces shredded
  braised ham-hock meat
1 to 2 cups ham-hock
  braising liquid
1/2 teaspoon thyme
White pepper
1 tablespoon finely
  sliced chives
1 tablespoon chopped
  parsley

For crêpe filling:
2 ounces Gruyère, grated
2 ounces mozzarella,
  grated
2 ounces chèvre, chopped

ARUGULA AND MÂCHE SALAD WITH LEMON BALSAMIC VINAIGRETTE *serves eight*

3 cups cleaned and dried
   arugula mixed with
   3 cups mâche
   (lamb's lettuce) or
   miner's lettuce

For vinaigrette:
2 tablespoons lemon juice
2 tablespoons balsamic
   vinegar
1 shallot, finely chopped
1/4 teaspoon salt
3/4 cup extra virgin
   olive oil

I suggest making this salad with arugula and mâche, or lamb's lettuce, which is available in a good many produce shops. For even better flavor, I recommend miner's lettuce, a tender green which grows wild in the California coastal woodlands.

To make vinaigrette, mix together first four ingredients. Let rest a couple of minutes. Whisk in oil until it is emulsified. If dressing is made ahead, whisk again before using. Dress the salad greens lightly, with just enough vinaigrette to barely coat the leaves.

CHOCOLATE PECAN CAKE WITH CHOCOLATE SAUCE AND BOURBON CREAM *serves eight to ten*

To make cake, combine butter, chocolate, and bourbon, and melt over hot water. Do not stir. Combine egg yolks and sugar, and beat until light. Add ground pecans, then the melted-chocolate mixture. Mix well. Beat the egg whites with pinch of salt until thick but not dry. Fold together and pour into a greased and floured 9-inch springform pan. Bake in 350° F oven for 25 to 30 minutes until set.

6 tablespoons butter
6 ounces semisweet
  chocolate
1/4 cup bourbon
8 eggs, separated
1 cup sugar
2 cups pecans, finely
  ground
Pinch of salt

For chocolate sauce, heat the cream to boiling in a heavy saucepan. Remove from heat and add chocolate, butter, and kirsch. Stir until smooth. Keep warm.

For chocolate sauce:
1/2 cup whipping cream
8 ounces semisweet
  chocolate, broken up
2 tablespoons butter
1 tablespoon kirsch

For bourbon cream, whisk cream until thick but not stiff. Add sifted powdered sugar and bourbon and whisk to desired thickness.

For bourbon cream:
1 cup whipping cream
1/4 cup powdered sugar
1/2 cup bourbon

Cut cake into 8 or 10 pieces. Cover each piece with chocolate sauce and a generous dollop of bourbon cream.

Timothy P. Maxson, Robert Freitag, and Michael Recchiuti

HERALDING THE SUMMER SOLSTICE

Grilled Moroccan Chicken Breast

Mango-Papaya Salsa

Black Bean and White Corn Salad with a Cumin Vinaigrette

Grilled Marinated Radicchio with Bocconcini

Rosemary Focaccia

Olallieberry Streusel Tart

Chocolate Truffle Shortbread Cookies

serves ten

Timothy P. Maxson is the founding chef of *Taste,* a flourishing San Francisco catering company that he started in 1979. Executive chef Robert Freitag has been with the firm for eight years, and Michael Recchiuti has been the pastry chef for five years.

We planned this menu to herald the summer solstice. Because weddings, anniversaries, and gala celebrations are a continual part of our business, we felt that a casual meal at the start of summer — a more relaxed and carefree time of year for us — was a comforting way to celebrate friendship and beginnings.

GRILLED MOROCCAN CHICKEN BREAST
serves ten

Bone chicken breasts into half breasts with skin on. Warm the oils in a non-aluminum saucepan and add the ground spices. Stir over low heat for a minute and remove from heat. Add the ginger, salt, and lemon juice and let cool. Marinate the chicken breasts in the mixture overnight.

Wipe off the excess marinade and grill the chicken breasts over medium heat, skin side down first, 3 to 5 minutes on each side. Serve warm or at room temperature with mango-papaya salsa.

5 whole chicken breasts
1/4 cup olive oil
1 teaspoon sesame oil
1 teaspoon ground coriander
1/4 teaspoon ground cinnamon
2 teaspoons ground cumin
1/4 teaspoon turmeric
1/2 teaspoon paprika
Pinch of cayenne pepper
1 tablespoon finely chopped ginger
1/2 teaspoon kosher salt
1 tablespoon lemon juice

MANGO-PAPAYA SALSA *yields four cups*

2 large, ripe mangoes
1 large, ripe papaya
3/4 pound ripe tomatoes
3 tablespoons minced
   crystallized ginger
1 jalapeño pepper
1 small red onion
1 small lime
3 tablespoons lime juice
2 rounded teaspoons
   mustard seed
2 rounded teaspoons
   poppy seeds
1/4 teaspoon ground
   cardamom
1 teaspoon ground
   cinnamon
1/4 teaspoon ground
   cloves
1 teaspoon ground
   coriander
2 tablespoons chopped
   parsley
1 teaspoon freshly
   cracked pepper
2 teaspoons kosher salt
3 tablespoons sugar
3 tablespoons champagne
   vinegar

Peel, seed, and cut the mangoes and papaya into 1/4-inch dice. Blanch, peel, seed, and cut the tomatoes into 1/4-inch dice, and place in colander to drain. Seed and mince the jalapeño. Cut the onion into 1/4-inch dice. Peel and finely chop the lime, saving as much juice as possible.

Combine all ingredients, except sugar and vinegar. Add these last, since the amount you will need depends on the sweetness of the fruit. The final mixture should not be too sweet or too soupy. Chill the salsa for several hours to allow the flavors to blend.

BLACK BEAN AND WHITE CORN SALAD WITH A CUMIN VINAIGRETTE *serves ten*

Sort through the black beans for pebbles. Rinse, and soak in water for 5 hours or overnight. Cook the beans in boiling unsalted water until tender but not mushy. Rinse with cold water and set aside.

Sear the chilies over the flame of a gas stove until evenly blackened. Put them in a paper bag and leave in the closed bag for 15 minutes. Peel, seed, and dice the chilies.

Cut the corn off the cob and blanch briefly, for less than a minute. Cool the kernels in cold water and drain well. Chop the scallions and cilantro. Toast and grind the cumin seeds (with a spice grinder or mortar and pestle). Combine the cumin, vinegar, mustard, pepper, and salt in a bowl. Slowly whisk in the oil.

In a large bowl, gently mix the beans, chilies, corn, scallions, cilantro, and cumin vinaigrette. Adjust the seasoning and chill before serving.

3 cups dried black beans
4 Anaheim chilies
4 ears fresh white corn
1 bunch scallions
1 bunch cilantro
1 tablespoon whole
  cumin seed
1/4 cup red wine vinegar
1 teaspoon Dijon mustard
1/2 teaspoon freshly
  ground black pepper
2 teaspoons kosher salt
3/4 cup olive oil

GRILLED MARINATED RADICCHIO
WITH BOCCONCINI *serves eight to ten*

1/3 cup balsamic vinegar
1/3 cup lemon juice
1 tablespoon Dijon
    mustard
2 teaspoons minced garlic
1½ cups olive oil
1 teaspoon kosher salt
1/2 teaspoon freshly
    cracked pepper
4 heads radicchio
1 pound bocconcini
    (small balls of fresh
    mozzarella)

Combine the vinegar, lemon juice, mustard, and garlic. Slowly whisk in the olive oil and season with salt and pepper to taste.

About 30 minutes before grilling, quarter the radicchio and marinate with two-thirds of the vinaigrette. Drain well (reserve the used vinaigrette), and grill over medium to low heat until the radicchio is wilted. After grilling, put the radicchio back in the vinaigrette and let marinate until ready to serve. Just before serving, drain the bocconcini (they come packed in water) and gently toss with the remaining one-third vinaigrette.

Cut the core off the quartered radicchio and arrange the leaves on a platter. Display the bocconcini on top of the radicchio and serve at room temperature. Serve with fresh-baked focaccia.

ROSEMARY FOCACCIA *makes two loaves*

In a large bowl, or the bowl of an electric mixer, combine the warm water, yeast, and sugar, and let proof until foamy. Stir in 1/3 of the flour, the olive oil less 2 tablespoons (reserve for brushing), 1 teaspoon salt, and the rosemary and scallions. Either by hand or in an electric mixer fitted with a dough-hook attachment, gradually incorporate the remaining flour until dough forms a slightly sticky ball (it could require more or less flour). Knead on a floured board until smooth and elastic. Form dough into a ball and let rise in a covered, oiled bowl for about 1 hour, or until dough doubles in size.

Punch down dough and divide into two pieces. Roll into two amoeba-shaped loaves 1/2 inch thick, and place on parchment-lined sheet pans sprinkled with cornmeal. Prick the loaves many times with a fork, brush with olive oil, and sprinkle with remaining salt. Let dough rest for 5 to 10 minutes. Bake in 425° F oven for 20 minutes, or until deep golden brown. Cool bread on racks.

1⅓ cups lukewarm water
2 teaspoons active dry yeast
2 tablespoons sugar
5½ cups all-purpose flour
2/3 cup olive oil
2 teaspoons kosher salt
3 tablespoons finely chopped fresh rosemary
1/2 bunch scallions, finely chopped
3 tablespoons cornmeal

OLALLIEBERRY STREUSEL TART
serves eight to ten

For tart shell:
1/2 cup unsalted butter, softened
1/3 cup sugar
1/8 teaspoon salt
1 egg yolk
1/2 tablespoon heavy cream
1/2 tablespoon vanilla extract
1 tablespoon chopped orange zest
1 cup flour

For tart filling:
2 pints olallieberries
1/4 cup brown sugar
1/2 teaspoon ground cardamom
1/8 teaspoon ground allspice
1 tablespoon cornstarch
1 teaspoon chopped orange zest
1/2 teaspoon vanilla extract

For streusel topping:
1 tablespoon plus 1 teaspoon granulated sugar
2 tablespoons brown sugar
1/4 cup plus 1 tablespoon flour
1 teaspoon ground cinnamon
4 tablespoons unsalted butter, chilled
1/4 cup chopped walnuts

To prepare the tart shell, use an electric mixer fitted with a paddle, and cream the butter with the sugar and salt. With the mixer on slow, blend in the egg yolk, cream, vanilla, and orange zest. With machine running, slowly add the flour until blended. Do not overmix. Wrap dough in plastic and refrigerate for at least 1 hour (or overnight).

Roll out pastry dough into a 12-inch circle. Line a 10-inch fluted tart pan with the pastry dough and chill for 1 hour. Line tart shell with aluminum foil and weight down with beans. Bake in a 325° F oven for 10 minutes, or until light gold. Let cool.

To make the tart filling, combine all the ingredients in a saucepan and mix well. Cook over medium heat until sugar is dissolved. Set aside.

To prepare the streusel topping, combine sugars, flour, and cinnamon. Cut chilled butter into flour mixture with a pastry cutter until crumbly. Toss with the walnuts. Chill for 1 hour.

To finish the tart, fill the partially baked pastry shell with the berry mixture and bake in a 325° F oven for 15 to 20 minutes, or until mixture starts to bubble. Remove the tart from oven and cover with the streusel topping. Return to the oven for 5 to 8 minutes. Cool on a rack.

CHOCOLATE TRUFFLE SHORTBREAD COOKIES *makes twenty-five cookies*

To prepare cocoa shortbread, sift together the flour, cocoa, and salt. Cream the butter and sugar in an electric mixer fitted with a paddle attachment. With the mixer set at slow speed, gradually add the sifted dry ingredients until just mixed. Add the vanilla. The mixture should be soft and malleable. Overmixing will make the dough tough.

On a floured board, roll out the dough to 1/8 inch thick. With a 1½-inch-diameter cookie cutter, cut 50 circles and place them on a cookie sheet lined with parchment paper. Bake in a 300° F oven for about 10 minutes. Cool on a rack.

To prepare the chocolate truffle batter, chop the chocolate into roughly 1/2-inch chunks and place in a large bowl. Cut up the butter and set aside to soften.

In a saucepan, heat the cream and powdered sugar to a rolling boil. Pour the hot liquid over the chopped chocolate and stir until dissolved. Beat in the softened butter and then the brandy and triple sec. Put the truffle batter in the refrigerator until it cools to a piping consistency.

Fill a pastry bag fitted with a medium (#4) star tip with the truffle batter. Pipe a rosette of truffle batter onto a shortbread cookie and gently press another cookie on top. Store in a cool place and dust with cocoa powder just before serving.

For cocoa shortbread:
2 cups all-purpose flour
2/3 cup cocoa powder
1/4 teaspoon salt
1 cup butter, softened
1 cup sugar
1/2 teaspoon vanilla
   extract

For chocolate truffle batter:
1/2 pound semisweet
   chocolate, preferably
   Belgian
1/2 cup unsalted butter
1/3 cup heavy cream
1 cup powdered sugar
1/3 cup brandy
2 tablespoons triple sec

Cocoa powder for dusting

Jane Benet

A REUNION IN JULY

Quail with Sage and Prosciutto

Polenta with Mushroom Sauce

Buttered Red Chard

Green Salad

Russian Cream with Fresh Berries

serves four

Jane Benet was food editor of the *San Francisco Chronicle* for 35 years, until 1988. She and her husband have since settled in Sebastopol in Sonoma County, where they raise their own fruits and vegetables and pursue careers as free-lance writers.

This meal originally served four as a joint birthday celebration in January, when chanterelles went into the mushroom sauce, and the dessert, profiteroles au chocolat, was my husband's birthday cake. It was more recently prepared for a reunion of friends on a cool day in July as the menu above.

If you have a microwave oven, by all means use it to make the polenta, which is lovely and smooth done this way. Otherwise, you have three things cooking on surface burners at one time. The dessert may be made a day ahead and kept in the refrigerator.

Make the mushroom sauce first. It takes the longest to cook. Then get the quail ready to roast and the chard ready to cook, and prepare the salad greens. About 40 minutes before sitting down, put the quail in the oven, make the polenta, and cook the chard. Drain and chop the chard and return it to the pan with a little butter and keep warm.

At serving time, pour the polenta onto the outer edges of a large serving dish, leaving a hollow in the center for the mushrooms. Arrange the quail, feet toward the center, evenly around the plate on top of the polenta. Pour sauce in the center and serve, accompanied by either a full-bodied Chianti or a well-aged Cabernet Sauvignon.

Serve the green salad between the entrée and dessert, dressing the chilled greens with a simple vinaigrette.

MUSHROOM SAUCE *serves four to six*

Put porcini in a bowl, cover with boiling water, and let soak until softened, about 15 to 20 minutes. Drain, reserving the liquid, and slice into long, thin strips. Set aside. Wipe fresh mushrooms with a damp cloth, brush, or paper towel. Remove any tough stems, and slice mushrooms. Leave oyster mushrooms in larger wedge-shaped pieces.

Heat olive oil in a heavy pan. Add garlic. Cook gently for a minute or two, then add all the cut-up mushrooms and stir to coat with oil. Add remaining ingredients, bring to a boil, then reduce heat and simmer, stirring occasionally, for 45 minutes to one hour. If sauce gets too thick, add a little hot water and simmer for a couple of minutes. Serve with polenta.

1 ounce dried porcini mushrooms
6 to 8 fresh shiitake mushrooms
6 to 8 fresh oyster mushrooms
6 to 8 fresh white mushrooms
2 tablespoons olive oil
2 large cloves garlic, minced
Porcini soaking liquid, about 1 cup
1 tablespoon tomato paste
1 cup dry red wine
1 cup chicken stock
Salt and pepper

QUAIL WITH SAGE AND PROSCIUTTO *serves four*

Rinse quail and pat dry with paper towels. Put 1 sage leaf in body cavity of each, then place 1 leaf along breastbone of each bird. Wrap each in a slice of prosciutto, going around the bird from wing to wing, with ends under the bird. Secure with a toothpick if desired. Heat oven to 400° F. Place birds on a rack in a roasting pan, breast side up, and roast for about 25 minutes, depending on size of quail.

8 quail
16 fresh sage leaves (dried will not do)
8 very thin slices prosciutto (preferably imported)

POLENTA IN THE MICROWAVE *serves four*

4 cups cold water
1¼ cups polenta
2 teaspoons kosher salt
3 teaspoons sweet butter
1/8 teaspoon freshly
    ground white pepper

Combine water, polenta, and salt, and cook at full power, uncovered, for seven minutes. Stir well, cover with a paper towel, and cook seven more minutes. Stir again and cook another 3 minutes. Remove from oven and stir in butter and pepper. Let stand five minutes. Stir and serve.

RUSSIAN CREAM *serves four to six*

1 envelope plain gelatin
1/4 cup cold water
1/2 cup sugar
3/4 cup boiling water
1 cup whipping cream
1 cup sour cream
1 teaspoon vanilla
Fresh berries

Soften gelatin in cold water, then add sugar and boiling water and stir until dissolved. Stir in whipping cream and chill until slightly thickened. Add sour cream and vanilla and whisk until bubbly. Pour into a 1-quart mold (preferably a ring mold) and chill until firm, at least 2 hours, or overnight. Unmold and serve with fresh berries. Strawberries are traditional, but ripe loganberries make this a sensational dessert.

Licia De Meo

A SUMMER BIRTHDAY WITH TREASURES OF THE GARDEN AND SEA

Spaghettini with Dungeness Crab, Rock Shrimp, Tomatoes, Corn, and Okra

Sautéed Salmon with Dill, Extra Virgin Olive Oil, and Beet Greens

Boiled Yellow Finn Potatoes

Baked Baby Beets with Sherry Vinegar

Black Mission Figs with Caprino and Taleggio Cheeses

serves six

Licia De Meo has been cooking in various restaurants in the San Francisco Bay area for eleven years. Her background is in traditional southern Italian cuisine with a contemporary California influence. She has been the chef at the *Clement Street Bar and Grill* in San Francisco for four years.

My grandfather Eugenio was a cook aboard the Marco Polo, *an Italian naval submarine, during World War I. Later, as a longshoreman in the Red Hook district of Brooklyn, he spent his Sunday mornings transforming vegetables from his garden and local seafood into festive meals that became prominent in the mythology of his eight children and eighteen grandchildren.*

This menu is in keeping with my grandfather's approach to cooking: revering the treasures of garden and sea.

With this meal, I recommend a dry, elegant white wine, Fiano di Avellino, from the region of Naples, and a Veuve Cliquot 1982 champagne.

SPAGHETTINI WITH DUNGENESS CRAB, ROCK SHRIMP, TOMATOES, CORN, AND OKRA *serves six*

1 pound spaghettini,
  preferably imported
  Italian
1 small red onion, sliced
3 tablespoons fruity
  olive oil
2 cloves garlic, minced
4 small dried red chilies
3 tablespoons chopped
  Italian parsley
3 large ripe tomatoes,
  peeled, seeded,
  and chopped
1/4 pound okra, sliced
  into 1/4–inch rings
Kernels cut from 2 ears
  of corn
1/3 pound rock shrimp
1/4 pound fresh crabmeat
Juice of 1 tart orange or
  Meyer lemon
Freshly ground black
  pepper and sea salt

Bring to a boil 4 quarts of salted water. Add the spaghettini, and stir periodically while cooking. Drain when al dente.

Meanwhile, sauté the onion in olive oil in a 10-inch sauté pan over gentle heat. When the onions are soft, add the garlic and whole chilies. Let cook 2 minutes, stirring once or twice. Stir in the parsley and tomatoes and simmer 12 minutes. Stir in the okra and cook until it turns a bright green. Add the corn and rock shrimp and cook for 2 minutes, circulating all the ingredients around the pan. Add the crabmeat. Squeeze the orange or lemon juice over the sauce. Add a few grinds of pepper and some salt. Gently heat through and toss with the hot spaghettini. Serve immediately.

SAUTÉED SALMON WITH DILL, EXTRA VIRGIN OLIVE OIL, AND BABY BEET GREENS *serves six*

Sauté the beet greens with 2 tablespoons olive oil, the garlic and chili flakes, and salt and pepper to taste. Use low heat, stirring every minute or so. When the greens are tender, add a squeeze of lemon and set aside.

Heat a sauté pan big enough to accommodate the fish. When the pan is quite hot, film the bottom with olive oil. Sprinkle salt on the salmon fillets and place them, rounded side down, in the pan. Sear the salmon over high heat for a few minutes, then lower the flame. Cook until the salmon is a little over halfway done, then turn and cook very briefly. Don't overcook. Watch it closely.

Serve each fillet on a dinner plate on a bed of beet greens. Squeeze some lemon juice over each fillet, then drizzle with extra virgin olive oil and sprinkle with fresh dill. Arrange sliced boiled yellow Finn potatoes and baked baby beets beside the salmon.

3 bunches beet greens, thoroughly washed, stems removed, and cut into 2-by-1-inch ribbons
Olive oil for cooking
1 small clove garlic, chopped
Pinch of chili flakes
Sea salt and freshly ground black pepper
1 lemon
6 salmon fillets, 5 ounces each, at room temperature
Extra virgin olive oil to drizzle over salmon
1/8 cup chopped dill

BOILED YELLOW FINN POTATOES *serves six*

Scrub the potatoes in cool water with a vegetable brush to remove dirt. Cook in salted water to cover, bringing water to a boil, then lowering the heat to a rapid simmer.

Test doneness after 12 minutes by squeezing gently between your thumb and forefinger. If potato yields slightly, remove from heat and drain. Since it continues to cook for a few minutes, let it sit a while before slicing and arranging on the salmon plate.

18 small yellow Finn potatoes
Salted water

BAKED BABY BEETS WITH
SHERRY VINEGAR *serves six*

6 baby golden beets
6 baby red beets
6 baby Chiogga beets
Sea salt
Sherry vinegar

Cut tops off beets. Scrub well with cool water and a vegetable brush. Put a single layer in a baking dish. Cover with water. Add 1 tablespoon sea salt and a good splash of sherry vinegar. Cover with foil and bake in a 400° F oven until tender and skins slip off easily. Drain off the water. Peel and keep warm until serving time. Arrange on plate with salmon.

BLACK MISSION FIGS WITH CAPRINO
AND TALEGGIO CHEESES *serves six*

12 fresh Black Mission figs, stems removed, and cut in half
4-ounce wedge of Caprino
4-ounce wedge of Taleggio

Caprino is a soft, creamy Italian goat cheese, and Taleggio, made from cow's milk, is a dessert cheese from Lombardy. They're ideal with fresh figs.

On a serving platter, arrange the fig halves around the two wedges of cheese. Pass it around the table.

Michel Laurent

A NOSTALGIC DINNER
IN THE COUNTRY

Cold Vichyssoise à Ma Façon

Warm Fall Salad with Goose Liver,
Lobster, and Apples

Noisettes of Veal with Chanterelles

Charlotte with Pear

serves six

Michel Laurent embarked on his career in
French cuisine in his native Reims, where he
served his apprenticeship at *La Chaumière*. In
Paris, he worked as chef at *Le Café de la Paix*
and *Maxim's* and operated his own restaurant,
Le Dômarais. Since 1986, he has been the chef
and co-owner with Joel Coutre of *Le Piano
Zinc* in San Francisco.

*A chef's life provides so few diversions that I usually spend the little free time
I have cooking for friends in the country. I particularly enjoy relaxing at a friend's
house where one can eat outdoors under an arbor of bougainvillea.*

*I sometimes fix a meal like this, made up of dishes that bring back happy
memories for me as a chef. I first made the vichyssoise at the* Normandie *restaurant in Deauville. The salad is my own invention. I did the veal noisettes at*
Maxim's *in Paris and the pear charlotte when I was an apprentice at* La
Chaumière *in Reims.*

COLD VICHYSSOISE À MA FAÇON *serves six*

1 tablespoon butter
4 leeks, cleaned and sliced
2 large potatoes, peeled
and sliced
2 cups heavy cream
Salt and white pepper
2 tablespoons thinly
sliced chives

Heat the butter and a tablespoon of water in a large pan, add the leeks and potatoes, and cook until the leeks are translucent. Add 2 quarts of water, and cook at a simmer for 45 minutes.

Transfer mixture in stages to a blender, and blend well. Strain through a china cap or sieve. Place in a mixing bowl over a larger bowl of ice. When cool, stir in the cream. Season with salt and pepper to taste. Serve with a garnish of chives.

WARM FALL SALAD WITH GOOSE LIVER, LOBSTER, AND APPLES *serves six*

10 ounces fresh goose liver, cut into 1/2-inch slices
2 apples, peeled and cut
into julienne-style strips
2 lobsters, 1½ pounds
each, blanched,
meat removed
and thinly sliced
1 medium shallot,
chopped
2 tablespoons sherry
4 cups mixed baby
lettuces, cleaned

For vinaigrette:
1 tablespoon red wine
vinegar
1/2 cup vegetable oil
Salt and pepper to taste
2 tablespoons chopped
chervil for garnish

Sauté goose liver in a skillet (without oil) for 1 minute each side. Remove to a plate and keep warm.

Sauté apple pieces in same skillet for 2 minutes. Remove and set aside.

Sauté lobster in same skillet for 1 minute. Remove and set aside.

Sauté chopped shallot in same skillet for 1 minute. Deglaze skillet with sherry.

Whisk together vinaigrette ingredients. Place lettuces in a large bowl. Toss with vinaigrette. Divide between six plates. Arrange goose liver, lobster, and apple on top. Spoon pan juices with shallot over salad. Garnish with chopped chervil.

NOISETTES OF VEAL WITH CHANTERELLES
serves six

Trim veal and cut into 1½-inch medallions. Heat butter in a large skillet, and sauté veal medallions, seasoned with salt and pepper to taste, about 5 minutes on each side. Remove to a warm plate.

Add chanterelles to the skillet and sauté 1 minute. Deglaze skillet with the cream. Add the dijon mustard, and simmer 1 minute.

Place veal on plates, with chanterelles and sauce on top. I suggest serving with a puree of carrots.

1 veal loin, or fillet, about two pounds
2 tablespoons butter
Salt and pepper
1 pound fresh chanterelle mushrooms, cleaned and, if large, cut up
1 cup heavy cream
1 tablespoon Dijon mustard

CHARLOTTE WITH PEAR *serves eight*

6 medium pears, peeled,
　halved, and cooked
　in water with 3
　tablespoons sugar until
　soft
2 dozen ladyfingers
1/3 cup apricot jelly,
　heated
8 egg yolks
1 cup plus 2 tablespoons
　sugar
2 cups milk
1 tablespoon gelatin
2 cups heavy cream,
　whipped soft
9-inch springform pan, or
　charlotte mold, lined
　with plastic wrap

When pears are cool, slice each half into six pieces. Set aside. Brush one side of ladyfingers with warm apricot jelly. Stand them close together against side of springform pan. The jelly will help them stand straight. Set aside.

Combine egg yolks and sugar. Bring milk to a boil. Add hot milk slowly to yolk mixture. Cook in a double boiler over simmering water until mixture is thick. Add gelatin and stir well. Cool over a bowl of ice.

Fold in whipped cream. Pour half of cream mixture into prepared springform pan. Arrange pear slices on top. Pour rest of mixture on top of pears. Chill for 2 hours. If you wish, decorate top of charlotte with fresh raspberries. Unmold and slice.

Rick Cunningham

AN INDEPENDENCE DAY DINNER

Tropical Fruit Punch and Rum Smoothies

Spiced Almonds

Assorted Cheeses, Fruits, and Vegetables with Lemon Dip

Seedy Breadsticks

Gazpacho with Roasted Cumin, Yogurt, and Avocado Slices

Grilled Chicken Breast with Red Pepper-Corn Sauce

Penne, Roma Tomato, and Basil Salad with Asiago

Peach and Mixed Berry Cobbler

serves six

A native of the Bay Area, Rick Cunningham studied home economics at Chico State College and was the regional chef for the *California Cafe* chain prior to assuming his present post in 1986 as the chef at *Ivy's* restaurant in San Francisco.

This menu for an Independence Day dinner came to mind as I was considering the ethnic diversity of our country. I decided to choose ingredients and spices which have their beginnings in other lands and are currently finding great success among American chefs. This resurgence of ethnic foods and flavors has found a home under the heading of New American Cuisine.

By choosing to develop an extensive menu for the occasion, I can give my guests the opportunity to sample the cultures and traditions of many people and lands. This, to me, seemed the perfect time to honor our neighbors and friends.

TROPICAL FRUIT PUNCH AND RUM SMOOTHIES *makes five quarts*

1 cup sugar
1½ cups lemon juice
1½ cups grapefruit juice
5 cups orange juice
6 cups unsweetened
  pineapple juice
2 cups apricot juice
3 cups cranberry juice
2 pints strawberries,
  hulled
10 kiwis, peeled and sliced
3 cups ginger ale
1 papaya, peeled, seeded,
  and diced
2 bananas, peeled just
  before using
1 pineapple, peeled,
  cored, and diced
Mint leaves
Crushed ice
1 pint rum
1 pint heavy cream

Make a simple syrup by boiling 1 cup sugar and 1 cup water for 5 minutes. Let cool. Mix together the fruit juices and chill overnight.

Make a strawberry-kiwi ice mold for the punch by placing some of the strawberries and sliced kiwis in a Jell-O mold with water. Freeze overnight. To assemble the punch, place the ice mold in a serving bowl. Add fruit juices and ginger ale. Garnish with mint leaves.

To make rum smoothies, ladle some punch into a blender with crushed ice, fresh fruit of choice, and 1½ ounces rum and 1½ ounces cream per drink. Blend until smooth.

SPICED ALMONDS *makes four cups*

4 tablespoons peanut oil
4 cups whole almonds
3/4 cup plus 2 tablespoons
  sugar
2 teaspoons salt
1 tablespoon ground
  cumin
1½ teaspoons red pepper
  flakes

Heat the oil in a large, heavy-bottomed sauté pan over medium-high heat. Add almonds and stir to cover completely with oil. Sprinkle on 3/4 cup sugar and continue stirring until the sugar caramelizes and coats the almonds.

Place the almonds in a bowl and toss with salt, cumin, red pepper flakes, and remaining 2 tablespoons sugar. Spread out on a cookie sheet and let cool. Don't touch. They're hot!

ASSORTED CHEESES, FRUITS, AND VEGETABLES WITH LEMON DIP
serves six or more

Cut off the pineapple top and place in the center of a large tray or cutting board. Decorate pineapple top with small flags and summer flowers. Peel, core, and slice pineapple. Arrange slices in a spiral from the center out. Arrange cheeses, fruits, and vegetables around pineapple slices. Garnish with fresh herbs and mint.

To make lemon dip, mix together ingredients and place in a serving dish.

1 pineapple
Assorted cheeses such as
  herbed Brie, spiced
  Havarti, or goat
  cheddar
Hulled strawberries,
  melon slices and pitted
  plums, nectarines and
  apricots
Blanched baby carrots,
  asparagus, and baby
  Blue Lake string beans
Fresh herbs and mint
  leaves for garnish

For lemon dip:
3/4 cup plain yogurt
3/4 cup sour cream
1/2 cup finely ground
  toasted pecans
Juice and zest of 1 large
  lemon
Pinch of salt
1/8 teaspoon freshly
  ground black pepper

SEEDY BREADSTICKS *makes five to six dozen*

1/4 cup warm water
  (105°-115° F)
1 package active dry yeast
Pinch of sugar
Olive oil
6 scallions, sliced
2 jalapeño peppers,
  seeded and
  finely chopped
1 tablespoon finely
  chopped oil-packed
  sun-dried tomato
2 teaspoons chili powder
1 cup milk
1/2 cup unsalted butter
1 cup yellow cornmeal
2 eggs
1½ teaspoons salt
3½ to 4 cups unbleached
  all-purpose flour
1½ cups grated garlic-
  flavored jack cheese
1 egg beaten with
  2 teaspoons water
  for egg wash
1/2 to 1 cup each, cumin
  seeds, fennel seeds, and
  sesame seeds

Place warm water in a small bowl. Stir in yeast and sugar. Let stand for 15 minutes.

In a sauté pan, heat 1 tablespoon olive oil over medium heat. Add the scallions, jalapeños, and sun-dried tomato, and cook for 10 to 15 minutes. Add chili powder and place mixture in a large bowl.

Heat the milk and butter until butter melts. Stir into scallion mixture.

With your fingers, washed, stir in the corn-meal, eggs, salt, yeast mixture, and 2 cups flour. Add jack cheese and enough flour so dough pulls away from side of bowl. Knead dough on flat surface for 10 minutes, adding flour if dough is sticky.

Coat a bowl with olive oil. Place dough in bowl and roll until completely coated with oil. Cover with a damp towel, set in a warm place, and let rise for 1 hour. Punch down and let rest for 5 minutes.

Break off small pieces of dough and roll out until approximately 8 to 10 inches long and 1/2 inch in diameter. Place on greased sheet pan and let rise for 45 minutes.

Preheat oven to 400° F. Brush breadsticks with egg wash. Sprinkle with fennel, sesame, and cumin seeds. Bake for 12 to 15 minutes. Let cool.

Can be prepared a day ahead and stored in an airtight container at room temperature until serving time.

GAZPACHO WITH ROASTED CUMIN, YOGURT, AND AVOCADO SLICES
serves six to eight

In a large bowl, mix together garlic, cucumber, red and yellow peppers, jalapeños, onion, tomatoes, Bloody Mary mix, tomato juice, lime juice, and olive oil. In a blender, puree half the mixture and return to the bowl with remaining half. Season with salt, pepper, and 1 tablespoon cumin. Chill for 24 hours, and adjust seasoning, if necessary, with salt, pepper, and cumin.

Mix 1 teaspoon cumin with yogurt and place in squeeze bottle (can be done previous day).

To serve, scoop out avocado slices from shell with large spoon and place 1 or 2 slices in each bowl of gazpacho. Squeeze design over top with squeeze bottle and serve.

1 tablespoon minced garlic
1 large cucumber, peeled, seeded, and diced small
1 red pepper, seeded and diced small
1 yellow pepper, seeded and diced small
3 jalapeño peppers, seeded and chopped
1 medium red onion, diced small
6 ripe large tomatoes, peeled, seeded, and diced
3 cups Bloody Mary mix
3 cups tomato juice
1/2 cup fresh lime juice
1/2 cup olive oil
Salt and freshly ground black pepper
2 tablespoons roasted cumin seeds, finely ground
1 cup low-fat yogurt
2 avocados, pitted and sliced in the peel

GRILLED CHICKEN WITH RED PEPPER-CORN SAUCE *serves six*

3 whole chicken breasts,
    preferably free-range
1/2 cup light olive oil
1 tablespoon minced
    garlic
2 to 3 tablespoons fresh,
    finely chopped
    lemon thyme
1 lime, sliced

For red pepper-corn sauce:
1/2 cup olive oil
8 red peppers, cored,
    seeded, and cut into
    1/2-inch dice
8 cloves garlic, cut in half
    lengthwise
2 tablespoons balsamic
    vinegar
1 tablespoon sugar
Pinch of red pepper flakes
Salt and freshly ground
    pepper
2 cups fresh corn kernels
3 tablespoons chopped
    oil-packed sun-dried
    tomatoes
20 fresh basil leaves

Rinse and split chicken breasts in half, remove bones and gristle, and trim excess skin and fat. Mix oil, garlic, lemon thyme, and lime slices, and coat chicken breasts. Marinate overnight.

To prepare red pepper-corn sauce, heat oil in a large sauté pan, add red peppers and garlic, and sauté for 5 minutes. Stir in vinegar, sugar, red pepper flakes, and salt and pepper to taste. Continue cooking for 15 minutes, stirring occasionally. Add corn, sun-dried tomatoes, and basil. Simmer 10 minutes. Serve hot.

Fire up charcoal at least 1 hour in advance of grilling time. Wipe excess marinade from chicken breasts, place on grill, and cook 6 to 7 minutes on each side. Be careful not to overcook. Serve topped with red pepper-corn sauce.

PENNE, ROMA TOMATO, AND BASIL SALAD WITH ASIAGO *serves six to eight*

Combine the tomatoes, goat cheese, garlic, basil, olive oil, 1/2 teaspoon salt, and pepper in a large bowl. Prepare at least 2 hours ahead, or the day before. If made the day before and refrigerated, bring back to room temperature before adding pasta.

Bring 5 quarts of water to a boil with dash of oil and 2 teaspoons salt. Add penne and cook until tender. Drain and toss with tomato-basil mixture. Serve at once with asiago.

8 Roma tomatoes, quartered
8 ounces goat cheese, crumbled
1 tablespoon minced garlic
1 cup basil leaves, julienned
1 cup olive oil
2½ teaspoons salt
1/2 teaspoon black pepper
1½ pounds penne
2 cups freshly grated asiago cheese

PEACH AND MIXED BERRY COBBLER
serves twelve

6 medium peaches
1/2 pint raspberries
1/2 pint blueberries
1/2 pint olallieberries
1/4 cup sugar

For cobbler batter:
1/2 cup unsalted butter, at
    room temperature
3/4 cup sugar
1 large egg, lightly beaten
1½ cups cake flour
2 teaspoons baking soda
1 teaspoon cream of tartar
1 teaspoon salt
1/2 cup buttermilk, room
    temperature

2 cups heavy cream,
    whipped (with a little
    powdered sugar and
    vanilla, if desired)

This is a version of Jim Dodge's cobbler, from his book, *An American Baker.*

Wash and dry the peaches. Split and discard pits. Cut each peach into chunks. Toss peaches with berries and sugar. Place in 2½-quart baking dish. Press down fruit to pack it in.

To prepare cobbler batter, beat the butter in an electric mixer fitted with a paddle. Slowly add sugar and continue beating for 10 minutes. Add the egg and beat well.

Combine flour, baking soda, cream of tartar, and salt. When the butter-sugar mixture is light, add a third of the flour mixture. Mix until smooth.

Turn off mixer and scrape down sides of bowl with a spatula. On low speed, add half the buttermilk, then a third of the flour mixture, rest of buttermilk, and rest of flour mixture. Mix until smooth after each addition, scraping sides and bottom of bowl several times. The mixture should be smooth and form a ribbon when paddle is removed.

Drop the batter in ribbons on top of the fruit until the whole surface is covered, except for a 1-inch strip around the edges. Do not spread the batter.

Bake in a 375° F oven for approximately 45 minutes, until the top is golden brown. It should be springy when touched, and there should be no wet batter under the crust.

Serve warm with whipped cream.

Rob Zaborny, Karen Smithson, and Patricia Unterman

A FOURTH OF JULY PICNIC

Patty's Cole Slaw

Rob's Baked Beans

Rob's Barbecued Chicken

Nora Belle Durbin's Corn Bread

Karen's Pecan Shortcakes with Peaches, Blackberry Sauce, and Crème Fraîche Ice Cream

serves twelve

The menu is a collaboration by the chefs at the *Hayes Street Grill* in San Francisco. Patricia Unterman is also co-owner of the restaurant and writes regularly about restaurants for the *San Francisco Chronicle*. She has co-authored four editions of the restaurant guide *Restaurants of San Francisco* for Chronicle Books.

Cooks rarely get a day off together, but the Hayes Street Grill *has always closed on the Fourth of July. For years, we communally ferried a picnic to Angel Island in San Francisco Bay. Then followed several baseball game-picnics, and last year we all went to Carmenet Vineyard in Sonoma. What doesn't change, year after year, is our favorite picnic dishes. We like the food to be American and hearty, easily transported and served.*

The method behind the barbecued chicken is worth some proselytizing because it produces smoky, crusty, tender, cooked-through chicken without charring it. Rob Zaborny, our kitchen manager, came up with the definitive recipe and sauce over the years, culminating in the preparation of four hundred quarters of barbecued chicken for box dinners prepared for AID and COMFORT II, the fund-raiser held in Berkeley.

Karen Smithson, our pastry chef, always drawn to new ways of putting seasonal fruits on the table, uses this shortcake recipe with endless variations. The simple cole slaw and cornbread recipes are respective family favorites of mine and Jacquelyn Buchanan, our executive chef. Rob's baked beans have more flavor than any I've tasted and are delicious just warm.

We guarantee the success of this picnic, any time of the year, indoors or out.

— Patricia Unterman

PATTY'S COLE SLAW *serves twelve*

1 large, heavy head of
  green cabbage
1 medium, heavy head
  of red cabbage
3 large carrots
1½ bunches scallions

For dressing:
2 cups mayonnaise,
  preferably homemade
2 cups yogurt
2 tablespoons malt or
  cider vinegar
1 teaspoon kosher salt
2 tablespoons prepared
  horseradish
1/4 cup light brown sugar,
  lightly packed

Cut cabbages in quarters, remove the cores, and thinly slice cabbages into shreds. Peel carrots and grate on the biggest holes of a box grater. Finely chop the white and green parts of the scallions. Toss all these ingredients together in a large bowl.

Put mayonnaise and yogurt in another bowl. Whisk in remaining ingredients. (If you use commercial mayonnaise, you may have to add more vinegar.) Pour over the vegetables and toss thoroughly.

ROB'S BAKED BEANS *serves twelve*

Soak lima beans overnight in water in a big pot or bowl.

Preheat oven to 375° F. Heat the olive oil in a large casserole. Add the bacon and sauté until some fat is rendered. Add the onions and garlic and sauté until translucent.

Drain the lima beans and add to the casserole with the rest of the ingredients. Stir well. Bring to a simmer and bake, covered, for 2 to 2½ hours. Adjust the salt when beans are cooked.

6 cups dried lima beans
18 cups water
1/4 cup olive oil
1/2 pound thickly sliced bacon, diced
3 cups chopped onion
6 cloves garlic, chopped
1 teaspoon salt
1 teaspoon freshly ground black pepper
2 tablespoons fresh thyme, finely chopped
6 cups canned Italian tomatoes, drained and pureed
1/4 cup Dijon mustard
2/3 cup brown sugar
8 cups chicken stock

ROB'S BARBECUED CHICKEN *serves twelve*

3 chickens, about
   3 pounds each

For marinade:
2 sprigs rosemary,
   finely chopped
Juice of 2 lemons
2 teaspoons kosher salt
2 teaspoons freshly
   ground black pepper
8 cloves garlic, thinly
   sliced
2 cups olive oil

For barbecue sauce:
4 cups ketchup
1 tablespoon curry
   powder
2 teaspoons cumin
1 teaspoon cayenne
2 tablespoons red wine
   vinegar
1 tablespoon
   Worcestershire sauce
1 teaspoon chopped garlic
4 tablespoons brown sugar
1 heaping teaspoon
   chopped rosemary
3 tablespoons unsalted
   butter

Wash and quarter the chickens. Pat dry. In a large bowl, combine the rosemary, lemon juice, salt, pepper, and garlic. Whisk in the olive oil. Toss chicken in the marinade and refrigerate overnight.

To prepare barbecue sauce, combine ingredients in a saucepan and cook over moderate heat for 30 minutes. Stir occasionally.

Preheat oven to 400° F. Remove chicken quarters from marinade and roast for 20 minutes. Toss warm chicken in barbecue sauce and let cool. Then, at the picnic site, heat a grill until the coals are completely red. Cook chicken over red coals until heated through and the skin becomes crusty, brushing with barbecue sauce at the end. The barbecue sauce can be warmed on the grill in a small metal bowl or saucepan.

NORA BELLE DURBIN'S CORN BREAD
serves twelve

The corn bread recipe came from chef Jacquelyn Buchanan's great-aunt and is therefore named for her.

Preheat oven to 350° F. Butter an 11-by-13-inch baking pan.

Mix the dry ingredients in a large bowl. Stir in the wet ingredients.

Transfer the batter to greased baking pan. Bake for 25 minutes, or until a toothpick comes out clean when stuck in the middle of the corn bread.

2 cups all-purpose flour
2 cups stoneground cornmeal
2 teaspoons salt
2 tablespoons baking powder
1/2 cup sugar
2 cups buttermilk
1/2 cup vegetable oil
2 large eggs

KAREN'S PECAN SHORTCAKES WITH PEACHES, BLACKBERRY SAUCE, AND CRÈME FRAÎCHE ICE CREAM *makes twelve*

To prepare the shortcakes, preheat oven to 425° F. Mix together the flour, sugar, and baking powder.

Cut in the butter until the largest pieces are the size of dried peas. (This can be done with two knives, in a food processor, or by rubbing the mixture with your fingers.) Stir in the chopped pecans, then the whipping cream. Knead the dough gently just until it comes together.

Roll out the dough to 3/4 inch thick, and cut 12 circles, using a sharp biscuit cutter or knife. The leftover dough can be gathered and rolled a second time.

(continued next page)

For shortcakes:
3 cups all-purpose flour
6 tablespoons sugar
4½ teaspoons baking powder
3/4 cup unsalted butter, cut into 1/2-inch dice
1 cup chopped pecans
1½ cups whipping cream

For crème fraîche ice cream:
1 quart whipping cream
1/4 cup buttermilk
2 vanilla beans, split lengthwise
3/4 cup sugar
8 egg yolks

For peaches:
2 quarts peeled and
    sliced peaches
1/2 cup sugar

For blackberry sauce:
3 cups blackberries
1/4 to 1/2 cup sugar

Place on an unbuttered sheet pan and bake for 15 to 20 minutes, until shortcakes are lightly browned and cooked through.

To prepare the crème fraîche, stir the cream and buttermilk together in a bowl. Cover and let stand at room temperature for 1 or 2 days, until it is the consistency of pudding. Refrigerate the crème fraîche until ready to make the ice cream.

To prepare the ice cream, scrape the vanilla beans and place in a nonreactive saucepan. Add the crème fraîche and sugar and heat to scalding. Remove from heat, cover, and allow to stand for 30 minutes while vanilla infuses. Reheat to scalding.

In a bowl, whisk the egg yolks while slowly adding about 1 cup of the hot cream mixture. Transfer the egg-yolk mixture to the saucepan and cook over low heat, stirring constantly, until the mixture thickens and coats the back of a spoon. Strain into a bowl. Cover and chill. Freeze in an ice-cream maker according to manufacturer's instructions. Makes approximately 1½ quarts.

To prepare the peaches, toss sliced peaches with sugar. If the peaches are very sweet or tart, adjust the amount of sugar.

To prepare the blackberry sauce, purée the berries with 1/4 cup sugar in a food processor. Taste and add more sugar if needed. Strain through a fine sieve to remove the seeds.

For final assembly, spread 3 tablespoons blackberry sauce on each plate. Split the shortcake in half crosswise and place the bottom half on top of the sauce. Place a scoop of ice cream on the shortcake. Spoon the peaches over the ice cream. Set the top of the shortcake off-center, like a little beret.

Alain Rondelli

A BASTILLE DAY DINNER

Crispy Polenta Tomatoes

*Pan-Roasted Veal Chops with
Potato-Sorrel Coulis*

*Warm Berry Mousse in Phyllo
Carnations with Mascarpone Sorbet*

serves four

Alain Rondelli was born in Tournant-en-Brie, outside Paris, and was barely out of his teens when he served as a chef for French president Valéry Giscard d'Estaing at the Palais de l'Elysée. He moved on to become the first assistant to Marc Meneau at his three-star restaurant, *L'Espérance*, in Saint-Père-sous-Vézelay in northern Burgundy. He came to the United States on cooking tours with Meneau, and then settled in San Francisco, where he is currently the executive chef at *Ernie's*.

With the onset of summer, we flock to the countryside for family celebrations. Strawberries, cherries, raspberries, and other red fruits of the season bring smiles to children's faces. And there is that fabulous sensation of biting right into the juicy flesh of apricots and peaches.

The warm weather invites us to eat vegetables, salads, and fresh herbs. Vibrant green and firm, the herbs of this season are perfect, almost unreal. We dine on a sunny terrace in the shade of a cherry tree. Fish and light meats are the centerpiece of our summer feast.

Then comes Bastille Day, the 14th of July, a celebration of freedom, with a bright show of fireworks. And we enjoy ourselves with more wonderful food, like the menu I present here.

CRISPY POLENTA TOMATOES *serves four*

For the polenta crust:
1/3 cup polenta
1/4 cup grated Parmesan
   cheese
2 cloves garlic, finely
   chopped
Coarse salt to taste

8 medium Roma
   tomatoes, ripe and firm
1 goat cheese, 11 ounces
3 tablespoons olive oil

To finish the dish:
2 tablespoons balsamic
   vinegar (the older, the
   better)
4 tablespoons extra virgin
   olive oil
2 tablespoons fresh
   chervil
2 tablespoons fresh chives,
   cut into 1-inch lengths
2 tablespoons fresh basil
   leaves, julienned
Salt and freshly ground
   pepper

This dish must be prepared at the last minute in order to preserve the crisp texture of the polenta crust.

Mix the polenta, Parmesan, garlic, and salt in a bowl. Set aside. Wash and dry the tomatoes. Cut them crosswise into even slices about 1/2 inch thick and set aside on a plate. Cut the goat cheese into 1/4-inch slices and set aside.

Just before serving, dip each tomato slice into the polenta mixture, evenly coating each side. In a medium sauté pan, heat the olive oil for 2 to 3 minutes over medium heat. Slide the tomato slices into the pan and cook for 2 to 3 minutes on each side, until both sides are golden brown.

Distribute the tomatoes on plates and drizzle evenly with balsamic vinegar and extra virgin olive oil. Arrange the goat-cheese slices attractively with the tomatoes and sprinkle generously with the herbs. Season with salt and pepper to taste.

PAN-ROASTED VEAL CHOPS WITH POTATO-SORREL COULIS *serves four*

To prepare the potato-sorrel coulis, wash the potato, wrap it in aluminum foil, and bake in a 350° F oven for 45 to 50 minutes. To test for doneness, pierce with a small knife. You should feel no resistance. Peel the potato and press it through a sieve to purée it. While the potato is still hot, add the milk and olive oil. The purée should have a slightly liquid consistency, so that it coats the back of a spoon. Set aside.

For the potato-sorrel coulis:
1 Idaho potato
1/2 cup milk
1 cup olive oil (not extra virgin, which would make the coulis too thick)
7 ounces (about 4 bunches) sorrel
Salt and pepper

To pan-roast the veal chops, heat the butter and vegetable oil for 1 to 2 minutes in a large sauté pan over medium heat. Place the chops in the pan, season lightly with salt and pepper, and cook for 4 to 5 minutes on each side. Remove to a plate and keep warm in a very low oven, 100° to 120° F.

4 large veal rib chops, 12 to 14 ounces each
1 tablespoon butter
3 tablespoons vegetable oil
Salt and pepper

To prepare the veal juice, pour the cooking fat from the pan. Add the onion and garlic and sauté until golden, then add the thyme, bay leaf, and veal stock. Cook over medium heat until reduced by two-thirds. Strain the juice through a sieve into a bowl, pressing with the back of a spoon to extract all the liquid.

For the veal juice:
1 medium onion, chopped fine
2 cloves garlic, peeled
1 sprig fresh thyme
1 bay leaf
1 cup veal stock

Rinse the pan and add the reserved veal chops and juice. Cook over low heat, reducing until the chop is glazed with the juice. Keep warm.

6 large, unblemished sorrel leaves for garnish

Meanwhile, finish the potato-sorrel coulis. First, place ice cubes and water in a bowl and set aside. Bring a large pot of salted water to a boil over high heat. Add the sorrel, boil for 1 to 2 minutes, drain immediately, and place in ice water until completely cold. (This re-

(continued next page)

moves any bitterness from the sorrel and fixes the chlorophyll, thereby retaining the color.)

Drain the sorrel thoroughly and chop roughly. Add to the potato mixture in a saucepan and cook over low heat for 5 minutes, stirring constantly with a wooden spoon. Season to taste with salt and pepper.

To assemble the dish, pour a small pool of the coulis onto each plate. Place a veal chop in the center, julienne the remaining sorrel leaves, and sprinkle around the chops as artistically as possible.

I would recommend serving the veal chops with seasonal mushrooms sautéed with shallots.

WARM BERRY MOUSSE IN PHYLLO CARNATIONS *makes four*

Prepare a marmalade with the fruit. First, rinse the fruit with cold water. Place in medium, heavy saucepan and cook over low heat, stirring every 10 minutes, until fruit begins to break down and dissolve. Continue cooking for 3 hours, stirring and scraping bottom every 15 minutes. Stir in sugar and cook for an additional 1/2 hour, stirring every 10 minutes. The marmalade should be thick and gelatinous. Remove to a bowl and let cool.

To prepare the phyllo carnations, lay one sheet of phyllo on flat surface. Brush entire surface with warm clarified butter. Lay another sheet of phyllo on top and brush again.

Cut out 4 6-inch circles from the phyllo. Place them on each flan ring or tart pan. Push center of each circle down, and press edges of phyllo around the inside of the ring (similar to a tart shell).

Lay out two more phyllo sheets, brushing with butter. Cut out 4 5-inch circles, and repeat above process. Ruffle the outer edges of dough to give carnation appearance.

Place 2 or so spoonfuls of marmalade into the pastry bag and pipe about 1/4 inch marmalade into each phyllo center. Set everything aside. Rewrap the phyllo. Keep butter warm.

Prepare the mousse. First, make a meringue by whipping the egg whites to soft peaks in an electric mixer. Add the sugar and continue whipping at high speed until the meringue is shiny and forms medium peaks.

(continued next page)

1½ cups red currants,
  stemmed
1½ cups blackberries
1 cup blueberries
1 cup Bing cherries, pitted
1 cup strawberries,
  stemmed
1/2 cup sugar

For phyllo carnations:
1 pound phyllo dough in
  12-by-17-inch sheets
1 cup clarified butter
Pastry or paintbrush,
  2½ inches wide
4 4-inch metal flan rings,
  or tart pans
Pastry bag with round tip

For meringue:
3 egg whites
5 tablespoons sugar

Powdered sugar for
  dusting

Fold a third of the meringue into the bowl with remaining marmalade. Once fully incorporated, add rest of meringue. Place mousse in pastry bag. Pipe about 1/3 cup mousse into each flower.

Lay out two more phyllo sheets, brushing with butter. Cut the phyllo into 1½-inch strips, top to bottom. Place the strips around the outer edge of the mousse, ruffling the phyllo every 1/2 inch to make it look like a carnation. Continue working strips around the edge, gradually moving to the center of the flower. It should take 5 strips of phyllo. Cut one strip of phyllo in two, roll it up loosely, and place it in center of the flower. Follow the same procedure with the other flowers. Put the flowers in the freezer for 4 hours.

Remove metal rings and place phyllo flowers on a sheet pan. Bake in a 350° F oven for about 15 minutes, until the phyllo is a dark golden color. Remove the flowers to plates with a spatula. Sprinkle with sieved powdered sugar. Serve with mascarpone sorbet.

MASCARPONE SORBET *makes about four cups*

1 cup sugar
1 cup water
1 pound mascarpone

Bring sugar and water to a boil in a saucepan and cook until sugar is completely dissolved. Cool to about 100° F. Using a whip, incorporate the mixture into the room-temperature mascarpone a little at a time. Transfer to an ice-cream maker and process according to manufacturer's instructions until the sorbet has the consistency of soft ice cream. Place in a container in the freezer until needed. Serve with the warm berry-phyllo carnations.

Alice Waters
MENU FOR A GARLIC DINNER

*Warm Olives with Garlic
and Thyme*

*Tomato, Green Garlic, and
Herb Soup*

*Charcoal-Grilled Chicken with
Garlic Purée*

White Peaches in Red Wine

serves four

Alice Waters is the founding chef and proprietor of *Chez Panisse* restaurant and *Cafe Fanny* in Berkeley, California. She is the author of the *Chez Panisse Menu Cookbook* (Random House, 1982), and coauthor of *Chez Panisse Pasta, Pizza and Calzone* (Random House, 1984) and *Chez Panisse Cooking* (Random House, 1988). She is currently writing a children's book about food and is a board member of the Land Institute, an ecological organization devoted to sustainable agriculture and stewardship of the earth.

There is an old Chinese proverb that says, "Garlic is as good as ten mothers." This sentiment has always appealed to me, because in addition to the delicious contribution garlic makes to cooking, it is wonderful because of its true nurturing and curative properties.

As a result of its double or even ten-faceted goodness, it seems to show up in great quantities in much of what we cook at Chez Panisse, *particularly in the time surrounding Bastille Day in July, when garlic makes its way into every course. This week-long festival celebrating California's annual garlic harvest first began seventeen years ago when we were inspired by a passionate group of Berkeley garlic believers, all part of a society known as the Lovers of the Stinking Rose. Their enthusiasm focused our attention on the subtleties of garlic, from its immature green stage (when it has yet to form cloves) to its late-winter sprouting. Consequently, we have learned to use garlic in different ways throughout the year, although it is always at its most irresistible right after it has been harvested in July.*

My affection for that moment has led me to make a menu best suited for that time of year, a time when the tomatoes and peaches are ripe and the smell of fresh garlic warming with olives and thyme brings everyone to the table for a cool glass of Provençal rosé and savory dishes of food.

WARM OLIVES WITH GARLIC AND THYME
serves four

3 whole cloves garlic
2 sprigs fresh thyme
1/2 cup Niçoise olives
2 tablespoons virgin
 olive oil

Peel the garlic cloves, cut them in half, and place in a small saucepan with the thyme and olives. Pour the olive oil into the pan and heat gently for about 5 minutes. Serve warm in a bowl as an appetizer.

TOMATO, GREEN GARLIC, AND HERB SOUP
serves four

Trim away the root of each garlic plant and
cut the shoot where it begins to open out into
dark green leaves. Remove one layer of the
outer skin of the shoot. Slice the garlic in half
lengthwise, then cut it into small pieces.

Combine the garlic and olive oil in a 3-quart
noncorroding saucepan. Salt and pepper it,
pour the water over it, and bring to a simmer. Cover the pan and cook for 20 minutes.
Add the tomatoes, reserved juice, and chicken
broth, bring to a simmer, and cook for 10
minutes.

Season the soup to your liking with salt, pepper, and a teaspoon or more of red wine vinegar. Stir in the herbs. Serve the soup with
slices of sourdough bread that have been buttered, sprinkled with grated Parmesan, and
baked.

15 green garlic plants,
   about 12 ounces
   (available in organic-
   produce shops)
2 tablespoons extra virgin
   olive oil
Salt and pepper
1 cup water
4 ripe tomatoes (1 pound,
   4 ounces), peeled,
   seeded, diced, juice
   strained and reserved
3 cups chicken broth
Red wine vinegar
2 tablespoons chopped
   fresh parsley and basil,
   or oregano

CHARCOAL-GRILLED CHICKEN WITH GARLIC PURÉE *serves four*

1 frying chicken, about
  3 pounds
2 heads garlic
1 cup virgin olive oil
Juice of 1 lemon
2 to 3 sprigs fresh thyme
Salt and pepper to taste

Cut the chicken into serving pieces. Peel 8 to 10 cloves garlic and chop them roughly. Marinate the chicken in 1/2 cup olive oil and the lemon juice with the chopped garlic and sprigs of thyme for 2 to 4 hours in the refrigerator.

Spread the remaining garlic cloves, with skins on, in a small baking dish in one layer and drizzle on the remaining olive oil. Sprinkle with salt and pepper and bake covered in a 300° F oven for 1½ hours, or until the garlic is completely soft. Purée the garlic through a food mill when it's done. Discard the skin and reserve the puree.

About an hour before cooking the chicken, remove it from the refrigerator. Prepare a medium-low charcoal fire. When the fire is ready, remove the chicken pieces from the marinade and season with salt and pepper. Cook the chicken on the grill, slowly, for about 35 minutes, turning frequently. The chicken should be nicely browned and juicy. Spread the garlic purée over the chicken while it is hot. Serve the chicken on a platter with oven-roasted potatoes and a green salad.

WHITE PEACHES IN RED WINE *serves four*

9 tablespoons sugar
1½ cups Zinfandel or
  other full-bodied, fruity
  red wine
4 to 6 ripe Babcock
  peaches, depending on
  their size

Stir the sugar in the wine until dissolved. Pit, peel, and slice the peaches about 3/8 inch thick and place in the wine. Let stand a few hours and serve in wineglasses with enough wine to cover. Serve with crisp cookies, such as langues-de-chat or lace cookies.

Barbara Tropp

A SUMMER LOVE
FEAST FOR TWO

*Pan-Seared Tuna with Roasted Red
Bell Pepper Sauce*

*Sautéed Green and Golden Zucchini
Ribbons*

Fresh Lemon Ice Cream

serves two

Barbara Tropp is the chef-owner of *China
Moon Cafe* in San Francisco. A scholar turned
Chinese cook, she was doing graduate work
in Chinese poetry and art history when her
interest shifted to cooking during a two–year
stay in Chinese homes in Taiwan. She is the
author of *The Modern Art of Chinese Cooking*
(Morrow, 1982) and the forthcoming *China
Moon Cookbook* (Workman).

    *This simple summer supper was served to a friend very dear to my heart. He
was Le Boyack, a large, warm bear of a man until his sickness with AIDS pro-
gressed, and a designer extraordinaire. Le (pronounced Lee; who knows why he
spelled it so oddly) could fill a space with light and pleasure like no one else. He
designed my little* China Moon Cafe *with a tenderness common only to very big
men with very big hearts, and he left a train of magic I still feel when the evening
has wound down, Billie Holiday is singing softly, and Le's spirit is wafting about
hungering for the flavors he adored.*
    *This is a nice menu for a lazy summer night. Much can be done in advance:
the ice cream, the sauce for the fish, the slicing of the zucchini. It is all easy work,
nothing intimidating. The ice cream is done without eggs, heavy cream, or cooking; just a simple swirl in a food processor is all that is required before freezing. As
for a starch to accompany the tuna, choose what pleases you at the moment. Rice,
fettuccine, or boiled little new potatoes would all be delicious.*

PAN-SEARED TUNA WITH ROASTED RED BELL PEPPER SAUCE *serves two to three*

1 pound fresh tuna, cut
    into triangular steaks,
    1/2 inch thick and 3 to
    3½ inches long

For marinade:
1/2 cup soy sauce
1 tablespoon ginger juice
    (squeezed from minced
    fresh ginger)
1/4 cup Chinese rice
    wine, or dry sherry
1 teaspoon sugar
2 teaspoons Japanese
    sesame oil
2 scallions, cut into 1-inch
    nuggets and smashed

For sauce:
3 medium red bell peppers
2 to 3 sun-dried tomatoes
    (not necessary if bell
    peppers are at peak of
    sweetness, but a good
    flavor booster if they
    are not)
1½ teaspoons finely
    minced garlic
1/2 cup unseasoned
    Japanese rice vinegar
2 tablespoons cider
    vinegar
1 tablespoon sugar
1 teaspoon fine sea salt
3 tablespoons Japanese
    sesame oil
1½ to 2 tablespoons
    chili oil
1 cup packed cilantro,
    chopped

Combine marinade ingredients and whisk to blend. Pour over tuna and marinate 15 minutes. If marinade doesn't completely cover tuna, turn once midway for even marination. Drain and discard marinade.

To make sauce, roast peppers in a 500° F oven, turning frequently until they blacken and blister. Put directly in a bowl, seal with plastic wrap, and set aside for 30 minutes. Peel, discarding skins and seeds; use your fingers and do not rinse the peppers lest the flavor wash away.

If using sun-dried tomatoes, cover with hot water. When soft, drain and mince.

Cut peppers into cubes and process along with tomatoes in a food processor fitted with the steel blade. Process until nearly smooth. Add minced garlic and pulse to blend.

Combine vinegars with sugar and salt and add to red pepper mixture with machine running. Combine oils and add slowly, continuing to run machine until the sauce emulsifies, another minute or two. Stop machine, add chopped cilantro, then pulse until combined and cilantro is minced small. (If doing in advance, add cilantro just a few hours before serving.) Taste and adjust seasoning with a bit more salt and vinegar if needed, depending on the flavor and sweetness of the peppers.

Heat a heavy-bottomed skillet over high heat until hot enough to sizzle a bead of water on contact. Add 1 tablespoon oil and swirl to glaze pan. When nearly smoking, add tuna steaks in a single layer with plenty of room between them. Panfry for 1 to 1½ minutes, or until golden brown. Turn and cook for another minute or so, or until tuna is medium rare.

Transfer steaks to heated serving plates and serve immediately topped with sauce and garnished with chives.

Corn or peanut oil for
  searing
1/2-inch segments of
  Chinese chives for
  garnish

SAUTÉED GREEN AND GOLDEN ZUCCHINI RIBBONS *serves two to three*

Heat a wok or large heavy skillet over medium-high heat until hot enough to evaporate a bead of water on contact. Add oil, swirling to thinly glaze bottom of pan. Heat oil until a sliver of red pepper sizzles immediately.

Add julienned pepper, tossing briskly for 1 minute, or until softened and curly at the edges. Add zucchini ribbons, stir-frying for 1 minute. Add wine-and-stock mixture and bring liquid to a boil. Cover pan, turn heat down low, and cook vegetables 1 to 1½ minutes, or until crisp-tender. Season to taste with salt and pepper, and serve immediately, or when tepid.

1½ tablespoons rendered
  chicken fat, or corn or
  peanut oil
1 small red bell pepper,
  cut into thin julienne
1 pound slender green and
  gold zucchini, cut into
  long, thin ribbons
1½ tablespoons Chinese
  rice wine, or dry sherry,
  combined with 2
  tablespoons unsalted
  chicken stock or water
Salt and pepper to taste

LEMON ICE CREAM *makes about 2 quarts*

**4 to 5 very large or 6 to 8
smaller lemons with
soft, unblemished skin
(to yield 1⅛ cups juice)**
2 cups sugar
4 cups half-and-half
2 pinches of salt

Wash lemons well in hot water with an abrasive and light soap. Rinse well and dry. Remove skin with a sharp vegetable peeler, taking care not to remove bitter white pith. Peel as many lemons as needed to obtain 1⅛ cups strained juice.

Combine lemon peel and sugar in the work bowl of a food processor fitted with the steel blade. Process until the peel is fine and the sugar slightly liquid, 3 to 5 minutes, depending on the sharpness of the blade.

Add lemon juice to work bowl and process briefly to combine, scraping sides down once or twice. Scrape the mixture into a non-aluminum mixing bowl. Add half-and-half and salt, then stir well to combine. Set aside for 15 to 30 minutes, stirring occasionally, to allow mixture to thicken and sugar to dissolve. At this point, the mixture may be sealed airtight and refrigerated up to several days before freezing.

Just before freezing, taste and adjust with more lemon juice and/or sugar and salt as required to get a very zippy lemon taste with a nice undertone of sweetness. Remember that the mixture should taste a bit too sweet at room temperature so it will taste perfect when frozen.

Freeze in an ice cream maker according to manufacturer's instructions. For best flavor, allow to ripen in the freezer for several hours before serving by packing the ice cream in a clean plastic container and sealing with a sheet of plastic wrap pressed directly on the surface. Serve slightly soft.

This ice cream keeps beautifully for about 4 days, after which the flavor begins to diminish.

Roland Passot

A SAINT'S DAY CELEBRATION

Mixed Green Bean Salad with
New Potatoes

Florida Red Snapper with a
Ratatouille of Garden Vegetables
and Lemon Vinaigrette

Peach Strudel

serves four

Roland Passot is a native of Lyons who left France in 1976 to work at *Le Français,* the noted restaurant near Chicago. He moved to San Francisco in 1980 to be the chef at *Le Castel* and opened his own restaurant, *La Folie,* in 1987. He chose to call it *La Folie,* the French word for madness, because he felt that one has to be mad to go into the restaurant business.

In France, we have an old tradition of celebrating our saint's day, if we are named after one. I can remember my grandmother's saint's day in July because we were always at our country home in Jujurieux, a small village outside Lyons. The garden was ready to harvest and my grandmother's saint's day menu always included haricots verts. A saint's day celebration was always a good excuse to get together with close friends and family and eat well, drink well, and, in our family, laugh well.

MIXED GREEN BEAN SALAD WITH NEW POTATOES *serves four*

1 pound purple or red
  new potatoes
1/4 cup vegetable oil
Salt and pepper
1 pound French haricots
  verts, or slender green
  beans
1 pound yellow wax beans
1/5 cup sherry vinegar
1 cup hazelnut oil
1/2 cup roasted pine nuts
1/2 cup minced shallots
1 carrot, cut into fine
  julienne
1/2 cup butter
2 bunches chives, chopped

Wash the potatoes, but do not peel them.
Coat a sheet pan with vegetable oil, place the
potatoes on it, and put pan in a 400° F oven
for 10 minutes, or until the potatoes are
tender. Turn the potatoes from time to time,
and check with a knife for doneness. Season
with salt and pepper. Set aside.

In the meantime, cook the green and yellow
beans separately in boiling salted water for 3
to 5 minutes, or until tender. Cool them in ice
water to keep them bright and crispy. Drain
well, and dry in towels.

In a bowl, combine the sherry vinegar with
salt and pepper. Add the hazelnut oil and mix
well. Put the beans, roasted pine nuts, shallots, and julienned carrot in the bowl and toss
with the vinaigrette.

Cut the potatoes into quarters. In a sauté pan,
melt the butter and sauté the potatoes until
golden brown. At the last minute, mix in the
chopped chives.

Arrange the bean salad in the middle of
4 large plates, and put the potatoes around
it. Serve immediately.

FLORIDA RED SNAPPER WITH A RATATOUILLE OF GARDEN VEGETABLES AND LEMON VINAIGRETTE *serves four*

Lay the snapper fillets on a table and pull out remaining bones with tweezers or small pliers. Marinate the fish for 2 hours in olive oil, rosemary, thyme, and garlic.

Fill a medium saucepan with water, and bring to a boil. Plunge the tomatoes in the water for a few seconds and remove to ice water. Peel the tomatoes and dice without squeezing out the seeds and juice, which have the best flavor. Heat some olive oil in a saucepan and add the diced tomatoes, garlic, and salt and pepper. Cook over high heat for 5 minutes, then simmer until the tomato liquid has evaporated completely, about 20 minutes. Set aside.

To make the ratatouille, heat some olive oil in a skillet and sauté the diced red and yellow bell peppers. Add zucchini, squash, and remaining crushed garlic. Season with salt and pepper. Separately, sauté the diced eggplant. Add the eggplant to the other sautéed vegetables. Set aside.

Prepare the lemon vinaigrette by mixing the lemon juice and olive oil in a bowl. Add the julienned basil and season lightly with salt and pepper. Set aside.

Season the snapper fillets with salt and pepper. Heat some olive oil in a nonstick skillet, and sauté the fish, skin side down, over high heat for a few minutes, until the skin is crispy. Cooking the fish only on the skin side

(continued next page)

2 Florida red snappers, 2½ pounds each, cleaned and filleted, with the skin on (and no scales)
1½ cups olive oil
Rosemary and thyme
3 to 4 garlic cloves, crushed
15 medium vine-ripe tomatoes
Salt and pepper
1 red bell pepper, diced
1 yellow bell pepper, diced
2 medium zucchini, diced
2 medium yellow squash, diced
1 medium eggplant, diced

For lemon vinaigrette:
1/2 cup freshly squeezed lemon juice
1 cup extra virgin olive oil
2 tablespoons julienned basil
Salt and pepper

will keep it moist. You may cover the fish briefly toward the end, but do not overcook it.

Put the warmed tomato sauce and ratatouille on plates. Place the fish on top, and spoon some heated lemon vinaigrette on the fish.

PEACH STRUDEL *serves four*

2 to 3 ripe peaches
1½ cups hazelnuts
1 package phyllo dough
1/2 cup melted butter
1/2 cup cinnamon sugar
   (1 part cinnamon to
   4 parts sugar)

Split peaches in half and remove the pits. Cut the peaches lengthwise in 1/4-inch slices, keeping the shape of the peach.

Toast the hazelnuts on a sheet pan in a 300° F oven for about 15 minutes. Let them cool. Place the nuts on a towel and rub off the skin. Put them in a processor and grind fine.

On a cool, dry table, remove phyllo dough from the package and lay out flat. Be patient working with this dough, as it tears and dries out easily. Take one sheet and set it on the table. Brush it with melted butter. Place another sheet on the first, and brush with butter. Repeat the process one more time. Sprinkle the third layer with cinnamon sugar and gound hazelnuts, covering the whole sheet. Add two more sheets of phyllo, buttering each layer. Cover the fifth sheet with cinnamon sugar and hazelnuts. Place one more phyllo sheet on top and brush with butter. You should have a total of six sheets. Using a sharp knife, cut the phyllo into 4 equal rectangular parts. Next, place peach slices at one edge of each rectangle. Fan out the slices a little. Carefully roll the phyllo layers over

the peach slices. Work fast until you've rolled
up all 4 strudels. Press together the ends of
each strudel, and brush the top with butter.

Place the strudels on a sheet pan, and bake in
a preheated 500° F oven. The strudel will
brown quickly on one side and will need to
be turned with a metal spatula so it will bake
evenly to a golden brown color on both sides.
The baking should take 12 to 15 minutes.

For presentation, trim the edges of the
strudels so they are flat and even. Cut each
strudel in half at an angle, and stand up both
pieces on a plate garnished with fresh peach
slices and brandied cherries dipped in chocolate. If you like, add cherry vanilla ice cream.

Jay Harlow

A MIDSUMMER BACKYARD BIRTHDAY PARTY

Roasted Peppers, Olives, Bread

Grilled Sea Bass with Roasted Garlic Marinade

Sliced Tomatoes

Stir-Fried Zucchini with Mint

Nectarine and Blackberry Cake

serves eight

Jay Harlow is a Berkeley resident who worked as a chef in such restaurants as the *Hayes Street Grill* and *Santa Fe Bar and Grill* before embarking on a career as a food writer. His weekly column on seafood appears in the *San Francisco Chronicle,* and his cookbooks include *The California Seafood Cookbook* (Aris Books, 1983), *The Grilling Book* (Aris Books, 1987), *Shrimp* (Chronicle, 1989), *The Art of the Sandwich* (Chronicle, 1990) and *Beer Cuisine* (Harlow & Ratner, 1991).

When you're celebrating a birthday, the food should be festive enough to make the guest of honor and the rest of the celebrants feel special, but not so elaborate that it steals the spotlight. Here's a simple grilled menu for a backyard birthday party in late July or August. Serve it with your choice of a summery white wine or, better still, an assortment of fine beers.

Start with a simple appetizer of finger foods: olives, perhaps some crudités, and strips of roasted and peeled sweet peppers drizzled with olive oil to drape over slices of crusty bread. In summertime, I use the grill a lot, so it's easy to roast the peppers for the hors d'oeuvres and garlic for the fish a day or two ahead of time. Of course, you can do both as the fire is getting started, but it's nice to keep last-minute chores to a minimum.

Use fillets of any firm, white, mild- to medium-flavored summer fish—sea bass, halibut, red snapper, grouper, yellowtail, whatever your fishmonger recommends among the catch of the day. I don't think this marinade does a lot for salmon, tuna, and other rich fish.

And what's a birthday celebration without a birthday cake? This one is not very sweet; instead, it relies on the flavors of two fresh seasonal fruits that go together marvelously. It's very much in the style of my friend Jim Dodge, my guru in pastry matters. Use any good yellow sponge or chiffon cake recipe.

GRILLED SEA BASS WITH ROASTED GARLIC MARINADE *serves eight*

While the fire is at the flaming stage, roast the heads of garlic near the edge of the grill, turning them occasionally and positioning them so the outside skin browns deeply but does not char. Cook until the outer cloves are soft when pressed gently and liquid bubbles out of the center, 15 to 20 minutes. Let cool slightly, then slice the heads crosswise through the thickest part to expose all the cloves.

Let the garlic cool just enough to handle, peel away any burnt skin, and squeeze the cloves out of each half into a bowl. Mash thoroughly with the back of a spoon. Stir in the oil, salt, and anchovy (if used).

Season the fish fillets with salt and pepper, and spread the marinade on both sides. Let stand until the fire is ready for cooking. Grill the fish, starting with the bone side down, until it releases easily from the grill, about 4 minutes. Turn, baste with a little of the remaining oil, and cook until a skewer easily enters the thickest part, another 3 to 4 minutes. Serve with slices of tomato and the stir-fried zucchini.

2 whole, firm heads garlic
4 tablespoons extra virgin olive oil
Pinch of salt
1 anchovy fillet, minced, or 1/2 teaspoon anchovy paste (optional)
8 diagonal slices of sea bass fillet, about 6 ounces each
Salt and pepper

STIR-FRIED ZUCCHINI WITH MINT *serves eight*

**2 pounds medium
   zucchini
2 tablespoons olive oil
Juice of 1 lemon or lime
1/2 cup loosely packed
   spearmint or
   peppermint leaves
Salt and pepper to taste**

Trim the ends of the zucchini and cut into fine shreds. A mandoline, or the shredding disc of a food processor, makes short work of this. If you have neither, slice the zucchini thinly on a diagonal into ovals about 2 inches long, stack a bunch of the slices, and slice lengthwise into matchstick shreds.

Heat the oil in a wok or lightweight skillet until a bit of zucchini sizzles on contact. You can do this on the stove, or right on the grill. Add the zucchini shreds, stirring to break them up, and cook just until heated through, about 1 minute. Add the lemon or lime juice, remove the pan from the heat, and toss in the mint leaves. Season to taste.

NECTARINE AND BLACKBERRY CAKE
serves twelve

Halve and pit the nectarines, but do not peel.
Slice all but one into thin wedges (about 16
per nectarine). Toss the slices with a little
lemon juice to keep them from turning
brown. Pick over the berries and discard any
with mold or underripe red sections. Set aside
12 perfect berries for garnish.

Trim the cake layers if necessary, leveling any
domed tops and peeling off any tough outer
layers. Whip the cream to soft peaks.

Place the bottom layer of cake on the serving
plate, spread with a thin layer of whipped
cream, and arrange the nectarine slices and
berries in a thick layer to within 1/2 inch of
the edge. Dot with spoonfuls of whipped
cream and spread with a spatula to fill in the
spaces between the fruits.

Top with the other layer of cake and spread
the remaining whipped cream evenly over the
top and sides of the cake. Cut the remaining
nectarine into 12 wedges and arrange them
like spokes with a berry alongside each one.
(If you want to leave space for writing and
birthday candles on top, arrange the fruits in
a ring around the outside.) Refrigerate the
cake until ready to serve.

4 medium nectarines
1 tablespoon lemon juice
1 pint blackberries
2 9-inch round yellow
  cake layers
1½ cups heavy cream,
  well chilled

Joey Altman

A LATE-SUMMER CARIBBEAN BARBECUE

Island Gazpacho

Hearts of Palm and Jicama Salad with Papaya, Tomato, and Green Onion-Coconut Dressing

Baked Yams with Sweet Onions and Ginger

Grilled Corn and Chayote Succotash

Jamaican Jerked Chicken and Pork

Tropical Fruit with a Coconut-Rum Sabayon

serves eight

Joey Altman started cooking at age fourteen in Catskill Mountain resort hotels. Traveling to France, he apprenticed in restaurants in Brittany and Lyons, and during visits to Jamaica, he developed an affinity for Island cuisine. He is currently the chef at San Francisco's popular Caribbean-style restaurant, *Miss Pearl's Jam House.*

I've chosen a Caribbean barbecue for a late-summer festivity since it's the season when fruits and vegetables are at their peak. The menu takes some work to prepare, but those who share my enthusiasm for spicy, exotic foods and enjoy cooking for friends will find it well worth their effort.

We start with an Island gazpacho, one of the best hot-weather soups I know. And in late summer, when tomatoes are at their best, it's just wonderful. We end with fresh tropical fruit with a coconut-rum sabayon, a delightfully light Caribbean adaptation of the classic French sauce and a perfect finish to a great, if filling, meal. To complement the food, I suggest serving big pitchers of rum punch.

ISLAND GAZPACHO *serves eight*

Combine the ingredients and season to taste.
Chill for a couple of hours and serve with a
garnish of julienned mint.

8 ripe tomatoes, cored,
  halved, seeded, and
  diced small
4 yellow tomatoes, cored,
  halved, seeded, and
  diced small
3 English cucumbers,
  peeled, seeded, and
  diced small
1 red bell pepper, seeded
  and diced small
1 yellow pepper, seeded
  and diced small
1 Anaheim chili, seeded
  and diced small
1 pasilla chili, seeded and
  diced small
2 jalapeño peppers,
  seeded and minced
1 large red onion, diced
  small
1 small jicama, diced
  small
1 mango, peeled and diced
  small
1 papaya, peeled and diced
  small
1 cup fresh lime juice
1 quart fresh tomato juice
  (10 tomatoes, pureed
  and strained)
1 teaspoon minced garlic
1/4 cup chopped cilantro
1 teaspoon freshly grated
  horseradish
1/2 cup olive oil
Salt and freshly ground
  pepper
10 mint leaves, julienned,
  for garnish

HEARTS OF PALM AND JICAMA SALAD WITH PAPAYA, TOMATO, AND GREEN ONION-COCONUT DRESSING *serves eight*

1 medium red onion,
  sliced into thin rings
1/2 cup lemon juice
1 cup large coconut chips
1/2 pound mixed baby
  lettuces
1 medium jicama, peeled
  and cut into 3-by-
  1/4-inch sticks
1½ pounds fresh hearts of
  palm or 2 cans, sliced
  into 1/4-inch rounds
2 papayas, peeled, seeded,
  and cubed
4 Roma tomatoes, sliced
  into 1/4-inch rounds

For lime vinaigrette:
Juice of 2 limes
6 tablespoons olive oil
1 minced shallot
Salt and pepper to taste

*For the green onion-coconut
  dressing:*
1 bunch green onions,
  green part only
1 cup unsweetened
  shredded coconut
1/2 cup lime juice
2 peeled shallots
1/4 teaspoon cayenne
  pepper
1 egg
1 tablespoon honey
2 tablespoons unsweetened
  coconut milk
1½ cups olive oil
Salt and pepper to taste

Marinate the sliced red onion in lemon juice for 15 minutes.

Toast the coconut chips in a 300° F oven until light golden.

Make a lime vinaigrette by whisking together the lime juice, olive oil, minced shallot, and seasoning to taste.

Prepare the onion-coconut dressing by placing all ingredients, except olive oil and salt and pepper, in a blender or food processor. Puree until smooth, then drizzle in olive oil, blending until thick and creamy. Season to taste. Toss the greens with lime vinaigrette in a salad bowl.

Toss the jicama and hearts of palm with green onion-coconut dressing and place on top of greens. Garnish with the papaya, tomatoes, red onion, and toasted coconut.

Note: Coconut chips are available in natural-food shops; fresh hearts of palm can be found in Latin markets; and unsweetened coconut milk can be found in Asian markets or the Oriental-food section of supermarkets.

BAKED YAMS WITH SWEET ONIONS AND GINGER *serves eight*

Preheat oven to 350° F. Layer the sliced yams in a buttered baking dish. Season with salt and pepper to taste.

In a skillet, sauté the onions and ginger in olive oil and butter until onions are golden brown. Stir with a wooden spoon frequently to prevent burning. Add the stock and cream and bring to a boil. Ladle over the yams and cover with foil. Bake for 1 hour.

6 yams, peeled and sliced into 1/2-inch rounds
Salt and pepper
2 sweet onions (such as the Maui, Vidalia, or Walla Walla variety), halved and julienned
4 tablespoons minced fresh ginger
1/4 cup olive oil
3 tablespoons butter
2 cups chicken stock
1 cup heavy cream

GRILLED CORN AND CHAYOTE SUCCOTASH *serves eight*

Grill the corn on all sides for about 2 minutes. When cool, peel off husks and silk, and cut kernels off the cobs.

Lightly oil the chayote slices, season with salt and pepper, and grill for a minute or two, just to get some color.

Grill the scallions and chop small.

Oil the red onion slices, season with salt and pepper, and grill until lightly charred. Dice small.

In a large skillet, heat 1/4 cup olive oil, add all the ingredients except for butter, and cook for 1 minute. Stir in butter, season to taste, and serve.

6 ears of corn with the husks on
6 chayote squash, sliced 1/4 inch thick
1 bunch scallions, trimmed
1 medium red onion, sliced 1/4 inch thick
Olive oil
Salt and pepper
1/4 cup chopped cilantro
4 cloves garlic, minced
2 large tomatoes, peeled, seeded, and chopped
1 cup chicken stock
4 tablespoons butter

JAMAICAN JERKED CHICKEN AND PORK
serves eight

2 large frying chickens,
   cut into 8 pieces
1 boneless pork-butt roast,
   about 2 pounds, sliced
   into 1½-inch steaks
1 bunch scallions,
   trimmed, for garnish

For jerk sauce:
5 bunches scallions,
   trimmed and roughly
   chopped
1 cup thinly sliced fresh
   ginger
1/2 cup chopped garlic
4 Scotch bonnet chilies
   (found in West Indian
   markets), or 10 jalapeño
   peppers, sliced, with
   seeds left in
1 cup lime juice
1½ cups soy sauce
1/4 cup ground allspice
2 teaspoons cinnamon
1 cup malt vinegar
1/2 cup brown sugar
2 tablespoons molasses
1/2 teaspoon nutmeg
1/2 teaspoon ground
   cloves
2 teaspoons fresh chopped
   thyme
1/2 cup olive oil
1 teaspoon black pepper

Jerk sauce is a classic Jamaican barbecue sauce-marinade. It has a marvelous complexity from blending the spicy with the sweet and sour and adding an uncommon combination of herbs and spices. The end result is truly unique.

To prepare the jerk sauce, place scallions, ginger, garlic, chilies, lime juice, and soy sauce in a food processor and purée until smooth. Transfer to a large mixing bowl and stir in remaining ingredients. Let stand 1/2 hour, and adjust seasoning to suit your palate with soy, lime, and brown sugar. The sauce should be spicy, gingery, and slightly sweet and sour.

Marinate the meats for 2 hours in just enough sauce to coat them well. Save remaining sauce to serve as an accompaniment.

Grill the marinated meat pieces over medium heat, turning frequently to avoid charring. When done, transfer to a serving platter, and grill the extra trimmed scallions to lay over the meat as garnish.

TROPICAL FRUIT WITH A COCONUT-RUM SABAYON *serves eight*

Mix the fruit and juices together and place in a serving bowl.

Place egg yolks, champagne, rum, sugar, and coconut milk in a large stainless-steel bowl. Place bowl over a pan of simmering water. With a large whisk, beat vigorously for 5 to 8 minutes, until mixture is thick to the point of soft peaks. Be careful not to overheat or yolks will burn and separate.

When done, place in refrigerator to cool. Whip the heavy cream and sugar to soft stiffness. Gently fold into cooled sabayon and serve over fruit.

1 mango, peeled, pitted, and cubed
1 papaya, peeled, seeded, and cubed
1 pineapple, peeled, cored, and cubed
2 bananas, peeled and sliced
1 pint strawberries, cleaned and sliced
1 pint raspberries
1/2 cup passion-fruit juice (available in gourmet shops)
1/2 cup pineapple juice
1/4 cup lime juice

For sabayon:
5 egg yolks
1/4 cup champagne
1/2 cup rum
1/2 cup sugar
1/4 cup sweetened coconut milk (found in Latin markets)
1 cup heavy cream, whipped with 2 tablespoons sugar

Marc Meyer

A SUMMER WEEKEND
SEAFOOD DINNER

Fresh Mint Marinated Salmon

Gulf Shrimp and Rice Salad

*Steamed Manila Clams with Green
Beans and Yellow Wax Beans*

Tropical Fruit Salad

serves six

Marc Meyer is a native New Yorker who
studied architecture at the University of California, Berkeley, and learned to cook during
a year as an apprentice chef in Rome, Italy.
He worked as sous-chef for five and a half
years at Manhattan's *An American Place* and
is currently the chef at the *Brasserie Savoy,*
a Parisian-style seafood restaurant in San
Francisco.

   *Festive occasions can often be somewhat spontaneous and not necessarily punc-
tuated by a seasonal holiday. A get-together with family or friends on a summer
weekend, for example, is a great opportunity to create a festive meal. The menu
that follows is ideal for casual dining because most everything can be prepared in
advance and served when needed.*

FRESH MINT MARINATED SALMON *serves six*

The night before your meal, prepare a mixture of the brown sugar, salt, and pepper, and sprinkle evenly over the surface of the salmon. If you have some seasoning left, just put it in a covered container until the next time. In another bowl, combine the orange zest, red onion, and mint, and pack onto the surface of the salmon. Wrap the dry marinated fish in plastic wrap, place it on a tray, and refrigerate.

The next day, unwrap the salmon and scrape the onion-mint mixture from the fish. Mince mixture finely, then blend with the olive oil. Set aside.

An outdoor barbecue is a great way to grill the marinated salmon, but your favorite cooking method (baked, or sautéed) will easily work as well. Either cook the whole fillet for 5 minutes or so on each side, or cut the fish into serving portions and proceed. The entire cooked fillet adds to a festive-looking table.

Spoon some of the olive oil–mint mixture over the cooked fish just before serving.

1 cup light brown sugar
1/2 cup kosher salt
3 tablespoons black
  pepper
4-pound piece of salmon
  fillet, pinbones
  removed
Grated zest of 2 oranges
1 red onion, thinly sliced
1 large bunch of fresh
  mint, roughly chopped
1 cup olive oil

GULF SHRIMP AND RICE SALAD *serves six to eight*

4 cups cooked rice
2½ pounds medium fresh
    Gulf shrimp, peeled and
    cooked
1 bunch chopped Italian
    parsley
1/4 cup toasted pine nuts
1/2 cup pitted chopped
    Niçoise olives
3 tablespoons chopped
    capers
Grated zest and juice of
    2 lemons
1 teaspoon minced garlic
2 minced anchovy fillets
2 cups olive oil
1/2 cup white wine
    vinegar
Salt and pepper

Most varieties of rice will work for this recipe. However, the stickier and more glutinous varieties, such as Arborio, or types used in Chinese cooking, are not advised. I recommend a basmati rice, a long-grain brown rice, or your favorite brand of converted rice.

Cook the rice until it is plump and tender. Spread it out on a tray, allowing it to cool. While the rice cools, prepare the other ingredients. Then, mix everything together and season to taste.

STEAMED MANILA CLAMS WITH GREEN BEANS AND YELLOW WAX BEANS *serves six*

Split the beans lengthwise and blanch in boiling salted water, about 3 minutes, until crisp-tender. Drain and rinse quickly in cold water.

Place in a large mixing bowl and drizzle on the beans a little olive oil and lemon juice.

Heat 5 tablespoons olive oil in a large, deep pan. Sauté the garlic, onion, and red pepper flakes. When the onion is translucent, add the tomato and the washed clams. Cover and cook for 5 to 6 minutes. When all the clams are open, pour over the beans, toss, and check for seasoning. Add salt, pepper, lemon juice, and olive oil to taste.

2 pounds green string beans
2 pounds yellow wax beans
1/2 cup olive oil
Juice of 1/2 lemon
2 cloves garlic, minced
1 small red onion, finely chopped
1/2 tablespoon red pepper flakes
1 tomato, peeled, seeded, and chopped
4½ pounds Manila clams, washed
Salt and pepper

TROPICAL FRUIT SALAD *serves six*

Mix together diced fruit. Toss with onion, pepper, jalapeños, cilantro, and lime juice. Season with salt and Tabasco to taste.

1 pineapple, peeled, cored, and medium diced
2 ripe mangoes, peeled, pitted, and medium diced
1 papaya, peeled, seeded, and medium diced
3 ripe kiwis, peeled and medium diced
1 small red onion, minced
1 red bell pepper, minced
2 jalapeño peppers, seeded and minced
1 bunch cilantro, chopped
Juice of 3 limes
Salt and Tabasco to taste

Chuck Phifer

AN END-OF-SUMMER SUPPER

End-of-Summer Tomato Soup

*Fontina-and-Apple-Stuffed
Pork Chops*

Apple Crisp

Tilly's Ice Cream

serves six

Nebraska-born Chuck Phifer grew up in
the Northwest and has resided in the Bay
Area for the past eleven years. A graduate
of the California Culinary Academy, he is
currently chef of *Eddie Rickenbacker's* in
San Francisco, where he features American-
heartland food.

One of our favorite celebrations comes around when brisk mornings and cooler
evenings begin to revive jaded summer appetites. The tomato season is waning, the
first apples of the year are coming down from Sonoma, and we start to crave heart-
ier meals again. It's time to round up our friends and have an end-of-summer supper.

END-OF-SUMMER TOMATO SOUP *serves six*

The success of this simple soup depends mostly on one thing: real tomatoes, preferably homegrown and definitely vine ripened. Better yet, overripe. Supermarket varieties just don't work. If you can't get wonderful tomatoes, make something else.

Rinse, core, and cut the tomatoes in halves or quarters. Place them in a 3-quart or larger kettle over high heat. If necessary, press down on the tomatoes to start the juices flowing. Reduce heat to medium.

Sauté the onion in 1 tablespoon butter until almost translucent, add the garlic, and continue to cook until the onion is clear and soft. Add this to the tomatoes. Return the tomatoes to a boil and cook over medium heat until reduced by a third.

Melt the remaining 2 tablespoons butter in a sauté pan, add the flour, and make a roux over medium heat, cooking until the flour turns light brown and smells nutty. Reduce heat and stir the half-and-half (or cream) into the roux. Turn heat to high, bring cream to a boil, and cook until slightly thickened. Add to the tomatoes and stir well. Continue to cook at a simmer for about 10 minutes. Remove from heat, let cool somewhat, puree and strain. Season with salt and pepper to taste. Adjust acidity with lemon juice, if necessary.

Reheat and serve with chopped chives, grated Parmesan cheese, basil whipped cream, or just by itself.

8 to 10 very ripe, large
   homegrown tomatoes
1 small onion, chopped
3 tablespoons butter
1 to 2 cloves garlic,
   minced
2 tablespoons flour
1 quart half-and-half or
   heavy cream
Salt and pepper
Juice of 1 lemon

FONTINA-AND-APPLE-STUFFED
PORK CHOPS *serves six*

4 tablespoons olive oil
1 small onion, finely
 chopped
1½ teaspoons, or more,
 chopped garlic
1 green apple, peeled,
 cored, and chopped
1/2 pound mild pork
 sausage
1 cup fresh bread crumbs
8 ounces fontina cheese,
 grated
1 teaspoon chopped
 fresh sage
6 pork chops, 8 ounces
 each, cut 1½ inches
 thick, with a pocket
1/2 cup white wine
1/2 cup Calvados
3 tablespoons butter
Salt and pepper to taste
12 to 18 whole sage leaves
 for garnish

Heat 1 tablespoon olive oil in a sauté pan and sauté the onion until almost translucent. Add garlic and cook until onion turns clear. Add chopped apple and cook a few minutes longer. Remove to a mixing bowl.

Place the sausage in the pan and cook until the pink is gone, breaking up the pieces quite small. Add to the onion mixture. Stir the bread crumbs into the mixture and cool. Mix in the fontina and chopped sage. Stuff the chops, dividing the mixture evenly, and secure openings with toothpicks.

Heat remaining 3 tablespoons olive oil in a large sauté pan and brown chops nicely on both sides. Remove to an ovenproof dish or pan large enough to hold chops in one layer. Bake at 400° F for about 20 minutes, or to desired doneness, turning once. Remove chops to a serving platter, and deglaze the pan over high heat with white wine. Scrape up all the browned bits. Add the Calvados and reduce liquid by one-half. Swirl in the butter and bring to a boil to emulsify. Adjust the seasoning with salt and pepper. Pour sauce over the chops. Serve immediately with garnish of whole sage leaves.

APPLE CRISP *serves ten*

Peel, core, and slice apples. Toss with sugar, flour, cinnamon, nutmeg, and cloves until dry ingredients are thoroughly moistened. Place in a 9-by-12-by-1½-inch pan and dot with butter. Set aside.

To prepare topping, work butter into the dry ingredients with your hands or in an electric mixer until mixture resembles coarse crumbs. Mixture should be lumpy, not powdery. If it seems too dry, work it a bit more until the crumbs are moist.

Sprinkle thickly over the top of the apple mixture and bake in 375° F oven until brown and bubbling. Remove and serve warm or cool. Serve with soft whipped cream or, better yet, homemade ice cream.

10 large Gravenstein or
   Jonathan apples
1½ cups sugar
3/4 cup flour
1/4 teaspoon cinnamon
1/4 teaspoon nutmeg
1/8 teaspoon ground
   cloves
2 tablespoons butter

For topping:
1 cup butter
1/2 cup brown sugar
1/2 cup granulated sugar
1 cup flour
1/2 teaspoon salt
1/2 teaspoon cinnamon

TILLY'S ICE CREAM *makes two quarts*

This ice cream is from an old recipe of my mother's. It is sweet and creamy, as ice cream should be. But unlike many of today's super-rich ice creams, it has a fresh, clean taste and doesn't coat the mouth with butterfat.

Beat the eggs and sugar together until light. Add the vanilla, half-and-half, and cream. Stir to mix well. Place in an ice-cream maker and process according to manufacturer's instructions. Store in freezer.

3 eggs
1 cup sugar
1 teaspoon vanilla
1½ quarts half-and-half
1 cup heavy cream

Stanley Eichelbaum

AN ELEGANT BRUNCH FOR LABOR DAY

*Crêpes Layered with Prosciutto,
Spinach, and Mushrooms*

*Sausage in Brioche with Eggs
Sarah Bernhardt*

*Wild Rice and Fruit Salad with
a Port Vinaigrette*

Cognac Brownies

serves four

Stanley Eichelbaum is a journalist and chef
who spent eighteen years as film and theater
critic of the *San Francisco Examiner* before en-
rolling for a professional chef's degree at the
California Culinary Academy. He operated
two San Francisco restaurants, *Eichelbaum &
Co.* and *Café Majestic,* and has since returned
to writing. He presently does a food column
for the *San Francisco Chronicle* and a restaurant
column for the *San Francisco Business Times.*

*You don't want to work on Labor Day. It's a lazy day, and an ideal occasion
for a relaxed, unhurried, elegant meal, perhaps an alfresco brunch that allows you
to eat on the lawn or deck in a last hurrah for the summer season.*

*Brunch is a meal that needs some forethought. You don't want to get up at
dawn, and it's a good idea to select dishes that can be done ahead, like those for this
menu, most of which can be prepared a day or so in advance.*

CRÊPES LAYERED WITH PROSCIUTTO, SPINACH, AND MUSHROOMS *serves four*

This recipe is based on a country dish of central France called Crépazes. I've adapted it for a hearty, delicious brunch or lunch dish.

To make the crêpe batter, whisk together the flour, eggs, salt, and sugar in a mixing bowl (or electric mixer), and slowly add the heated milk, whisking until the mixture is smooth. Add the melted butter, whisking until it is incorporated. Let the batter stand for a couple of hours. It should be the texture of heavy cream, but if it becomes too thick, add more milk.

Use a 10-inch nonstick frying pan or a crêpe pan to make the crêpes. Coat the bottom with a few drops of oil and heat the pan. When the pan is quite hot, ladle a small amount of crêpe batter into the pan, tilting and turning it to spread the batter evenly. It should lightly coat the pan bottom. You want the crêpes to be as thin as possible.

Cook over moderate heat until the outer edges begin to brown. Turn with a thin plastic spatula, and let the other side brown slightly. Remove the crêpe to a plate. Repeat the process until you have no more batter, stacking the finished crêpes on the plate. It helps to place a strip of waxed paper between the crêpes to keep them from sticking. You should have 8 to 10 crêpes.

To prepare the spinach filling, blanch the spinach leaves in lightly salted boiling water for 1 minute. Remove and drain well, preferably by squeezing out the water through a

(continued next page)

For the crêpes:
1/2 cup flour
3 eggs
1/4 teaspoon salt
Pinch of sugar
1½ to 2 cups milk, heated
2 tablespoons butter, melted
Vegetable oil for frying

For spinach filling:
1 bunch spinach, cleaned, with stems removed
1 tablespoon butter
2 tablespoons flour
1 cup milk, scalded
1/4 teaspoon salt
1/8 teaspoon pepper
1/8 teaspoon nutmeg

For mushroom filling:
Butter and vegetable oil
2 tablespoons shallots, minced
1/2 pound mushrooms, thinly sliced
Salt and pepper

1/2 pound prosciutto, thinly sliced
2/3 cup heavy cream
1/2 cup grated Gruyère cheese
1/3 cup toasted, coarsely chopped pistachios

kitchen towel. Chop the spinach by hand or in a processor.

In a saucepan, melt the butter over low heat and stir in the flour to make a roux. Slowly add the hot milk, and whisk until the mixture thickens. Season with salt, pepper, and nutmeg. Stir in the chopped spinach. Set aside.

To prepare the mushroom filling, heat some butter and oil in a sauté pan and add the shallots. Sauté for 1 or 2 minutes, then add the sliced mushrooms and cook for 10 minutes, until the mushroom juices have evaporated. Lightly season with salt and pepper. Set aside.

To assemble, use the 10-inch skillet or an ovenproof dish the same diameter as the crêpes. Lightly butter the bottom, and lay in a crêpe. Cover the crêpe with sliced prosciutto. Dribble over it a teaspoon of cream. Lay another crêpe on top of the prosciutto. Spread with some spinach filling. Dribble on some cream. Cover with another crêpe. Spread with a layer of sliced mushrooms and some cream. Lay on another crêpe, and repeat with the prosciutto. Continue stacking until you have no crêpes or filling left. Spoon remaining cream over the top. Place the skillet with the stacked crêpes in a 375° F oven and bake for 15 minutes, until liquid starts to bubble. May be made ahead to this point and refrigerated, covered with plastic wrap.

Before serving, sprinkle the top crêpe with a few drops of cream, the grated Gruyère cheese, and the chopped pistachios. Place under a broiler for 5 minutes, until the cheese is melted. Cut into 4 wedges and serve.

SAUSAGE IN BRIOCHE WITH EGGS
SARAH BERNHARDT *serves four*

The sausage in brioche, which should be made ahead, is a fine accompaniment for these garlic-flavored scrambled eggs. The name eggs Sarah Bernhardt is my own, having been told some time ago that the noted chef Auguste Escoffier made these eggs for actress Sarah Bernhardt. The story may be apocryphal, but the eggs, with just a hint of garlic, are truly delicious.

Poach the sausages in simmering water for 15 minutes. Drain and set aside.

To prepare the brioche dough, mix together the yeast, sugar, and warm water, and let stand until softened and bubbly. In an electric mixer, combine the yeast mixture, melted butter, salt, flour, and eggs. Beat until smooth, elastic, and satiny, about 10 minutes. Place in a greased bowl, covered, set in a warm, draft-free spot, and let rise until double in size, about 1 hour. Punch the dough down and refrigerate, covered with plastic wrap, for 2 to 3 hours.

Remove the chilled dough, divide it in 4 pieces, and roll out on a floured surface to 1/4 inch thick. Place a sausage in the center of each piece of dough, brush the edges with egg wash, and enclose the sausage by neatly folding the ends of dough under it. Place the sausages in brioche, seam side down, on a parchment-lined sheet pan and brush the brioche surface with egg wash. Let rise for 10 minutes. Bake in a 400° F oven until brioche is golden brown, about 15 to 20 minutes. If made ahead, reheat in a 300° F oven for 15 minutes before serving.

(continued next page)

For brioche dough:
1½ tablespoons (or packages) active dry yeast
2 tablespoons sugar
1/2 cup warm water
1 cup melted butter
1½ teaspoons salt
4 cups all-purpose flour
4 eggs
1 egg, beaten, for egg wash

4 Italian sausages, mild or hot, according to your taste
1 lage clove garlic, peeled
10 to 12 eggs
Salt and pepper
Clarified butter for frying
Sliced chives or chopped parsley for garnish

To prepare the eggs Sarah Bernhardt, stick the garlic clove on the tines of a fork. Attach it securely, since you'll be using it to stir the eggs.

Place the eggs in a lage bowl and whisk well. Season with salt and pepper to taste. In a large skillet, heat some clarified butter over low heat. Add the beaten eggs, and stir constantly with the garlic-clove fork. Cook the eggs to your taste, creamy and moist, or somewhat dry. Serve with a sausage in brioche that's been sliced in two and arranged on a plate between a mound of eggs. Garnish with sliced chives or chopped parsley.

WILD RICE AND FRUIT SALAD WITH A PORT VINAIGRETTE *serves four to six*

Wash the rice in a colander, place in a bowl, pour boiling water over it, and soak for 30 minutes. Drain and place in a saucepan with 4 cups water and 1/2 teaspoon salt. Bring to a boil and simmer, covered, for 30 to 40 minutes, until the pods open and the kernels are swollen and tender. Drain and set aside.

Soak the dates, apricots, figs, and currants in port wine for 30 minutes. Drain off the wine and reserve. Combine the dried fruit, scallions, celery, pecans, and wild rice in a large bowl.

Remove zest from the orange and chop. Make the vinaigrette by mixing together the reserved port wine, orange zest, lemon juice, vinegar, and salt and pepper. Whisk in the walnut oil. Toss the wild-rice mixture with the vinaigrette. Just before serving, peel the orange, cut into segments, and add to salad. Peel and core the apple or pear, and cut into bite-size pieces. Add to the salad with the grapes. Sprinkle with chives and parsley and serve on a curled lettuce leaf.

3/4 cup wild rice
1/2 teaspoon salt
1/3 cup pitted dates, cut up
1/2 cup dried apricots, cut up
1/2 cup dried figs, cut up
1/2 cup dried currants
2/3 cup port wine
4 scallions, thinly sliced
3 ribs celery, diced
1/3 cup toasted pecans, coarsely chopped
1 navel orange
Juice of 1 lemon
1 teaspoon balsamic vinegar
Salt and pepper to taste
1/2 cup walnut oil
1 tart apple or ripe but firm pear
2/3 cup seedless grapes
Sliced chives and chopped parsley
Red-leaf lettuce for garnish

COGNAC BROWNIES *makes thirty-two*

9 ounces unsweetened
  chocolate
1 cup plus 2 tablespoons
  butter
9 large eggs
4½ cups sugar
1 teaspoon vanilla
2 to 3 tablespoons cognac
2¼ cups all-purpose flour
1¼ teaspoon salt
2½ cups roughly chopped
  walnuts or pecans

Make ready an 11-by-17-inch jelly-roll pan by lining with aluminum foil. Grease the foil with butter.

Melt the chocolate and 1 cup butter in the top of a double boiler over moderately low heat. Let cool somewhat.

Beat the eggs and sugar in an electric mixer until light and fluffy. Add the vanilla and cognac and blend well. Stir in the melted chocolate and butter.

Combine the flour and salt and fold into the chocolate mixture, stirring with a spatula. Do not overmix. Stir in the chopped nuts.

Spread the brownie batter evenly in the prepared baking pan, using a rubber spatula to fill out the corners and smooth the surface.

Place the pan in a 325° F oven and bake for 35 minutes. Test with a skewer for doneness. The cake should be moist but set. Let cool.

When cool, turn the pan upside down on a work surface. Remove pan and peel off foil. Using a warm knife, cut the cake in half, then in half again, and continue cutting in half until you have 32 pieces. If not served that day, the brownies may be wrapped in plastic and refrigerated or frozen for future use.

Serve with ice cream.

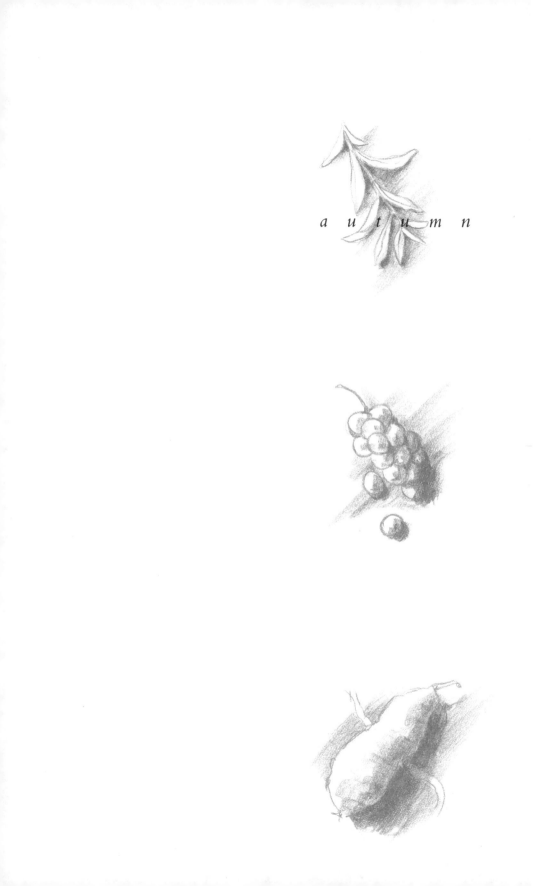

a u t u m n

Annie Somerville

A ROWING PARTY'S PICNIC BREAKFAST

Black Mission Figs and Cantaloupe

Open-Faced Sandwiches with Herbed Goat Cheese and Marinated Tomatoes with Roasted Peppers, Garlic, and Basil

Freshly Squeezed Orange Juice

Champagne on Ice

Chocolate-Pine Nut Biscotti

Hot Coffee from a Thermos

serves six

Annie Somerville started cooking at the Zen Center in San Francisco and continued her training at Tassajara Zen Mountain Center in Carmel Valley. She is currently executive chef at San Francisco's renowned vegetarian restaurant, *Greens*.

This is a delicious, simple breakfast that I shared with friends in late September, on an early morning row on San Francisco Bay. The day was warm and clear, the bay was glassy, and the company was exceptional. We rowed to an island at the northern end of the bay, carried the wooden boats ashore, and thoroughly enjoyed our morning meal in a sea cave looking out toward Marin County.

I chose the tastiest ingredients my neighborhood bakery and grocery had to offer, knowing that the best of the season was available to me. Time was also a factor, since there was very little time for preparation so early in the day.

OPEN-FACED SANDWICHES WITH HERBED GOAT CHEESE AND MARINATED TOMATOES WITH ROASTED PEPPERS, GARLIC, AND BASIL *serves six*

1 loaf crusty sourdough
    bread, thickly sliced

*For marinated tomatoes with
    roasted peppers, garlic,
    and basil:*
3 ripe tomatoes
1 red and 1 yellow pepper,
    roasted, peeled, and
    thickly sliced
2 cloves garlic, chopped
1/3 cup basil, coarsely
    chopped
1/2 cup extra virgin
    olive oil
Few drops balsamic
    vinegar
Salt and freshly ground
    black pepper to taste

For herbed goat cheese:
12 ounces creamy
    goat cheese
1 small shallot, diced
1 tablespoon freshly
    chopped herbs (any
    combination of
    marjoram, thyme,
    parsley, and chives)
Freshly ground black
    pepper to taste

It's best to make the marinated tomatoes a few hours, or a day, in advance. Cut the tomatoes in half, core, and squeeze out the juice and seeds. Chop the tomatoes and toss with the peppers, garlic, basil, and olive oil. Season to taste with balsamic vinegar, salt, and pepper. Don't be shy with the garlic and basil. Add more if you like.

To prepare the herbed goat cheese, cream the goat cheese and add the shallots, herbs, and pepper to taste.

Spread on thickly sliced sourdough bread and pile the marinated tomatoes and peppers on top.

CHOCOLATE-PINE NUT BISCOTTI
makes fifty pieces

This is *Greens'* variation of Lindsey Shere's *Chez Panisse* biscotti recipe.

Toast pine nuts in a 350° F oven until golden, about 5 minutes. Cool and chop coarsely. Set aside.

In a mixing bowl or electric mixer, cream butter and sugar. Beat until fluffy. Beat in eggs until mixture is smooth. Mix in cognac and vanilla.

Combine flour, baking powder, and salt, and stir into mixture until just combined. Stir in grated chocolate and pine nuts.

On a lightly floured board, roll dough into logs 1 inch in diameter and the length of your baking sheet. Set rolled dough on parchment-lined baking sheet about 2 inches apart. Bake in a 325° F oven for 25 minutes, or until set and lightly browned. Cool the rolls on a rack for 5 minutes, then slice them diagonally 1/2 inch thick.

Lay the slices back on the baking sheet and bake for another 5 minutes to dry them. Turn over the slices and bake for another 5 minutes. Cool and store in a tightly sealed container.

1/2 cup pine nuts
1/2 cup soft butter
3/4 cup sugar
2 eggs
2 tablespoons cognac
1 teaspoon vanilla extract
2 cups plus 2 tablespoons flour
1½ teaspoon baking powder
1/4 teaspoon salt
1 cup grated semisweet chocolate

Mark Malicki

A HARVEST LUNCH
AT THE WINERY

*Duck "Hams" with Fig Chutney
and Corn Cakes*

*Braised Lamb Shanks with
Leek Confit*

Potato and Garlic Purée

*Garden Salad with Lemon Verbena
and Sparkling Wine*

*Goat Milk Yogurt Cheese with
Pistachios and Saffron*

*Pears Poached in Ginger with
Ginger Cookies*

serves twelve

Mark Malicki moved to Sonoma County, California, five years ago from New York, where he worked at the *River Café* and *Le Périgord*. In 1987, he opened *Truffles* restaurant in Sebastopol and sold it three years later. He is currently the chef at *Iron Horse Vineyards* in Sebastopol.

I think my favorite time of year at the winery has to be the harvest. The gardens are literally overflowing with fruits and vegetables, all of which we use for harvest lunches. Another reason I like this time of year is that my wife Jenny and I get to work together, at which point I realize where I get all my great ideas.

DUCK "HAMS" WITH FIG CHUTNEY AND CORN CAKES *serves twelve*

Remove skin but not fat from the duck breasts, then combine salt and sugar and place in a medium-sized bowl with duck breasts. Rub mixture evenly on breasts. Place breasts on a sheet pan, and spread remainder of salt-sugar mixture over breasts.

Remove leaves from thyme sprigs, combine with peppercorns and coriander, and distribute over duck breasts. Cover with foil, weight down, and place in refrigerator overnight.

Remove breasts from refrigerator, scrape off seasoning, and sprinkle with crushed black pepper. Cut 16 rectangles of cheesecloth, 1 by 2 feet. Place 4 layers of cloth on top of each other, and put a breast, fat side down, on corner of cloth. Fold breast in half, so it has the shape of a log, then start rolling from the corner of cloth. Roll tightly, and when breast is 1/3 covered, fold opposite corners of cloth toward each other and fold tightly over breast. Tie with butcher's twine, wrapping it around cloth from one end to the other, and securing ends tightly. Leave a few inches of extra twine at one end so you can hang the breast. Repeat process with other breasts.

Hang duck breasts in a cool, dark, draft-free place, and age for two or three weeks. When ready to serve, remove twine, unwrap, and slice thinly, as you would prosciutto.

To prepare fig chutney, place garlic and ginger with half the vinegar in bowl of a food processor and puree until smooth. Set aside.

(continued next page)

For duck "hams":
4 boneless duck breasts, preferably Muscovy, 12 to 14 ounces each
1 cup rock salt
1/2 cup sugar
2 bunches fresh thyme
2 teaspoons black peppercorns
2 teaspoons coriander seeds
2 teaspoons crushed black pepper
Cheesecloth and butcher's twine

For fig chutney:
2 whole heads garlic, peeled and coarsely chopped
3 tablespoons ginger, coarsely chopped
1½ cups balsamic vinegar
4 pounds fresh figs, washed and stems removed
1½ cups sugar
1½ teaspoons salt
1 teaspoon cayenne pepper
1/2 cup Pinot Noir

For corn cakes:
4 medium eggs
1 cup flour
2 tablespoons clarified
    butter
1 small onion, chopped
1½ cups fresh corn
    kernels
1/2 cup pine nuts
Salt and pepper to taste
1 tablespoon peanut oil

In a 4-quart heavy-bottomed pan, combine figs, remaining vinegar, sugar, salt, and cayenne. Bring to a boil, add garlic-ginger puree, lower heat, and simmer uncovered for about an hour. Add the wine and continue cooking for approximately 1 hour more, until chutney is consistency of honey. Remove from heat and let cool; then refrigerate. Bring to room temperature before serving.

To prepare corn cakes, beat the eggs into the flour in a medium bowl. Add the clarified butter, onion, corn, pine nuts, and salt and pepper to taste. Stir until well blended.

Place a skillet with peanut oil covering bottom over medium heat, and when hot, drop the batter a tablespoon at a time into pan. The pancakes should be about 3 inches in diameter. Cook for about 3 minutes on one side, or until golden brown, flip, and cook for 2 more minutes. Remove from pan and place on warm platter. Serve with fig chutney and slices of duck "ham."

BRAISED LAMB SHANKS WITH
LEEK CONFIT *serves twelve to fifteen*

To prepare leek confit, slit leeks in half lengthwise and wash under cold running water to remove sand. Drain. Slice leeks thinly crosswise.

Use a mortar and pestle or herb mill to pound dried shrimp with chilies to a paste or powder.

Heat peanut oil in a large, heavy skillet. When oil is hot but not smoking, add leeks and, stirring occasionally, brown slightly. Add ground shrimp and chilies, turmeric, and salt, and cook, covered, over low heat for 15 to 20 minutes, stirring occasionally. Leeks are done when oil has been absorbed and leeks are caramelized. When done, set aside for lamb.

Meanwhile, place raw peanuts in a heavy skillet and cook over medium heat, shaking constantly, until golden brown. Remove from pan, let cool, and chop. Set aside for garnish.

To prepare lamb shanks, heat oil in a large enamel pot. Season lamb shanks with salt and pepper and brown on all sides. Remove shanks, add vegetables and garlic, and cook for about 5 minutes. Return shanks to pot, along with Kaffir lime leaves and lemon grass. Add vegetable stock and cook at a simmer for 2 hours, tightly covered and undisturbed. Add 1 cup leek confit and cook for 1/2 hour longer. Remove shanks and place on platter. Puree pan liquid, pour over shanks, and serve with remaining leek confit and peanut garnish.

For leek confit:
2 dozen leeks
4 tablespoons dried
  shrimp (available in
  Asian markets)
2 to 3 small fresh or dried
  chilies (Thai or
  serrano), seeded
1/2 cup peanut oil
1 teaspoon turmeric
1 teaspoon salt

1/2 cup raw peanuts, for
  garnish

For lamb shanks:
3 tablespoons olive oil
1 dozen lamb shanks, cut
  in half crosswise
Salt and pepper
6 carrots, diced
3 yellow onions, diced
4 stalks celery, diced
24 garlic cloves, thinly
  sliced
4 Kaffir lime leaves
  (available in Asian
  markets)
3 tablespoons chopped
  lemon grass
1½ quarts vegetable stock
1 cup leek confit

POTATO AND GARLIC PURÉE *serves twelve*

2 heads garlic
4 pounds russet potatoes,
   washed
Bouquet garni of fresh
   herbs, such as thyme,
   sage, and rosemary, plus
   2 tablespoons whole
   black peppercorns
Salt
Fruity extra virgin
   olive oil

Preheat oven to 350° F. Cut garlic heads
crosswise and roast until soft, about 35
minutes.

Put potatoes in a large heavy pot and cover
with cold salted water. Bring to a boil and
cook about 20 minutes, until tender. Drain
potatoes, remove jackets, and return to empty
pot. Squeeze out roasted garlic pulp and add
to potatoes. Drop in bouquet garni and add
about 2 cups of water to cover. Bring to a
boil, reduce heat, and simmer for 10 to 15
minutes. Remove bouquet garni, season with
salt to taste, and let cool about 15 to 20 minutes.

Working in small batches, ladle potato mixture into a food processor and purée, but only
until smooth and consistency of thick batter.
Pour in heavy ribbons into serving bowl, removing any large lumps. Drizzle olive oil on
potato purée before serving with lamb shanks.

GARDEN SALAD WITH LEMON VERBENA AND SPARKLING WINE *serves twelve*

1 head deer's tongue
   or butter lettuce
1 head lollo rosso or
   red-leaf lettuce
1 handful each of interesting
   greens, such as Japanese
   mustard, fennel tops, ama-
   ranth, purslane, mint,
   anise, hyssop, arugula,
   chervil, and nasturtiums
1 bunch lemon verbena
   (or 2 teaspoons dried)
1/2 cup sparkling wine
Salt and pepper

Wash and dry greens separately, then combine
them. For dressing, bring 1/2 cup water to a
boil, add the lemon verbena, turn off heat
and let steep for 1/2 hour. Remove lemon verbena. Let cool and toss with the greens, along
with 1/2 cup sparkling wine and salt and pepper to taste.

GOAT MILK YOGURT CHEESE WITH PISTACHIOS AND SAFFRON *makes three cups*

The night before, line a colander with two layers of cheesecloth. Put 1 quart yogurt in colander without stirring. Tie 4 corners of cloth together and hang over sink or other undisturbed area with a bowl underneath. Make certain it's high enough so liquid doesn't touch cheese. Repeat process with other 2 quarts of yogurt.

The next morning, place a pan on the stove over medium heat and toast saffron threads until reddish brown in color. Soak saffron in 1 tablespoon milk.

Remove seeds from cardamom pods and grind them with mortar and pestle.

Gently unwrap cheese and place in a nonreactive bowl. Strain saffron threads out of milk and add saffron milk to cheese. Add cardamom powder and sugar, stirring just until blended. Refrigerate for at least 1 hour. Serve with sprinkling of pistachios and fruits that are sweet and acidic, such as tangerines or pomegranates.

Cheesecloth
3 quarts goat-milk yogurt
20 threads of saffron
1 tablespoon milk
4 cardamom pods
2 tablespoons sugar
1/4 cup shelled unsalted pistachios, toasted and roughly chopped

PEARS POACHED IN GINGER *serves twelve*

12 Seckel pears, peeled
Juice of 1 lemon
1 cup sugar
1/4 pound ginger, peeled
   and thinly sliced
   crosswise
1 bottle sparkling wine

After peeling pears, place in bowl of cold water with lemon juice. Put sugar in a large enamel pot over medium heat until sugar caramelizes. Add pears and ginger, mixing well to coat pears with caramel. Add sparkling wine and cook over low heat for about 20 minutes.

Remove pears with slotted spoon and place on platter. Cook down poaching liquid to a syrup. Pour over pears with ginger slices and serve warm or cold.

GINGER COOKIES *makes thirty cookies*

1 cup unsalted butter
1/2 cup powdered sugar
2 cups flour
2 teaspoons powdered
   ginger
1/4 teaspoon salt
1/4 teaspoon baking
   powder

Preheat oven to 350° F. Cream butter (in an electric mixer, if you wish), then add sugar, beating well. Mix together the flour, ginger, salt, and baking powder. Add to butter–sugar mixture.

Roll out dough on floured surface to 1/4 inch thick. Cut into rectangles, about 2 by 2 inches. Place on ungreased sheet pan and bake for 20 to 25 minutes, or until light brown around edges. Serve with ginger pears.

Jacquelyn Buchanan

FEASTING IN THE VINEYARD

Spit-Roasted Whole Pig

Two Salsas: Tomatillo and Avocado

Pinto Beans

Grilled Corn and Grilled Jalapeños

Mixed Green Salad

Bread Pudding with Dark Rum

serves fifteen

Jacquelyn Buchanan received her chef's training at the California Culinary Academy in San Francisco and started her career at the *Union Hotel* in Benicia, California. She has since worked in San Francisco at the *Post Street Bar and Cafe* and currently as executive chef at the *Hayes Street Grill*.

My husband and I have the good fortune to live on the grounds of Carmenet Vineyard, where he is the vineyard manager, on Moon Mountain Drive in Sonoma. The terrain is steep and rocky, the views spectacular, and the grapes are as special as the dirt and the people who farm it.

The harvest celebration is held as close as is practical to the last day of picking. It is a joyful occasion and everyone contributes. Families are always included. Horseshoes are pitched, and there is always dancing to a Spanish station playing loudly on a car radio.

SPIT-ROASTED WHOLE PIG *serves fifteen*

Salt and pepper
Olive oil infused with
   garlic and herbs (e.g.
   thyme, rosemary, and
   oregano), for basting
Garlic and herbs for the
   stomach cavity
1 pig, about thirty-five
   pounds

In a grill designed for spit roasting, start an oak fire 2 to 3 hours ahead to establish a good bed of coals. Add grape wood to the fire before cooking, to increase the heat.

Salt, pepper, and oil the pig. Place herbs and garlic in the stomach cavity and sew closed.

Spit the pig and roast it 4 feet above the fire for 6 hours. Baste frequently with oil. Keep adding grape wood to the fire. When the pig is done, slice it up and serve with salsa and warm tortillas.

TOMATILLO SALSA *makes one quart*

5 pounds tomatillos,
   husked, grilled, and
   roughly chopped
5 pasilla chilies, grilled,
   peeled, and chopped
2 large red bell peppers,
   grilled, peeled, and
   chopped
2 bunches cilantro,
   chopped
3 to 5 jalapeño peppers,
   chopped
1 red onion, chopped
Juice of 3 to 5 limes
Salt to taste

Combine ingredients. Mix and season with salt to taste.

AVOCADO SALSA *makes three cups*

Peel and cube the avocados. Toss with lime juice. Toss with other ingredients, and moisten with olive oil. Season with salt to taste.

6 avocados
Juice of 3 limes
2 bunches cilantro
1/4 cup Cuervo gold tequila
3 fresh cayenne peppers, grilled, peeled, and chopped
2 bunches scallions, sliced
2 tablespoons light olive oil

PINTO BEANS *serves fifteen*

Rinse the beans and soak them for eight hours. Drain and rinse. Place in a large pot and cover with water. Add lard, onions, salt, and epazote. Partially cover pot, and simmer slowly (do not let boil), stirring occasionally. Add more water when top layer of beans becomes dry. Cook until tender.

8 cups pinto beans
8 tablespoons lard
3 onions, diced
Salt to taste
3 to 4 sprigs epazote (Mexican herb, available in Latin markets)

GRILLED CORN AND GRILLED JALAPEÑOS
serves fifteen

15 ears of corn, left in husks

12 or so jalapeño peppers, skewered

When the pig is done, grill the corn in husks and skewered jalapeños over a slow fire for 15 minutes.

BREAD PUDDING WITH DARK RUM *serves eight*

3/4 cup unsalted butter

4 cups day-old bread, cut into cubes (sweet French bread works best)

4 eggs

2 egg yolks

1 quart heavy cream

1/2 cup sugar

2 tablespoons dark rum

This recipe would have to be doubled to serve fifteen.

Melt the butter and toss with the bread cubes. Place in a Pyrex baking dish. Mix together the whole eggs, yolks, cream, sugar, and rum. Pour mixture over the bread cubes. Put the baking dish in a pan of hot water, and transfer to a 325° F oven. Bake for 1 hour, or until custard is set in the middle.

Charles Saunders

A GRAPE HARVEST DINNER

*Sweet White Corn Chowder with
Dungeness Crab Cakes*

*Spinach Salad with Asian Pear,
American Blue Cheese, and Toasted
Hazelnut Vinaigrette*

*Chicken and Wild Mushroom
Strudel with Lemon Yogurt Sauce*

*Sebastopol Apple Cake with Warm
Caramel Sauce*

serves eight

Charles Saunders is a graduate of the Culinary Institute of America in Hyde Park, New York. He also trained in Switzerland and was the private chef to the U.S. ambassador in Bern. He came to California in 1988 and spent two and a half years as executive chef at the *Sonoma Mission Inn & Spa,* developing recipes for healthy, organic spa food. He has since traveled across the country and into Canada on guest-chef assignments.

I thought this meal would exemplify the spirit of the grape harvest. The warmth of the chowder, crispness of the salad, contrast of the strudel, and comforting feeling of the apple cake and caramel sauce are part of the celebration of the end of the summer's toil and contemplation of the success of the harvest. Will our dreams of a perfect wine be realized? The meal satisfies the inner soul with a variety of colors, flavors, and textures of the fall season.

SWEET WHITE CORN CHOWDER *yields one quart*

5 ears white corn
2 tablespoons unsalted
  butter
1/4 pound each onion,
  carrot, and celery,
  roughly chopped
1/2 cup Sauvignon Blanc
1 quart chicken stock
1/4 cup roasted garlic
  cloves, peeled
1 cup canned corn,
  drained
1/2 cup polenta
1 pint half-and-half
2 tablespoons fresh thyme,
  roughly chopped
1/4 cup dry sherry
Salt, white pepper, and
  cayenne to taste

Roast the ears of corn in 350° F oven for
45 minutes. Shuck them, and, using a sharp
knife, remove the kernels. Reserve the cobs.

Heat the butter over moderate heat in a
heavy-bottomed soup pot and sauté the
chopped vegetables until tender. Add the
stripped cobs and pour in the wine, chicken
stock, roasted garlic, and all the corn kernels.
Allow to simmer for 30 minutes.

Add polenta and simmer for 20 minutes.
Remove and discard cobs. Puree in a blender.
Add the half-and-half to adjust consistency,
and strain through a large-holed china cap or
sieve. Finish the chowder with thyme and
sherry. Adjust seasoning.

Serve with crab cakes.

DUNGENESS CRAB CAKES *makes thirty-two*

1/2 pound Dungeness
  crabmeat
1/4 cup finely chopped
  onion
1/4 cup finely diced celery
Olive oil
1/2 pound fresh white
  bread crumbs (no crust)
1 egg
1 tablespoon Dijon
  mustard
1 teaspoon chopped
  thyme
2 teaspoons chopped
  Italian parsley
Salt and pepper to taste
Butter

Squeeze crabmeat to remove excess moisture.
Sauté the onion and celery in a small amount
of olive oil and drain well. Add vegetables to
the crabmeat. Toss in half the bread crumbs,
the egg, mustard, herbs, and seasoning. Form
into 1-tablespoon-size crab cakes.

In a cast-iron skillet, heat some olive oil and
butter. Roll each crab cake in remaining
bread crumbs and sear on both sides. Place
the golden brown cakes on paper towels to
drain.

Pour corn chowder into preheated bowls with
4 crab cakes per serving.

Serve immediately.

SPINACH SALAD WITH ASIAN PEAR, AMERICAN BLUE CHEESE, AND TOASTED HAZELNUT VINAIGRETTE *serves eight*

To prepare the vinaigrette, mix all ingredients and allow to stand several hours before serving.

To assemble salad, the spinach leaves should be tossed in a chilled bowl with 1/8 cup vinaigrette per person. The pear slices should be added at the last minute. Place the dressed salad on plates and crumble blue cheese over it. The flowers can be chopped and placed over the salad, or left whole as a garnish.

1 pound spinach leaves, stemmed and washed
2 Asian pears, cored and thinly sliced
1/2 pound American blue cheese
8 edible flowers (optional)

For hazelnut vinaigrette:
1/4 cup hazelnuts, toasted, skinned, and chopped
3/4 cup fresh orange juice, reduced by half and cooled
1/4 cup rice vinegar
1/4 cup Chardonnay
3/4 cup olive oil
1/8 cup hazelnut oil
2 tablespoons finely chopped red onion
2 tablespoons chopped Italian parsley
Salt and pepper to taste

CHICKEN AND WILD MUSHROOM STRUDEL WITH LEMON YOGURT SAUCE *serves eight*

1 free-range chicken, 3 to
3½ pounds

For chicken seasoning:
Salt and black pepper to
taste
1 tablespoon roughly
chopped sage
1/2 onion, 1 carrot, and
1 stalk celery, medium
diced

For wild mushrooms:
2 tablespoons olive oil
1 pound assorted wild
mushrooms (shiitake,
oyster, field, chanterelle,
etc.), thinly sliced
1 shallot, peeled and
finely chopped
1 clove garlic, peeled and
finely chopped
Salt and pepper to taste

For couscous:
1 cup couscous
2 tablespoons each finely
diced celery, red onion,
red bell pepper, yellow
bell pepper, and carrot
3 cups chicken stock with
1/4 teaspoon curry
powder
Salt and pepper to taste
Juice of 1 lemon
2 teaspoons chopped mint
2 teaspoons chopped
Italian parsley
2 teaspoons chopped basil

Place the seasoning mixture in the cavity of chicken and put in a roasting pan. Roast chicken in 350° F oven for 1 hour, or until juices run clear. Allow to cool. Pull skin off chicken and discard, then remove all meat from bones. Shred the meat with your hands. Set aside.

To prepare wild mushrooms, heat olive oil in a sauté pan, and sauté mushrooms, shallots, and garlic over high heat, tossing quickly. Season with salt and pepper. Remove from pan and allow to cool.

To prepare couscous, combine couscous with diced vegetables. Heat chicken stock to boiling. Pour over couscous. Cover tightly with plastic wrap and allow to stand for 10 minutes. Fluff up with a fork, adjust seasoning, and add lemon juice and fresh herbs.

To make lemon yogurt sauce, combine all ingredients and allow to stand in refrigerator several hours prior to serving.

To prepare chicken filling, combine shredded chicken meat, sautéed mushrooms, couscous, and hard-boiled eggs. Toss but do not overmix.

To make strudel, spread a sheet of phyllo dough on a clean, dry dish towel, the long side toward you. Brush with melted butter to coat sheet completely. Place several mint leaves and Italian parsley leaves on the sheet. Lay another sheet of phyllo on the first one, brush with butter, and place leaves on it. Continue layering procedure until 4 sheets are stacked up.

Spread half the chicken mixture down the middle of the phyllo. Take the end of layered phyllo sheets nearest you and roll on top of chicken mixture, lifting dish towel to help guide the phyllo. Continue to roll, then place filled phyllo roll, seam side down, on a buttered baking sheet. Brush the phyllo with egg wash. Repeat the procedure with remaining chicken mixture and phyllo dough.

Bake strudel in center of 375° F oven for 15 to 20 minutes, until phyllo is golden brown. Allow to cool for 10 minutes. For best results, use serrated knife to slice. Serve with lemon yogurt sauce.

For lemon yogurt sauce:
1 cup mayonnaise
3/4 cup plain yogurt
1/2 teaspoon minced garlic
1/2 teaspoon grated ginger
1 teaspoon wasabi powder
Juice of 1 lemon
1 tablespoon shredded coconut, toasted
1 teaspoon honey
Salt and white pepper to taste

3 eggs, hard-boiled and roughly chopped
1 package phyllo dough, frozen or fresh
1/2 cup unsalted butter, melted
1/4 bunch whole mint leaves
1/4 bunch Italian parsley leaves
1 egg, beaten, for egg wash

SEBASTOPOL APPLE CAKE WITH WARM CARAMEL SAUCE *serves ten*

1/4 cup vegetable oil
4 large eggs
1½ cups light brown
 sugar, firmly packed
1½ teaspoons vanilla
 extract
2 cups all-purpose flour
1 teaspoon freshly grated
 nutmeg
1 teaspoon cinnamon
1½ teaspoons baking soda
1/2 teaspoon salt
1 pound apples
 (Gravenstein, Jonathan,
 or Rome), peeled,
 cored, and finely
 chopped
1¼ cups walnuts, toasted
 and coarsely chopped
1¼ teaspoons grated
 orange zest

For caramel sauce:
1 cup heavy cream
1 cup sugar
1 cup water
1 egg
1 egg yolk
1 teaspoon vanilla extract
2 tablespoons strong
 coffee, preferably
 espresso
2 tablespoons butter

Preheat oven to 350° F. In a large bowl, whisk together the oil, eggs, brown sugar, and vanilla. Add the flour, nutmeg, cinnamon, baking soda, salt, apples, walnuts, and orange zest, and stir the mixture until it is just combined. Pour the batter into a lightly buttered and floured 10-inch springform pan. Bake in the middle of oven for 50 minutes, or until a tester inserted in the middle comes out clean.

To prepare caramel sauce, heat the cream in a saucepan.

Combine sugar and water in a stainless-steel saucepan and mix thoroughly. Cook over moderate heat, stirring once with a wooden spoon, then, with a pastry brush that has been dipped in water, keep rim of pan clean. Remove from heat when sugar is a rich golden brown.

Add hot cream to caramelized sugar. Return to heat for 3 minutes, being careful not to let mixture boil over. Cool for 15 minutes. Stir in egg, egg yolk, vanilla, and coffee. Stir in butter and let cool before transferring to a storage container.

Remove cake from pan and cut into wedges. Lightly reheat caramel sauce and spoon warm sauce onto each plate. Set cake wedge on sauce. Garnish with dollop of whipped cream and chopped toasted walnuts.

John Ash

A DINNER TO RENEW
AN OLD FRIENDSHIP

*Fresh Mussels with Serrano Chilies
and Fresh Mozzarella*

Fettuccine with Braised Rabbit

*Salad of Fennel, Pears, Persimmons,
and Pecans with a Prune Vinaigrette*

Hazelnut Biscotti

serves six

John Ash's restaurant, *John Ash and Company,* in Santa Rosa, California, is considered one of the best in the wine country. As a chef with a fine-arts background, he regularly writes, teaches, and lectures about food and has done "festivals" of California food and wine in several Japanese cities. He is currently working on a book about contemporary game cooking and was recently appointed culinary director of *Fetzer Vineyards' Food and Wine Center* in Valley Oaks, California.

I would call this a celebration to renew an old friendship. It was a meal that I did for close friends whom I hadn't seen in a long while. They returned to California in the fall from living abroad, and this was the dinner they requested, which reminded them of fall in the wine country.

FRESH MUSSELS WITH SERRANO CHILIES AND FRESH MOZZARELLA *serves six*

1/4 pound bacon
2 tablespoons finely
   minced garlic
2 tablespoons finely
   minced scallions
1½ teaspoons stemmed,
   seeded, and finely
   minced fresh serrano
   chilies
4 tablespoons extra virgin
   olive oil
2 tablespoons finely
   minced parsley
6 tablespoons dry white
   bread crumbs
36 large mussels, poached,
   top shell removed,
   liquor reserved
6 ounces fresh mozzarella
   cheese
1 large bunch spinach,
   washed well and stems
   removed, and 6 cooked
   crayfish or grilled
   prawns for garnish
   (optional)

In a sauté pan, cook the bacon until crisp. Drain well and chop finely. In a separate pan, briefly sauté the garlic, scallions, and chilies in 2 tablespoons olive oil until just soft. Do not brown. Combine the bacon, garlic mixture, and parsley in a bowl and set aside. In another small bowl, lightly coat the bread crumbs with drops of olive oil.

Divide the bacon mixture evenly on top of the mussels and moisten with a few drops of the reserved poaching liquor. Slice the mozzarella very thinly and cover each mussel. Sprinkle the oiled bread crumbs evenly over each mussel. If not serving immediately, cover and refrigerate.

To serve, place the mussels on a bed of rock salt or crumpled foil to keep them level. Place in a 425° F oven or under a broiler, until the cheese just melts. In a sauté pan, lightly wilt the spinach leaves in a few drops of olive oil. Serve immediately on warm plates. Place a circle of mussels on top of the spinach and garnish with a crayfish or prawn.

FETTUCCINE WITH BRAISED RABBIT
serves four to six

Season rabbit pieces liberally with salt and pepper. Heat the olive oil in a heavy-bottomed casserole and quickly brown the rabbit. Remove, and sauté the mushrooms, onion, garlic, carrots, and celery, in batches if necessary, until very lightly browned.

Return the rabbit to the casserole, add the sun-dried tomatoes, red wine, fresh tomatoes, herbs, and 2 cups stock, and bring to a simmer. Cover and simmer for 45 to 50 minutes, or until the meat is tender and begins to pull away from the bone easily. Remove rabbit, separate the meat from the bone, discard bones, and cut meat into small pieces. Return the meat to the casserole with the vegetables and simmer for another 15 minutes. Correct seasoning and add additional stock, if necessary, for a nice sauce consistency. Stir in the parsley and basil just before serving.

Cook the pasta al dente in 6 quarts of boiling salted water. Drain in a colander and toss with the rabbit sauce. Garnish with the basil sprigs and cheese.

1 large rabbit, 4 pounds, cut into quarters
Salt and freshly ground pepper
1/3 cup olive oil
1/2 pound fresh chanterelle or shiitake mushrooms
1 cup finely sliced yellow onion
3 tablespoons slivered garlic
1/2 cup finely diced carrots
1/2 cup celery, cut into thin slices on the bias
1/4 cup sun-dried tomatoes in oil, drained and roughly chopped
1 cup hearty red wine
2 cups seeded, diced fresh ripe tomatoes
1 teaspoon each minced fresh thyme and sage
2 to 4 cups rich rabbit or chicken stock
1/3 cup finely chopped parsley (preferably Italian)
1/4 cup chopped fresh basil (or substitute 1 tablespoon chopped fresh mint)
1 pound fresh fettuccine
Fresh basil or mint sprigs and freshly shaved asiago and Parmesan cheese for garnish

SALAD OF FENNEL, PEARS, PERSIMMONS, AND PECANS IN A PRUNE VINAIGRETTE

serves six

For prune vinaigrette:
1/4 cup black currant or raspberry vinegar
1/4 cup champagne vinegar
1/3 cup fresh orange juice
1 tablespoon minced shallot
1 teaspoon fresh minced tarragon
1/2 cup light olive oil
Salt and freshly ground pepper
1/4 cup pitted prunes, cut into eighths lengthwise
2 cups spicy greens such as arugula, watercress, tat tsoi, endive, and/or radicchio
2 firm fuyu persimmons, sliced thinly into rounds
2 ripe pears, sliced in wedges
1 medium bulb fresh fennel, thinly sliced
1/4 cup pecan halves, lightly toasted

To prepare the vinaigrette, combine vinegars and orange juice in a small saucepan and reduce by one-third over moderate heat, about 5 minutes. Cool and quickly whisk in the shallot, tarragon, and olive oil. Season with salt and pepper to taste. Stir in the prunes and allow to sit for at least 1 hour for the flavors to develop.

Place the greens on chilled plates, separating the types. Attractively arrange the fruits and fennel on top and drizzle the vinaigrette over. Top with pecans and serve.

For a more substantial salad, place paper-thin slices of prosciutto or coppa attractively on top.

HAZELNUT BISCOTTI *makes approximately two dozen*

Preheat oven to 350° F. Coarsely chop hazel-nuts. Combine sugar, butter, liqueur or brandy, nuts, and eggs. Mix well.

Stir in flour, baking powder, and salt. Knead briefly and form into a long loaf about 2 inches in diameter. Place on a nonstick or parchment-lined cookie sheet and bake for 25 minutes, or until firm. It will have a cakelike texture. Remove from oven and cool.

Slice diagonally into 1/2-inch slices and lay out on the sheet pan. Bake for 20 minutes more, turning once until both sides are lightly browned and toasted. Cool and store in an airtight container. Serve with good coffee.

1 cup hazelnuts, lightly toasted and skinned
1 cup sugar
1/2 cup unsalted butter, melted
4 tablespoons hazelnut liqueur or brandy
3 whole eggs
3 cups flour
2 teaspoons baking powder
1/4 teaspoon salt

Peter M. DeMarais

A COMMEMORATIVE AUTUMN MENU

*Pear and Sweet Potato Soup
with Ginger*

*Pasta Pinwheels with Apple,
Chanterelles, and Thyme Beurre
Noisette*

*Ahi Tuna Seared Rare in Pumpkin-
Seed Crust with Roasted Pepper
Salad*

Rose Petal Sorbet

*Medallions of Venison on Braised
Fennel and Endive with Huckleberry
Vinaigrette*

*Fig Mousse in Walnut Chocolate
Tuiles*

serves six

Peter M. DeMarais is a native San Francis-
can descended from a long line of chefs. His
great-grandfather, Pierre Epinot, came from
Lyons to be the chef at San Francisco's *Palace
Hotel,* where DeMarais is currently the executive sous-chef. Prior to that, he was the chef
at the *Café Majestic.* He is a competitive mara-
thon runner and twice won first prize for
recipes entered in a health-food contest organ-
ized by the Cancer Education and Prevention
Center of Oakland.

I created this autumn menu in memory of my good friend, the Reverend Wade Egbert, of Mill Valley, California, who died of AIDS in October 1988. His birthday was also in October. Through the Marin County AIDS Support Network, I became Wade's care-giver and daily companion during his illness.

Toward the end, Wade could no longer eat. To pass the time, I would describe to him my favorite recipes and specialties I prepared at the restaurant. Wade loved the autumn and the fiery colors found in the foods of the season, such as red peppers, orange pumpkins, violet figs, and golden pears. Some of these foods are part of my autumn menu.

PEAR AND SWEET POTATO SOUP WITH GINGER *serves six*

Heat olive oil in a large pan and sauté onion, celery, leeks, shallots, and ginger until translucent. Add pears (reserve some pear for garnish), sweet potatoes, and chicken stock. Stir and bring to a boil. Reduce heat and allow to simmer for 45 minutes. Season with salt and pepper. Puree the soup in a blender or food processor. Set aside and chill.

When the soup is cold, whisk in the yogurt. Serve cold, garnished with a dollop of yogurt, a slice of pickled ginger, and some diced pear.

1 tablespoon olive oil
1 onion, sliced
3 ribs celery, sliced
3 leeks, mostly whites, cleaned and sliced
3 shallots, chopped
1/4 cup peeled, chopped ginger
4 pears, peeled and cored
4 sweet potatoes, peeled and cut into small pieces
4 cups chicken or vegetable stock
Salt and white pepper to taste
1/2 cup low-fat yogurt
Pickled ginger for garnish

PASTA PINWHEELS WITH APPLE, CHANTERELLES, AND THYME BEURRE NOISETTE *serves six*

2 sheets fresh pasta
  (9 by 12 inches)
8 ounces ricotta cheese
2 tablespoons chopped
  fresh thyme
1/4 cup chopped fresh
  basil
12 ounces fresh
  chanterelles, sliced and
  sautéed
2 cups peeled, sliced green
  apple, lightly sautéed
1/2 cup walnuts, toasted
  and roughly chopped
Cheesecloth and twine
Olive oil
Chicken broth

For beurre noisette:
2 tablespoons butter
1 tablespoon chopped
  shallot
1 tablespoon Calvados
1 tablespoon chopped
  fresh thyme
Salt and pepper

Lay out pasta sheets on a work surface. Spread with a layer of ricotta. Sprinkle with thyme and basil. Arrange the cooked chanterelles in three lines on each sheet, top to bottom. Place cooked apple slices between lines of chanterelles. Sprinkle with walnuts. Lay out length of cheesecloth, then roll up pasta tightly, side to side. Rub surface of pasta roll with olive oil and encase in cheesecloth. Tie both ends of cloth tightly with twine.

Cook pasta pinwheels in simmering, lightly salted chicken broth (or water) for 20 minutes. Remove cloth carefully.

To prepare beurre noisette, brown the butter with the shallots in a sauté pan over moderate heat. Do not let burn. Add the Calvados and thyme, salt and pepper. Serve with slices of pasta pinwheel.

AHI TUNA SEARED RARE IN PUMPKIN-SEED CRUST WITH ROASTED PEPPER SALAD *serves six*

Season tuna pieces with salt and pepper. Coat them with pumpkin seeds. Set aside.

To prepare pepper salad, roast peppers and pearl onions in a 400° F oven for 20 minutes. Place in covered container for 20 minutes. Peel pearl onions. Peel and seed peppers. Cut into strips and place in bowl with pearl onions.

Add garlic, anchovies, shallots, cilantro, olive oil, and balsamic vinegar. Toss together. Season to taste.

Heat olive oil in a skillet and sear tuna pieces a couple of minutes on each side, until pumpkin seeds begin to turn from green to gold. Pat dry and serve on top of pepper salad.

12 ounces Ahi tuna, cut into 2-ounce portions
1/2 teaspoon salt
1/2 teaspoon white pepper
1 cup toasted chopped pumpkin seeds
2 red bell peppers
2 yellow bell peppers
1 cup pearl onions
3 tablespoons virgin olive oil

For pepper salad dressing:
2 cloves garlic, finely chopped
2 tablespoons chopped anchovies
2 tablespoons chopped shallots
1/4 cup chopped cilantro
4 tablespoons virgin olive oil
2 tablespoons balsamic vinegar
Salt and pepper to taste

ROSE PETAL SORBET *makes 6 cups*

Bring sugar and 1½ cups water to a boil, stir, and simmer for 5 minutes. Let cool. Wash rose petals thoroughly. Pour syrup and cold champagne over petals. Let stand, covered, for 3 hours, or overnight. Strain through cheesecloth. Freeze.

1½ cups sugar
1½ cups water
2 quarts rose petals (must be organic)
2 cups cold champagne

MEDALLIONS OF VENISON ON BRAISED FENNEL AND ENDIVE WITH HUCKLEBERRY VINAIGRETTE *serves six*

1 loin venison (about
  30 ounces)
4 tablespoons olive oil
2 tablespoons chopped
  shallots
2 tablespoons chopped
  tarragon
3 cups thinly sliced fennel
1 cup thinly sliced strips
  Belgian endive
1/2 teaspoon salt
1 teaspoon black pepper
2 tablespoons Pernod
1/4 cup hazelnuts, roasted,
  cleaned of skins, and
  chopped

For vinaigrette:
1/2 cup hazelnut oil
2 tablespoons chopped
  shallots
1/4 cup crème de cassis
1/8 cup sherry vinegar
2 tablespoons chopped
  tarragon
1½ cups fresh
  huckleberries
Salt and pepper to taste

Panfry the venison in 2 tablespoons olive oil, browning all sides. Transfer skillet to 400° F oven for approximately 20 minutes (for rare). Place venison on warm platter and set aside.

To the same pan add shallots, tarragon, fennel, endive, salt, and pepper. Sauté 5 to 10 minutes with more olive oil. Deglaze with Pernod. Sprinkle with hazelnuts. Set aside.

To prepare vinaigrette, place hazelnut oil and shallots in saucepan over low heat for a few minutes. Whisk in cassis and vinegar. Stir in tarragon and huckleberries. Season to taste.

Slice venison into six medallions. Serve on a bed of fennel-endive mixture. Ladle huckleberry vinaigrette over venison.

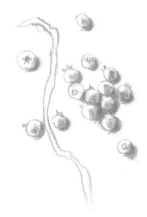

FIG MOUSSE *serves six*

Whip the cream and set aside. In a saucepan, cook the sugar, cassis, brandy, and vanilla bean to syrup consistency, about 5 minutes. Remove vanilla bean. Add chopped figs and stir. Let cool.

Whip egg whites until stiff. Fold in fig mixture. Fold in whipped cream. Keep chilled.

When ready to serve, spoon fig mousse into walnut tuiles. If you wish, garnish with a chocolate-dipped whole fig and walnut half.

2 cups heavy cream
1/3 cup sugar
1/4 cup crème de cassis
1/8 cup brandy
1 vanilla bean, split in half
2 cups fresh, finely chopped Black Mission figs
1½ cups egg whites

WALNUT CHOCOLATE TUILES *makes six*

Lightly grease a baking sheet, or line it with parchment paper.

In a saucepan, bring sugar, butter, and honey to a boil. Off heat, stir in vanilla, nuts, flour, and cinnamon. Immediately pour 6 thin circles onto the baking sheet. Bake at 350° F for 6 to 8 minutes.

Quickly remove tuiles from pan with a spatula and shape over inverted coffee cups. Remove from cups when they've crisped. Dribble melted chocolate over the tuiles to form stripes. Serve with a mound of fig mousse in each tuile.

4 tablespoons brown sugar
4 tablespoons butter
5 tablespoons honey
1 teaspoon vanilla
1/8 cup ground walunts
1/2 cup flour
1/4 teaspoon cinnamon
3 ounces semisweet chocolate, melted

Donna Nicoletti

AN OLD-FASHIONED COLUMBUS DAY DINNER

Escarole Soup

Stuffed Artichokes

Fusilli with Ricotta Cheese and Black Pepper

Chicken Vesuvio

Zabaglione

serves four

Donna Nicoletti is a graduate of the California Culinary Academy. She is the chef and part owner of San Francisco's *Undici* restaurant, where she re-creates dishes of her southern Italian heritage.

There was a time when Columbus Day was celebrated on October 12. This, of course, was before it became the Monday of just another three-day weekend. Then, it was clearly an Italian-American holiday that no one could deny us. So we honored the great sailor, Christopher Columbus, an honest-to-God Italian who discovered America, the land our parents and grandparents worshiped.

So what that Columbus sailed for the queen of Spain (a mostly forgivable transgression), or that he actually landed on an island in the Caribbean, or that he thought he had landed in India (a confusion often attributed to lack of pasta on his long journey). The bottom line was that he was Italian and discovered America.

Columbus Day meant a cool autumn day of parade watching and dinner with the family in a nice, home-style Italian restaurant. Although the conversation was purely American, the food was purely Italian. It was restaurant food at its best — no different really than the food we ate at home, except that you could get anything you wanted from a menu several pages long. Here are some of those menu selections.

ESCAROLE SOUP *serves four*

In a large pan, sweat the onion with garlic, salt, bay leaves, oregano, and just enough olive oil to coat the onion. Add the escarole and cook until just wilted.

Heat the chicken stock separately, then add it to the pan with the vegetables. Cook until they become soft, about 1/2 hour. Serve with Parmesan cheese and black pepper.

1 large onion, diced
1½ cups medium-diced celery
1 head escarole, cut into coarse pieces
3 cloves garlic, minced
8 cups chicken stock
2 bay leaves
1 teaspoon dried oregano
Olive oil
Salt and black pepper
Grated Parmesan cheese

STUFFED ARTICHOKES *serves four*

4 globe artichokes
1½ cups bread crumbs
1½ cups grated Parmesan
  cheese
3 teaspoons dried oregano
Pinch of salt
1 teaspoon black pepper
4 bay leaves
Rind of 1/2 lemon
Olive oil

Mix together the bread crumbs, Parmesan, oregano, salt, and pepper. Cut off stems of artichokes. Slice 1/2 inch off tops and snip off tips of the leaves. Spread the leaves out and rinse them on the inside. Drain upside down for a few minutes.

Brush the insides of the leaves with olive oil to keep the artichokes moist. Starting from the outer leaves, carefully pull back each leaf and drop in some bread-crumb mixture. Do not overstuff. When you have gotten as many leaves as possible stuffed, transfer the artichokes to a pot.

Add enough water to the pot to come one-fourth up the side of the artichokes. Add the lemon rind and bay leaves.

Cover well and simmer about 30 minutes, checking occasionally for evaporation. Add more water, if necessary, during cooking. The artichokes are done when a knife easily pierces the heart.

Serve immediately with a bit of cooking liquid. Make sure your guests eat the heart. It's the best part.

FUSILLI WITH RICOTTA CHEESE AND BLACK PEPPER *serves four*

In an electric mixer fitted with the paddle attachment, mix the ricotta, eggs, salt, and pepper. Beat well for 4 to 5 minutes, until the mixture becomes fluffy. On slow speed, gradually add the cream, and beat until incorporated. The mixture should be thick but saucelike.

Cook the pasta in boiling, salted water until al dente. Drain the fusilli of all but a bit of cooking water (a little will keep the pasta moist). Transfer to a bowl. Quickly toss with the ricotta mixture and parsley. Serve with Parmesan cheese.

4 cups ricotta cheese
2 eggs
3/4 teaspoon salt
3/4 teaspoon black pepper
1 cup cream
12 ounces fusilli
4 tablespoons finely
  chopped parsley
Grated Parmesan cheese

CHICKEN VESUVIO *serves four*

2 pounds small roasting
   potatoes, cleaned and
   cut in half
Olive oil
3 teaspoons chopped
   garlic
2 teaspoons dried oregano
Salt and pepper
2 frying chickens, 2½
   pounds each, cut up
   into thighs, drumsticks,
   half breasts, and wings

So named, we think, because the Neapolitans, who lived in the shadow of Vesuvius, brought the recipe to America.

On a baking sheet, toss the potatoes with olive oil, 1 teaspoon garlic, 1 teaspoon oregano, and a good amount of salt and pepper. The olive oil should lightly coat the potatoes. Bake in a 400° F oven for 30 minutes, occasionally turning the potatoes with a metal spatula.

Heat some oil in a sauté pan. Season the chicken pieces with salt and pepper, and sear, skin side down. Toss in remaining garlic. Sprinkle oregano on the chicken, making sure not to drop it in the oil, as it will burn. Turn the chicken and sear the other side. Transfer to a baking pan and roast in a 400° F oven, 20 minutes for the breasts and 30 minutes for the drumsticks, thighs, and wings. Serve with the potatoes.

ZABAGLIONE *serves four*

6 egg yolks
1/2 cup sugar
3/4 cup Marsala

Of course, in a restaurant, the waiter prepared this at the table, over a Sterno burner.

In an electric mixer fitted with a whisk attachment, beat the egg yolks and sugar until they reach the ribbon stage. Transfer mixture to a copper or stainless-steel bowl.

Place the bowl over a pan of simmering water and add the Marsala. Whisk the mixture by hand until it becomes soft and fluffy, 7 to 10 minutes. Serve immediately, by itself, over fruit, or, better yet, over ice cream.

Edward Espe Brown

A FESTIVE VEGETARIAN
MENU FOR AUTUMN

*Frisée and Radicchio Salad with Roasted Walnuts and
Grilled Red Pepper Sauce*

Potatoes Baked in Parchment with Fresh Herbs

Spaghetti Squash in a Spicy Tomato Sauce

Nut Loaf in Phyllo Pastry

Carrot Salad with Grapefruit, Raisins, Ginger, and Mint

Red Bartlett Pear Tart

serves four

Edward Espe Brown learned to cook at the
Tassajara Zen Mountain Center in Carmel
Valley, California, and was manager of the
renowned San Francisco vegetarian restaurant
Greens for five years. He is the author of *The
Tassajara Bread Book, Tassajara Cooking,* and
The Tassajara Recipe Book (Shambhala/Zen
Center, 1970, 1973, 1985) and coauthor of
The Greens Cookbook (Bantam, 1987). He
currently conducts cooking classes and studies
Chinese medicine to explore the healing
effect of food and herbs.

    *This is a festive vegetarian menu that was prompted by a joyous occasion in
October, when two friends received their licenses for acupuncture. The recipes originally included Chinese medicinal herbs, but I decided to leave them out, since they
are not readily available and their use would require explanation beyond the scope
of this book.*
    *Even without the Chinese herbs, this is a fine menu for an autumn celebra-
tion, perhaps even Thanksgiving or Christmas. I like dividing up the meal into*

courses like this. The food is spread out over time, allowing ample opportunity to appreciate and savor the virtues of each dish, as well as occasion to visit, chat, and digest. An appropriate wine may be picked for the dishes being served, and I would end the meal with a brandy like Armagnac.

FRISÉE AND RADICCHIO SALAD WITH ROASTED WALNUTS AND GRILLED RED PEPPER SAUCE *serves four to six*

1 head frisée or 1/2 head
   curly endive
1 head radicchio
1/4 cup walnuts
4 red bell peppers
3 cloves garlic
5 tablespoons olive oil
2 teaspoons balsamic
   vinegar
Salt and freshly ground
   black pepper

This is an attractive and colorful dish, with the roasted red pepper sauce pooled around the green and purple of the frisée and radicchio, both of which have been lightly cooked to soften and sweeten them.

Wash the frisée and radicchio, then cut the larger leaves into two or three pieces. Roast the walnuts in a 350° F oven for about 8 minutes and then chop them coarsely.

Roast the red peppers over a gas burner, or charcoal grill them until blackened all over (or optionally, slice in half lengthwise and broil cut side down until well blackened). Place in a closed container and let steam 5 to 10 minutes. Remove the blackened skins, stems, seeds, and veins. Slice 2 of the peppers into strips and set aside. Purée the other 2 peppers in a blender to form a sauce with a light seasoning of 1 clove garlic, a tablespoon or so of olive oil, a teaspoon or so of balsamic vinegar, salt, and pepper.

Mince the other 2 cloves garlic and put in a bowl with the frisée and radicchio. Heat 3 to 4 tablespoons olive oil in a large skillet, then pour it over the frisée and radicchio while tossing with tongs. Place clumps of the greens back in the hot skillet to cook lightly, just so they soften slightly but do not entirely

lose their shape. Season with a few drops
balsamic vinegar, salt, and pepper.

To assemble the salad, mix most of the pepper strips and walnuts (saving some for garnish) with the frisée and radicchio. Place the
mixture in the middle of plates and surround
with the red pepper sauce. Garnish with
remaining pepper strips and walnuts.

POTATOES BAKED IN PARCHMENT WITH FRESH HERBS *serves four*

The parchment for this dish is an unwaxed
paper available in most supermarkets. To be
able to unwrap the potatoes at the table makes
this a fun dish.

1 pound new potatoes
1 head garlic
Olive oil
**Salt and freshly ground
    black pepper**

Cut the potatoes into bite-size pieces and separate the head of garlic into cloves. Peeling
the garlic is not necessary, but extra-large
cloves should be cut in half.

**4 short sprigs rosemary,
    about 3 to 4 inches**
Parchment paper

Tear off four pieces of parchment paper, 12 to
15 inches long. Place a fourth of the potatoes
and garlic in the middle of one half of each
piece of paper. Sprinkle on a few drops of
olive oil, some salt and pepper, and a sprig
of rosemary. Fold the other half of the paper
over the potatoes. Then fold the edges of the
paper to form a packet. One way to do this is
to form a half-moon shape, but any shape
will do as long as the edges are sealed to
retain the steam while baking.

Bake in a 375° F oven for about 30 minutes.
The potatoes are done when their bouquet
permeates the room when you open the oven
door. If you want, open a package and check
to see if the potatoes are soft.

SPAGHETTI SQUASH IN A SPICY TOMATO SAUCE *serves four to six*

1 spaghetti squash
1 teaspoon cumin seed
2 teaspoons dried oregano
2 tablespoons olive oil
1 yellow onion, diced
2 cloves garlic, minced
1 dried ancho chili or
   negro chili
1 can (1 pound, 12 ounces)
   stewed tomatoes,
   pureed
1/2 teaspoon minced
   chipotle chili
Red wine vinegar
Salt
Fresh thyme or oregano
   for garnish

Spaghetti squash is fun because it appears to be something (spaghetti) that it isn't. This gives the dish a somewhat mysterious quality and lets everyone in for a few surprises. The sauce is seasoned with the ingredients of what usually constitutes chili powder, so if you aren't up to getting all that together, use a chili powder of your choice.

Bake the spaghetti squash in a 350° F oven for about 50 minutes, until it is fork-tender. Remove from the oven and let cool.

While the squash is baking, you can assemble the tomato sauce. Roast the cumin seeds in a dry frying pan until aromatic and slightly colored. Add the oregano briefly, until it, too, is aromatic. Grind these in a spice grinder. If using a whole dried chili, roast in a 350° F oven for about 3 minutes, and then remove stem and grind in a spice mill.

Heat the oil in a large skillet and sauté the onion until it is translucent. Add the garlic, cumin, oregano, and chili, and continue to sauté for another minute. Add the pureed tomatoes and simmer 10 to 15 minutes.

Finish the seasoning with the chipotle chili, a few drops of vinegar, and salt, if needed. (If the chipotle chili is not available, add more of the other seasonings to intensify the flavors to your own satisfaction.)

Cut the squash open and remove the string and seeds, then scoop out the flesh with a spoon so that it forms spaghettilike strands. Add these to the tomato sauce and simmer until serving time, or place in a casserole in a low oven to keep warm. When serving, garnish with fresh thyme or oregano, whole or minced.

NUT LOAF IN PHYLLO PASTRY *serves six to eight*

The cheese and nut loaf filling gives this phyllo pastry a substantial, somewhat "meaty" nature, yet the pastry is light and flaky. Overall, the dish is festive and the crispy brown pastry gives it an appealing look.

Most phyllo dough comes frozen, so give it a couple of hours to thaw, then remove the sheets you need (you may have to cut them in half for the 9-by-13-inch size you want) and reseal and refreeze the rest.

Heat the olive oil and sauté the onion for several minutes until it is translucent. Add the mushrooms, garlic, dried herbs, and some salt and pepper. Cook for several minutes, until the mushrooms shrink and brown slightly. If they release a lot of juice, raise the heat and cook off the excess liquid.

Remove to a bowl and add the rice, walnuts, eggs, cheese, and fresh herbs. Mix together and adjust the seasoning.

Using a pastry brush, butter the bottom of a 9-by-2-by-13-inch pan. Put in a sheet of phyllo dough and brush it with butter. Repeat for 7 layers, then spread the filling over the phyllo. Cover with the remaining phyllo sheets, brushing each layer with the melted butter.

Cut the completed pastry into 12 square pieces, then cut each square in half diagonally. The pastry may be chilled for 20 to 30 minutes first to make cutting easier.

(continued next page)

16 to 20 sheets phyllo dough, 9 by 13 inches (about 1/2 pound)
2 tablespoons olive oil
1 onion, diced
1/2 pound mushrooms, halved and sliced
3 cloves garlic, minced
1 teaspoon each dried thyme and marjoram
1/2 teaspoon dried sage
Salt and freshly ground black pepper
1½ cups cooked brown or wild rice
1½ cups walnuts, finely chopped
3 eggs, beaten
3/4 pound grated cheese: cheddar, Gruyère, fontina, Parmesan, or provolone (one or more kinds, but include some Parmesan)
1/2 cup minced mixed fresh herbs (e.g., parsley, thyme, marjoram)
3/4 to 1 cup unsalted butter, melted
Sprigs of fresh herbs for garnish

Bake in a 375° F oven for 50 to 60 minutes, until the top is golden brown. Let sit for a few minutes to firm up, then remove from pan to a serving platter and garnish with sprigs of fresh herbs. May be served hot or at room temperature.

CARROT SALAD WITH GRAPEFRUIT, RAISINS, GINGER, AND MINT *serves four to six*

3 large carrots
1/2 cup raisins
2 ruby grapefruit
1 tablespoon freshly
    grated ginger
1/2 cup fresh mint cut
    into julienne strips
Whole mint leaves, for
    garnish

Fresh, juicy, sweet, tart, and pungent, as well as brightly colorful, this salad is a refreshing contrast to the phyllo pastry.

Cut the carrots diagonally into ovals, then cut the ovals into narrow strips — a kind of julienne where each piece has a pale, orange-yellow center and darker orange tips. Blanch the carrots for about 1 minute in boiling water and drain.

Cover the raisins with boiling water and let sit to plump up.

Cut the peel off each end of the grapefruit and then cut the peel off the sides. Using a sharp knife, cut each segment away from its sheath.

Combine the grapefruit and carrots with the ginger and mint. Drain the raisins and mix them in. Check the taste to see if you might like a little more sweetness (say, honey) or tartness (perhaps lemon juice).

May be mixed up ahead of time and allowed to sit for an hour or more before serving. Garnish with whole mint leaves.

RED BARTLETT PEAR TART *serves four to six, or even eight*

To prepare the tart dough, combine the flours with the sugar and lemon peel. Cut in the butter until it is in pea-sized pieces. Add the vanilla and water and mix in lightly. Although this is called dough, it does not really need to come together in a piece, as it will be pressed into the tart pan. Keep it on the dry side.

Press the tart dough into a 9-inch tart pan, starting with the sides and then filling in the bottom. Press to a thickness of about 1/4 inch, and be careful to press into the corners of the pan so the dough is not too thick there.

To prepare the filling, cut the butter and sugar into the flour along with the spices. Distribute over the tart dough.

Quarter the pears, core them, and cut into diagonal slices. Arrange the slices decoratively in the tart pan, fanning them out or placing them in concentric circles, skin side up, starting from the outside. Or . . . you figure it out. If you wish, sprinkle a little sugar on top.

Bake in a 375° to 400° F oven for about 35 to 40 minutes, until the sides of the tart are nicely browned and the pears are tender.

For tart dough:
1/4 cup whole wheat flour
1 cup all-purpose flour
2 tablespoons sugar
1 teaspoon grated lemon peel
1/2 cup unsalted butter
1 teaspoon vanilla extract
1 tablespoon water

For the filling:
2 tablespoons unsalted butter
2 tablespoons sugar
1/4 tablespoon all-purpose flour
1/8 teaspoon ground cardamom
1/8 teaspoon anise seed
2 to 3 Red Bartlett pears

Christopher L. Majer

A FALL EQUINOX MENU

Oysters with White Truffle
Mignonette

Butternut Squash and Sage Ravioli
with Red Chard and Brown Butter

Roast Rack of Lamb with
Chanterelle Risotto and
Pommery Mustard Sauce

Pear Sorbet with Lemon Crisps,
Caramel Sauce, and
Armagnac Cream

serves four

Christopher L. Majer began his culinary career in New York in such restaurants as the *Gotham Bar & Grill*, *Arcadia*, and *The Quilted Giraffe*. In 1987, he came to San Francisco as executive sous-chef at *Campton Place*. He is presently the chef at *Splendido's*, doing his own interpretation of Mediterranean cuisine.

The first day of fall is a change. It's a time to place the summer behind and look forward to good things. The weather turns cooler, the trees start to turn color, and the season hastens one to move indoors and drink a bottle of fine red wine.

The foods of autumn start to arrive, and soon turn bountiful. Dreams of game, wild mushrooms, pumpkins, truffles, oysters, and chestnuts can now be realized, along with an abundance of grapes, apples, pears, cranberries, and huckleberries.

OYSTERS WITH WHITE TRUFFLE MIGNONETTE *serves four*

Shuck the oysters and place them on 4 plates on a bed of chopped ice, seaweed, rock salt, or anything else that will keep them steady. Combine all other ingredients except the truffle, and let sit 20 minutes. Spoon equal portions of mignonette on oysters, and, if used, top with sliced white truffle.

2 dozen oysters
1½ tablespoons white truffle oil
5 tablespoons white wine
1 tablespoon champagne vinegar
1/2 tablespoon finely chopped shallots
1/4 teaspoon kosher salt
2 tablespoons cracked white peppercorns
1/2 ounce white truffle, thinly sliced (optional)

BUTTERNUT SQUASH AND SAGE RAVIOLI WITH RED CHARD AND BROWN BUTTER *serves four*

Make pasta dough by combining semolina, flour, and salt on work surface. Form a well in the middle. Add eggs and olive oil. Knead into a ball. If dough is hard or dry, add some water. Cover with plastic wrap and chill for an hour or more.

Preheat oven to 400° F. Cut squash in half lengthwise and scoop out seeds. Brush with butter, season with salt and pepper, and bake until completely soft. Scoop out meat and chop roughly.

Heat 1 tablespoon butter in a nonstick sauté pan. Lightly cook the garlic and sage. Add

For pasta dough:
1 cup semolina
1 cup all-purpose flour
1 teaspoon salt
2 large eggs
2 teaspoons olive oil
Water, if necessary

1 butternut squash, approximately 1½ pounds
1/2 cup plus 2 tablespoons unsalted butter
Salt and pepper
1 teaspoon chopped garlic

(continued next page)

1 tablespoon chopped
   fresh sage
1 tablespoon grated
   Parmesan cheese
1 tablespoon lemon juice
1/4 teaspoon nutmeg
1 bunch red chard,
   cleaned
1 egg, lightly beaten, for
   egg wash

the squash and heat through. Add Parmesan
and 1/2 teaspoon lemon juice. Season with
nutmeg and salt and pepper to taste. Cool.

On a floured work surface, or in a pasta
machine, roll out pasta dough as thinly as
possible (1/16 inch or so). Lay out dough in
rectangular sheets. On half the sheets, place a
scant teaspoon of squash mixture at 1-inch
intervals.

Brush remaining sheets with egg wash, and
lay over first sheets. Press around mounds of
filling with your finger. With a ravioli wheel,
cut 1-inch squares, making sure to seal the
edges. Place raviolis in one layer on floured
sheet pan and refrigerate until ready to use.

Bring a large pot of salted water to a boil.
Drop in raviolis and let cook for 2 to 3
minutes. Drain.

Meanwhile, heat 2 tablespoons butter in a
skillet. Add red chard and wilt lightly. Place
on 4 plates. Add remaining butter and brown
lightly. Sprinkle on remaining lemon juice,
and salt and pepper to taste. Place cooked
raviolis on wilted chard and top with brown
butter.

ROAST RACK OF LAMB WITH CHANTERELLE RISOTTO AND POMMERY MUSTARD SAUCE
serves four

Preheat oven to 450° F. Place chanterelles and 2 tablespoons butter, cut into small cubes, in a small roasting pan. Add garlic and thyme, and season with salt and pepper. Cover with aluminum foil. Roast in oven for 15 to 20 minutes. Remove foil, thyme, and garlic. Reserve any juices. Set aside.

To prepare risotto, heat olive oil and 2 table-spoons butter in a large saucepan. Add onions and cook without coloring until soft, approximately 10 minutes. Add rice and stir until well coated. Sauté lightly for 1 or 2 minutes. Add 1/2 cup warm chicken stock and stir constantly. When liquid is almost absorbed, add more stock to just cover rice, and stir. Repeat this process for 15 minutes, or until rice is almost tender.

Add mushrooms, reserved juices, and a bit more stock, and cook until rice is al dente, about 5 minutes. Stir in remaining butter, cheese, and herbs. Season with salt and pepper.

(continued next page)

2 lamb racks, each with
    8 chops, thoroughly
    trimmed
Salt and pepper
2 tablespoons olive oil

For risotto:
12 ounces chanterelle
    mushrooms, cleaned
    and, if large, cut up
5 tablespoons unsalted
    butter
4 cloves garlic, peeled and
    lightly mashed
3 sprigs fresh thyme
Salt and pepper
2 tablespoons olive oil
1 medium onion, finely
    diced
1½ cups Arborio rice
5 cups chicken stock,
    heated
2 tablespoons freshly
    grated Parmesan cheese
1/2 teaspoon each
    chopped tarragon, mint,
    chives, basil, and Italian
    parsley

For Pommery sauce:
5 tablespoons unsalted
   butter
2 cloves garlic, peeled and
   sliced
2 shallots, peeled and
   sliced
1/4 cup white wine
3/4 cup reduced lamb
   stock or veal stock
3 tablespoons Pommery
   mustard
Salt and pepper

To make Pommery mustard sauce, melt 1 tablespoon butter in a saucepan, add garlic and shallots, and cook without coloring over medium-low heat for 2 minutes. Add white wine and reduce by half. Add reduced lamb stock and simmer for 5 to 10 minutes. Gently whisk in remaining butter. Strain through a fine strainer or cheesecloth. Stir in mustard. Season with salt and pepper.

Preheat oven to 450° F. Season racks of lamb with salt and pepper. Heat olive oil in a large skillet. Brown lamb lightly on all sides, and place skillet in the oven; make sure bones do not extend over the sides of the skillet, as they will burn. Roast for approximately 20 minutes, until the internal temperature reaches 125° F. The lamb will be rare. If you desire it better done, let it cook a few more minutes. Allow the racks to rest 10 minutes.

Slice the racks so each person will receive 3 chops, one double chop and two single chops of approximately the same width. Divide the risotto evenly in the middle of 4 plates. Place the chops around the risotto and gently spoon the sauce around the plates.

PEAR SORBET WITH LEMON CRISPS, CARAMEL SAUCE, AND ARMAGNAC CREAM
serves four

For pear sorbet:
1¾ pounds ripe pears
1/3 cup sugar
Pinch of salt
Juice of 1/2 lemon
A few drops of Armagnac
   or pear liqueur

To prepare pear sorbet, peel, core, and cut up pears. Cook with a bit of water until soft. Puree. Whisk in sugar and flavorings to taste. It may not need all the sugar if pears are very sweet. Chill in an ice-cream maker according to manufacturer's instructions. Store in freezer.

To make lemon crisps, beat butter with lemon zest until light in color, about 3 to 4 minutes. You may use an electric mixer. Beat in sugar until well blended. Beat in egg whites gradually, scraping sides of the bowl. Fold in the flour. Cover and chill overnight.

Preheat oven to 325° F. On a nonstick or buttered baking sheet, spread out batter into 6- to 8-inch rounds. The rounds should be almost transparent when spread on pan. Bake about 5 minutes, until golden brown.

Remove from baking sheet with a spatula and form into cones by wrapping around a dowel. If cookies become too brittle, return to oven briefly, and they will soften again.

To prepare Armagnac cream, whip cream to soft peaks, add sugar and Armagnac, then whip until stiff.

To make caramel sauce, cook butter and sugar in a heavy saucepan over moderate heat until sugar caramelizes. When medium dark, pour in cream and bring back to a boil, whisking occasionally. Thin with water if necessary. Serve warm.

To assemble plate, fill each lemon–crisp cone with pear sorbet. Spoon warm caramel sauce onto plate. Lay filled cone on side of plate, and place Armagnac cream beside it. If you wish, garnish with raisins.

For lemon crisps:
1¼ tablespoons unsalted butter, softened
1¼ teaspoons grated lemon zest
1/2 cup sugar
3 egg whites
3 tablespoons flour

For Armagnac cream:
1/2 cup whipping cream
2 teaspoons sugar
2 teaspoons Armagnac

For caramel sauce:
1/2 cup butter
1 cup sugar
1/2 cup cream
Raisins for garnish

Peggy Knickerbocker

AN AUTUMN
BIRTHDAY PRESENT

My Mother's Meat Loaf

*Mashed Potatoes with Parmesan
and Garlic*

Warm Cabbage Salad

Wine Jelly

or

*Grapes with Sour Cream and
Brown Sugar*

serves four

Peggy Knickerbocker was born in San
Francisco and opened her first restaurant at
Mooney's Irish Pub in North Beach. She then
ran a catering business, the *Cooking Company*, for fifteen years and was the chef and
co-owner of a popular waterfront restaurant,
Pier 23, until she sold out to her partner in
1989. She is presently doing free-lance writing, mostly about food.

*I love to ease into the fall season with warm, hearty food as the weather be-
gins to cool. This happens to be a season when a lot of my friends have birthdays.
I give this meal as a birthday present. Either I invite friends to my house, or go to
the location of the birthday celebration and bring the food. Cooking for friends is
my favorite way to pay my respects and show my love.*

MY MOTHER'S MEAT LOAF *serves four to six*

Heat olive oil in a sauté pan and cook the garlic, onion, celery, scallions, peppers, and bay leaf until onion is soft and translucent. Combine the mixture with the meat and remaining ingredients. Mix well and place in a loaf pan. It will enhance the flavors if you let it stand overnight (but don't add the egg until the last minute). Bake in a preheated 350° F oven for 40 to 50 minutes.

To prepare the barbecue sauce, heat all the ingredients in a heavy saucepan, stirring to combine. Serve the meat loaf hot with barbecue sauce and mashed potatoes, or serve cold as open-faced sandwiches with mustard and cabbage salad (warm or at room temperature).

2 tablespoons olive oil
6 cloves garlic, chopped
1 yellow onion, chopped
2 stalks celery, thinly sliced
4 scallions, chopped
1/2 red bell pepper, chopped
1/2 yellow or orange bell pepper, chopped
1 bay leaf, crumbled
1¼ pound lean hamburger meat
1/2 pound lean ground pork
1 tablespoon Worcestershire sauce
1 cup bread crumbs
1½ teaspoons cumin
1 tablespoon paprika
1 tablespoon dried thyme
1 tablespoon cinnamon
1 tablespoon white pepper
1 tablespoon black pepper
1 teaspoon cayenne
1 tablespoon salt
1 tablespoon Dijon mustard
2 ounces ketchup
1 egg

For barbecue sauce:
1/2 cup prepared spicy barbecue sauce
1¼ cup red wine
1/4 cup meat-loaf drippings
1 tablespoon Worcestershire sauce
2 tablespoons ketchup
2 tablespoons tomato salsa (optional)

MASHED POTATOES WITH PARMESAN AND GARLIC *serves four to six*

6 boiling potatoes, peeled
    and cut into chunks
1/4 teaspoon salt
4 tablespoons butter
3 cloves garlic, chopped
1/2 cup milk
1/8 teaspoon white pepper
4 tablespoons grated
    Parmesan cheese

Place potatoes in a heavy saucepan with salted water to cover. Bring to a boil and cook until tender, about 20 minutes.

Heat the butter in a sauté pan and lightly brown the garlic.

Drain the potatoes and return them to the saucepan. Mash them with a potato masher. Add the butter and garlic. Beat in the milk a little at a time. Add the pepper and Parmesan and stir until well blended. Serve hot with the meat loaf.

WARM CABBAGE SALAD *serves ten*

This salad is lusty with colors and flavors. It is good the second day or longer. The point is to get as many colors involved as possible.

Cook bacon until crisp and drain, reserving 2 tablespoons of the fat. Chop the bacon and set aside.

Whisk together ingredients for soy-balsamic vinaigrette and marinate sliced cabbage and julienned carrot in it for an hour or so.

Sauté the onions and garlic in the bacon fat until lightly browned. Add the marinated cabbage and carrot.

Just before serving, toss in the other vegetables (add the peas at the very last moment so they'll keep their color and crispness). The raw vegetables will soften somewhat in the heated cabbage. Toss in the cheese and bacon, Japanese vegetables, and chopped parsley. Serve warm or at room temperature with the meat loaf.

1/2 pound bacon
1 medium head red
  cabbage, thinly sliced
2 carrots, julienned
2 large white onions,
  sliced
6 to 8 cloves garlic,
  chopped

For soy-balsamic vinaigrette:
1/4 cup soy sauce
1/4 cup balsamic vinegar
1/2 cup olive oil
4 cloves garlic, chopped
6 tablespoons
  Worcestershire sauce
2 tablespoons brown sugar
3 tablespoons sweet
  mustard
2 tablespoons dried
  oregano
1 tablespoon coarsely
  cracked black pepper
Dash of Tabasco sauce

1/2 cup each yellow and
  red cherry tomatoes
1/2 red and 1/2 orange
  bell pepper, julienned
1/4 pound snow peas or
  snap peas
1/2 pound blue cheese,
  crumbled
Japanese pickled
  vegetables (available in
  Japanese markets)
Italian parsley, chopped

WINE JELLY *serves four*

2 tablespoons (2
   envelopes) gelatin
1/2 cup cold water
1 cup boiling water
3/4 cup sugar
1⅔ cups dry sherry
1/3 cup lemon juice
1 cup softly whipped
   cream
Zest of 1 orange

I like to serve a light dessert because the meal is filling. A ripe persimmon served on a dark green ivy leaf is another good choice.

Soak gelatin in cold water until soft, then dissolve in boiling water. Add the sugar, sherry, and lemon juice. (You can flame the sherry if you wish to exclude the alcohol.) Pour into serving bowl and refrigerate until set, about 3 to 4 hours. Serve with whipped cream and orange zest on top.

GRAPES WITH SOUR CREAM AND BROWN SUGAR *serves six*

3 cups Thompson
   Seedless grapes (or any
   combination of seedless
   grapes)
Juice of 1 orange
1/2 cup sour cream
2 tablespoons dark rum
   (optional)
1/4 cup brown sugar
Zest of 1 orange
Fresh mint sprigs

Mix grapes, juice, sour cream, and rum in a bowl and chill for an hour. Transfer to a serving dish and sprinkle with brown sugar and orange zest. Garnish with mint sprigs. Serve with biscotti and espresso.

Jeremiah Tower

THE EPITOME OF DECADENCE: ROAST BEEF WITH CHÂTEAU D'YQUEM

Risotto with White Truffle

Roast Beef with Château d'Yquem

Caramelized Apple Tart

serves six

After studying architecture at Harvard University, Jeremiah Tower changed his focus and entered the culinary field as chef and partner at *Chez Panisse* in Berkeley, California. Since then, he has been spectacularly successful as the owner of two San Francisco restaurants, *Stars* and *690,* and co-owner of the *Peak Cafe* in Hong Kong. He is the author of *New American Classics* (Harper & Row, 1986).

Everyone has theories on divine decadence. Mine stems from a remark made by Prince Youssoupov, an aristocratic Russian friend of my uncle. "The epitome of decadence," he said, "is to drink Château d'Yquem with roast beef."

I served it myself when I was at Harvard, during the raging heat of the summer of 1964. I invited my closest friends, and it was over 100 degrees in the kitchen. The combination of the tastes and the heat sent everyone into a rapturous, if silent, swoon.

Later, when I was at Chez Panisse, *I gave a second Sauternes dinner, to see if it had been the heat the first time that had caused such raptures. I wanted not only to explore the ultimate gastronomic test of one's palate but to persuade my restaurant regulars, despite their skepticism, that the sweet wines of Sauternes were often perfect with food other than desserts and foie gras. On this occasion, the temperature was only 50 degrees, and we established once again that the greater the wine, the greater the range of its marriage with food. And for me, there is no sweet wine like a great d'Yquem with a great hunk of old-fashioned, well-marbled beef.*

I decided to give yet another Sauternes and roast beef dinner recently on my birthday in November. Among those who shared the meal at my house were my Stars' managers — Mark Franz, Noreen Lam, and Steve Vranian. We drank Château d'Yquem 1967 throughout the meal, and it was indescribably wonderful. Let me share the menu with you.

RISOTTO WITH WHITE TRUFFLE *serves six*

6 tablespoons sweet butter
1 large onion, finely chopped
2 cups Arborio rice
8 cups chicken stock
1 tablespoon chopped garlic
Salt and freshly ground pepper
1½ ounces fresh white truffle

Melt 2 tablespoons butter in a heavy frying pan over low heat. Add the onion and sweat it, covered, until translucent, about 5 minutes. Do not let it brown.

Add the rice and sauté over medium heat, stirring constantly until all the rice is coated with the butter.

Add the stock, a cup at a time, and cook the rice over medium heat, stirring constantly. Keep adding more stock a cup at a time as it is absorbed by the rice. When the rice is just tender, after about 15 minutes, add the garlic. Cook until rice is al dente, 5 to 7 minutes. Season with salt and pepper. Add the remaining butter and stir until incorporated. With a truffle cutter or sharp paring knife, shave off pieces of truffle and sprinkle on the rice.

ROAST BEEF WITH CHÂTEAU D'YQUEM
serves six to eight

Rub the rib roast all over with the vodka.
This begins to break down the fat and makes
the meat flavorful and tender. Rub in the salt
and pepper. Cut small pockets evenly in the
fat and slip in the bay leaves. Let sit at room
temperature for 2 hours.

Preheat oven to 425° F. Put the beef in a roasting pan and roast for 30 minutes. Then turn
down the heat to 325° F and cook 12 to 15
minutes per pound, or until internal temperature reaches 125° F. The meat will be rare to
medium rare, at which point the juices will
run slightly pink when you stick a skewer or
fork into it. When the beef is cooked, let it sit
in a warm place (on the oven door, or in the
oven with the door open) for 30 minutes, so
the meat can soften and reabsorb all the juices
that would run out if meat were cut now.

Place the bread under the roast before carving, and serve the juice-soaked bread with the
beef.

Slowly carve before your guests and serve
with the Château d'Yquem.

1 beef rib roast of 3 to
 5 ribs, about 5 to
 9 pounds
1/2 cup vodka
3 tablespoons salt
1 tablespoon freshly
 ground pepper
12 bay leaves
4 slices stale bread
To be served with a bottle
 of Château d'Yquem

CARAMELIZED APPLE TART *serves eight*

For tart pastry:
2 cups all-purpose flour
1/4 cup sugar
1/2 teaspoon salt
1 cup unsalted butter,
    cut in pieces
1/4 cup cold water

8 large green apples
    (pippin or Granny
    Smith)
1 cup sugar
Pinch of salt
4 tablespoons butter
1 cup softly whipped
    cream

This is the famous French tarte Tatin, the se-cret of which is in the apples giving up their juices in the cooking process, combining with the sugar and butter, and caramelizing.

To prepare the tart shell, combine 2 cups flour, sugar, and salt in a bowl. Mix the but-ter quickly into the flour by hand or with the paddle attachment of a mixer until the butter is in small, crumbly pieces. Add the water and blend together, gathering the mass into a ball. Wrap in plastic and refrigerate until needed.

Place chilled pastry dough on a lightly floured table. Shape it into a flattened circle. Dust the top with flour, turn over, dust again, and roll out the dough 1/4 inch thick into a 9-inch round.

Peel and core the apples and cut them in sixths. Toss them in a bowl with the sugar and salt. Spread 2 tablespoons butter in a heavy 10-inch nonstick skillet. Place the apples side by side in the skillet and dot with the remaining butter. Place the pastry over the apples, leaving a 1/2-inch gap all around between the pastry and the edge of the pan.

Bake in a 375° F oven until the apples are tender and the crust is golden and cooked through, about 45 minutes.

Look along the sides of the tart to see if the juices have started to caramelize. If they are a deep golden brown, the tart can be left to cool for 5 minutes and then turned over onto a plate. If not, put the pan over medium heat and cook, moving the pan slowly around the burner, for 5 to 10 minutes to let the juices caramelize. Let cool for 5 minutes and turn out onto a platter. Serve with soft whipped cream.

Udo Nechutnys

A SIMPLE, UNIQUE THANKSGIVING MEAL

Spicy Squash Soup

Steamed Fish with Napa Cabbage, Shiitake Mushrooms, and Ginger Black Beans

Quince Tart with Cinnamon Ice Cream

serves six

Udo Nechutnys left has native Germany at age fourteen to pursue a culinary career in France. He trained under Paul Bocuse in Col-longes-au-Mont-d'Or, worked at *Maxim's* in Paris, and made his way to Hong Kong to cook at the *Mandarin Hotel* and to Osaka, Japan, to teach French cuisine at the Tsuji Restaurant and Hotel School. A California resident since 1977, he settled in the Napa Valley, first as the chef at *Domaine Chandon* in Yountville. He then ran his own restau-rant, *Miramonte,* in St. Helena, and is pres-ently the executive chef at *Auberge du Soleil* in Rutherford.

My wife, Mei, and I live in a restored vintage farmhouse nestled in the foot-hills of the Napa Valley. Together, we grow beautiful fruits and vegetables, and tend to the six acres of gardens and orchards that surround our home. I spend the rest of my free time doing construction on our house, while Mei nourishes her passion for pottery. Her work embodies her strong Chinese background. She has a delicate touch and a beautiful, distinctive style.

We lead a simple life and eat simple, undiluted food, like this menu for a unique Thanksgiving meal, which reflects my French culinary training and the influence of the time I spent in China and Japan.

SPICY SQUASH SOUP *serves six*

1 winter squash (e.g.,
   butternut)
2 yellow onions, chopped
1 minced jalapēno or
   milder chili pepper,
   according to your taste
1 tablespoon butter
1 quart chicken stock
1 tablespoon cumin seeds
Salt and pepper
1 cup heavy cream, lightly
   whipped
1/2 cup pine nuts, toasted

Cut the squash in half and discard seeds and pulp. Place the squash halves face down in a roasting pan with enough water to coat the bottom and bake in a 375° F oven until soft. When done, peel off skin. Reserve juice from the baking pan.

In a soup pot, sweat the onions and chili pepper in butter over low heat. Add the squash flesh and reserved juice. Add chicken stock and bring to a simmer.

Toast cumin seeds to golden brown in a hot, dry pan. Grind the seeds to a fine powder and add to soup with salt and pepper to taste. Let the soup simmer for 40 minutes. Allow to cool and purée in batches. Serve hot, garnished with a dollop of whipped cream and sprinkling of toasted pine nuts.

STEAMED FISH WITH NAPA CABBAGE, SHIITAKE MUSHROOMS, AND GINGER BLACK BEANS *serves six*

On pieces of parchment paper, place a few cabbage leaves with fish on top and mushrooms around. Transfer parchment and contents to a steamer, and steam over simmering water until fish is cooked, about 5 to 10 minutes. Lift out parchment and arrange fish and vegetables on plates. Season lightly with salt and pepper.

In a sauté pan, heat olive oil and add shallots, garlic, ginger, and black beans. Cook for 5 minutes. Drizzle over and around fish. Garnish with sliced scallions and cilantro.

1 head Napa cabbage, trimmed and pulled apart
6 pieces, 6 to 7 ounces each, flounder, halibut, or other flatfish
8 ounces shiitake mushrooms, quartered
Salt and pepper
1/3 cup olive oil
2 tablespoons chopped shallots
2 cloves garlic, chopped
1 teaspoon finely grated ginger
3 tablespoons Chinese fermented black beans, washed and chopped
2 scallions, sliced, and cilantro for garnish

QUINCE TART WITH CINNAMON ICE CREAM *serves six*

For ice cream:
1 pint half-and-half
1 pint heavy cream
1 vanilla bean, sliced in
　half and scraped
5 to 6 cinnamon sticks
1 slice lemon peel
12 egg yolks
3/4 cup sugar

For tart dough:
1/2 cup sugar
2¼ cups flour
1/2 cup plus 2 tablespoons
　butter
Pinch of salt
2 to 3 egg yolks

6 ripe quinces

To prepare ice cream, place half-and-half, cream, vanilla bean, cinnamon sticks, and lemon peel in a large saucepan over medium heat. Bring to a simmer, reduce heat, and let steep 15 to 20 minutes. Lightly beat egg yolks, add sugar, and temper with some of the hot cream mixture. Add to saucepan with rest of cream mixture and cook over low heat, stirring, until thick. Strain, and cool over a bowl of ice. Freeze in an ice-cream maker according to manufacturer's instructions.

To make tart dough, sift together dry ingredients and cut in butter until well blended. Add egg yolks and blend in. Avoid overmixing. Cover dough with plastic wrap and refrigerate for at least 1 hour.

Peel quinces, slice in half, and scoop out seeds. Slice thinly, keeping the halves together. Grease a baking sheet with some butter and sprinkle with sugar. Place the sliced quince halves in the pan, pressing to fan them out slightly. Place a dollop of butter on the quince halves and sprinkle with sugar. Bake in 325° F oven until cooked but firm.

Roll out chilled pastry dough to 1/8 inch thick and cut out circles somewhat larger than the quince halves. Place pastry circles on parchment-lined baking sheet, prick with a fork, and bake in a 350° F oven until golden brown.

With a spatula, lift quince halves and turn onto pastry circles, arranging them attractively. Sprinkle with sugar and caramelize with a hot iron or under a broiler. Serve with cinnamon ice cream.

Patrizio Sacchetto

AN ITALIAN-FLAVORED THANKSGIVING DINNER

Pumpkin Tortelli with Sage Butter

Turkey Cutlets Filled with Prosciutto, Fontina, and White Truffles

Toasted Nut Tart with Espresso Coffee Ice Cream

serves six

Patrizio Sacchetto received his chef's training at the Maggia Culinary Academy in Stresa, Italy, and worked summers under prominent European chefs. Since coming to San Francisco in 1984, he has taught at the California Culinary Academy and served as chef at *Umberto's, Harry's American Bar & Grill,* and the *Blue Fox.* He is currently the chef-owner of *Teatro* restaurant.

For the first Thanksgiving in our new home in Petaluma, I had planned to serve a traditional dinner. But we had the unexpected pleasure of a visit by my family from Italy, and the holiday became a perfect opportunity to create a menu based on American tradition with an Italian flavor. The result was beyond my greatest expectation. The dinner was the beginning of a new Thanksgiving tradition for my family.

PUMPKIN TORTELLI WITH SAGE BUTTER
serves six

1 small pumpkin
1¾ cups freshly grated
   Parmesan cheese
10 Amaretti cookies,
   finely crumbled
Salt and freshly ground
   pepper
1¾ cups all-purpose flour
3 eggs
2 tablespoons olive oil
1 egg, lightly beaten, for
   egg wash
6 tablespoons butter
1/4 cup sage

Tortelli are like ravioli, only different in shape.

Using a sharp knife, cut the pumpkin into large pieces. Remove seeds and place the pumpkin on a foil-lined baking sheet. Bake in a preheated 350° F oven for 30 minutes. Let cool. Remove skin from pumpkin, and purée 1½ cups of the flesh in a food processor.

Mix the pumpkin purée with half the Parmesan and the crumbled Amaretti cookies. Season with salt and pepper.

To prepare the pasta, heap the flour on a board and make a well in the center. Break the eggs into the well and add the olive oil. Work eggs and oil into the flour to form a dough. Knead until smooth and elastic. Roll out dough into 2 sheets of equal size, 1/32 of an inch thick, i.e., as thin as possible, since you will be using 2 layers of pasta. You may roll out dough in a pasta machine, if you wish.

Place 1/2 teaspoon of pumpkin mixture on the first pasta sheet in small mounds about 2 inches apart. Brush the pasta lightly with egg wash. Top with second sheet and press gently around each mound of filling. Cut out tortelli with a 2-inch round cookie cutter with fluted edge, and pinch edges closed.

Bring a large saucepan of salted water to a boil. Drop in tortelli and cook al dente, about 2 to 3 minutes.

Melt the butter in a small saucepan and add the sage. Drain the tortelli. Place on a serving plate with remaining Parmesan and drizzle with sage butter. Serve hot.

TURKEY CUTLETS FILLED WITH PROSCIUTTO, FONTINA, AND WHITE TRUFFLES *serves six*

With a meat pounder or the side of a cleaver, pound the turkey cutlets between sheets of plastic wrap until very thin (approximately 1/4 inch) and about 9 by 3 inches.

Arrange 1 slice prosciutto, 2 slices truffle, and 1 slice fontina on each of the six cutlets.

Brush the edges of the cutlets with egg white, then fold in half lengthwise to close. Press down along the edges to seal.

Dredge each cutlet in flour. Lightly beat together the eggs and water. Dip cutlets into egg mixture and coat with the bread crumbs.

Heat the olive oil in a large skillet, and sauté the cutlets to golden brown over medium to high heat, turning once. Serve with a garnish of lemon wedges and parsley.

6 turkey cutlets (thin slices turkey breast, 3 ounces each)
6 thin slices prosciutto, 2 by 3 inches
12 thin slices white truffle
6 thin slices fontina, 2 by 3 inches
2 tablespoons egg white
3/4 cup flour
2 eggs
1/4 cup water
2 cups fine dry bread crumbs, preferably from Italian bread
6 to 8 tablespoons olive oil
12 lemon wedges
6 parsley sprigs

TOASTED NUT TART *serves eight to ten*

2/3 cup pecan halves
2/3 cup blanched sliced
  almonds
1/2 cup hazelnuts
2 large eggs, lightly beaten
1/3 cup dark brown sugar
2/3 cup light corn syrup
1/8 teaspoon salt
1 teaspoon vanilla extract
2 teaspoons flour
2 tablespoons unsalted
  butter, melted and
  cooled

For tart shell:
1/2 cup plus 1 tablespoon
  unsalted butter
1/4 cup sugar
1 large egg
1½ cups all-purpose flour

To prepare pastry dough for tart shell, cream the butter and sugar in an electric mixer fitted with a paddle attachment. Add the egg and mix. Add the flour and mix. Don't overmix. Remove dough, shape into a ball, wrap in plastic, and chill. When firm, roll out on a floured surface to 1/8 inch thick. Fit into a 9½-inch tart pan with removable bottom. Cover dough with a round of parchment paper or aluminum foil. Weight down with beans or lentils. Bake in a preheated 400° F oven for 15 minutes. Cool on wire rack. Remove beans and paper. Fill in sides of shell that may have shrunk with leftover dough. Keep chilled.

Reduce oven to 350° F. Roughly slice pecans and place with sliced almonds on a baking sheet. Toast lightly in oven. Then toast the hazelnuts. Remove from oven and place hazelnuts in a metal colander with large holes. Rub nuts against colander to remove as much of skins as possible. Slice hazelnuts in half.

Adjust oven to 375° F. In a medium bowl, combine eggs, brown sugar, corn syrup, salt, and vanilla. Stir until well blended. Stir in flour, melted butter, and nuts.

Pour filling into partially baked tart shell to within 1/8 inch of top. Bake until filling is just set, about 30 minutes. Cool on wire rack. Remove from tart pan and serve with espresso ice cream.

ESPRESSO COFFEE ICE CREAM
yields three and a half cups

Bring the milk to a boil and add the coffee. Stir, cover, and let steep off heat for about 5 minutes. Strain through filter paper or fine sieve. You should have about 1 cup coffee extract.

Mix the coffee extract with 1 cup cream in a saucepan, and bring to a boil. Meanwhile, whisk together egg yolks and sugar until mixture is thick and reaches ribbon consistency. This may be done in an electric mixer. Temper the egg-sugar mixture by stirring in some hot coffee-cream mixture. Place in a saucepan with rest of hot mixture and cook, stirring, until it thickens and reaches 180° F. Be careful not to overcook, since it will curdle at too high a temperature.

Pour the remaining cup of cream into a clean bowl and strain the hot mixture directly into it, using a fine strainer. Cool to room temperature. Pour into an ice-cream maker, and freeze according to manufacturer's instructions.

Serve with slices of the nut tart.

1¼ cups milk
1/3 cup finely ground
   espresso coffee beans
2 cups heavy cream
5 egg yolks
1/2 cup sugar

Rick O'Connell

DESSERTS FOR THANKSGIVING

Apples Baked in Cranberry Juice

Lemon Squares

Wild Rice–Maple Syrup Pie

Pumpkin Pie

serves eight

Rick O'Connell is a San Francisco chef who has worked at *Rosalie's* and *Raf*. She is currently the consulting chef at various Bay area restaurants and the author of *365 Ways to Cook Italian* (HarperCollins, 1991).

My family's favorite holiday has always been Thanksgiving. We love the flavors and excitement of harvest food. The day is a wonderful coming together, minus the gift-giving and fanfare of other holidays. We continue to try to eliminate things to make the dinner simpler, but it never works. The menu has become a cliché, and we love it that way. Having friends drop in later for dessert is a special part of the day. Therefore, I offer you this dessert menu for family and friends.

APPLES BAKED IN CRANBERRY JUICE
serves eight

Preheat oven to 350° F. Core apples, removing the stem and seeds but leaving the bottoms intact by at least 3/4 inch.

Place apples in a glass baking dish just big enough to hold them. In a small bowl, combine the sugars, cinnamon, walnuts, and raisins.

Stuff sugar mixture into the cores of the apples. Pour cranberry juice around the apples. Dot with butter.

Cover with foil and bake for 30 to 40 minutes, depending on the size of the apples, until tender.

Carefully remove apples from the baking dish and place on a serving plate. Pour juice into a small saucepan and boil to reduce to about 3/4 cup, until it becomes a little syrupy. Drizzle over apples. Serve slightly warm or chilled.

8 small to medium cooking apples, Granny Smith or pippin
1/2 cup granulated sugar
1 cup brown sugar
1 teaspoon cinnamon
1/2 cup coarsely broken walnuts
1/2 cup golden raisins
1½ cups cranberry juice
2 tablespoons unsalted butter

LEMON SQUARES *makes sixteen squares*

For shortbread:
2 cups all-purpose flour
1/2 cup powdered sugar,
   plus extra for dusting
1 cup unsalted butter,
   melted

For lemon curd:
2 large lemons
2 cups sugar
1 tablespoon unsalted
   butter, melted
4 large eggs

Preheat oven to 350° F. To prepare shortbread, sift together flour and sugar in a medium-sized bowl. Add melted butter and work with hands to form a dough. Press dough into an 8-by-8-inch baking pan until flat and even. Bake for 15 minutes.

In the meantime, prepare the lemon curd. Carefully grate the zest from the lemons, being sure not to include any of the bitter white pith. Squeeze juice from lemons and set aside.

In a medium bowl, whisk together sugar, butter, eggs, juice, and zest. As soon as the shortbread has baked for 15 minutes, pour the lemon mixture over it and level with a spatula.

Bake 20 to 25 minutes, until the curd is set. Dust with sifted powdered sugar. When cool, cut into 2-inch squares. These are delicious with soft whipped cream or lemon sorbet.

AMERICAN PIE DOUGH *makes two pie shells*

When making American pie dough, you can handle it as much as possible while cutting the butter into the flour. It should resemble a fine cornmeal, not polenta. Once you add the liquid, you should handle it only long enough to pull it together into a workable dough.

Combine 2 cups flour, salt, shortening (or lard), and butter in a bowl. Using a pastry blender, your hands, or a food processor, cut the shortening into the flour until it forms a fine, even meal.

Add ice water a tablespoon at a time, and pull mixture into a dough, using your hands. Knead 4 or 5 times only, and then divide into two pieces.

Flatten each piece to a 4- to 5-inch disc on a piece of plastic wrap. Wrap each piece in plastic and chill for 1/2 hour in the refrigerator.

Flour a work surface and roll dough out to 1/4 inch thick. Fit into 9-inch pie plate. Trim and crimp the edges. Cover with plastic, and refrigerate or freeze until ready to use. Repeat for second pie shell.

2 cups all-purpose flour
1/8 teaspoon salt
1/2 cup vegetable shortening or lard
4 tablespoons unsalted butter, cut into small bits
4 to 5 tablespoons ice water

WILD RICE–MAPLE SYRUP PIE *serves eight to ten*

1/2 cup wild rice
1/2 cup brown sugar
2/3 cup maple syrup
Pinch of salt
3 large eggs, fork beaten
1/2 recipe American pie
   dough, rolled out and
   fitted into a 9-inch pie
   plate

Wild rice and maple syrup are both native American foods. Wild rice is native to Minnesota and Wisconsin but is now cultivated in California, in the Sacramento Valley, from the Mt. Shasta area to Sutter County.

In a medium saucepan, bring 4 cups of water to a boil. Add the wild rice and return to a boil. Cover partially and allow to cook for 1 hour, or until all the grains have popped open. Add more boiling water if needed. Drain and set aside. You should have 2 cups cooked wild rice.

Preheat oven to 350° F. In a large bowl, combine the brown sugar, maple syrup, salt, and eggs. Stir to combine. Stir in the cooked wild rice.

Pour wild-rice filling into the prepared pie shell. Bake for 45 minutes, or until the filling begins to puff. Serve with unsweetened whipped cream.

PUMPKIN PIE *serves eight*

Some of the best pumpkin pies are made from the back-of-the-can recipe, but you may cook your own pumpkin if you wish. I would advise you to cut the pumpkin into wedges, removing the stem and seeds. Place the wedges on a cookie sheet and cover with foil. Bake at 350° F for anywhere from 30 minutes to 1 hour, or until the flesh is tender. The time will differ with the type, age, and thickness of the pumpkin. Scoop the flesh from the skin, and purée in a food processor.

Preheat oven to 450° F. In a large bowl, stir pumpkin purée with rest of ingredients. Beat lightly to combine. Pour pumpkin mixture into prepared pie shell. Bake for 10 minutes at 450° F. Lower heat to 325° F and bake 50 minutes, or until set. Serve slightly warm or chilled.

2 cups cooked fresh or
  canned pumpkin
1 cup milk
1 cup heavy cream
1/2 cup dark brown sugar
1/2 cup granulated sugar
1½ teaspoons cinnamon
1 teaspoon powdered
  ginger
1/2 teaspoon nutmeg
1/4 teaspoon cloves
1/4 teaspoon salt
1 tablespoon flour
2 large eggs, fork beaten
1/2 recipe American pie
  dough, rolled out and
  fitted into a 9-inch pie
  plate

Barbara Karoff

A SOUTH AMERICAN–INSPIRED THANKSGIVING DINNER

Ceviche Pan-American

Spicy Avocado: Colombia

Pumpkin Soup: Argentina

Marinated Turkey: Chile

Kale Greens: Brazil

Corn-Tomato Pudding: Ecuador

Potatoes with Chilies and Cheese: Peru

Corn Bread: Paraguay

Grapefruit-Cucumber Salad Carioca

Fruit Cake: Brazil

serves four

Barbara Karoff is a free-lance food and travel writer who lives in San Francisco. She is the author of *South American Cooking: Foods and Feasts from the New World* (Addison-Wesley, 1989) and has conducted cooking demonstrations on cargo-passenger ships sailing around South America.

A South American-inspired Thanksgiving dinner is not as odd as it may seem, because a surprising number of foods we associate with our national holiday are indigenous to South America. These include the festive bird itself, a native of Peru, as well as pumpkins, squash, and potatoes.

Although avocados, tomatoes, corn, and chilies are not as frequently included in our traditional Thanksgiving feast, they, too, are products of the New World and were unknown elsewhere until the Europeans arrived in the Western Hemisphere five hundred years ago.

CEVICHE PAN-AMERICAN *serves four*

Combine the citrus juices. Blanch the onion rings in boiling water for 1 minute. Drain and refresh immediately under cold water. Add to the juices. Add the crushed chilies and salt.

Cut the fish into bite-size pieces, removing all skin and bones. Place in a shallow glass or stainless-steel dish and cover with the marinade. Allow to stand at room temperature for 4 to 6 hours. (If the weather is very warm, marinate in the refrigerator.) The fish is "cooked" and ready to serve when the flesh becomes opaque.

Serve as an appetizer, arranging fish pieces on lettuce leaves with a garnish of olives and sprigs of parsley or cilantro.

Juice of 1 orange
Juice of 1 lemon
Juice of 4 limes
1 red onion, thinly sliced into rings
2 ancho chilies or other mild dried chilies, stems and seeds removed, and crushed
1/2 teaspoon salt
2 medium fillets (6 ounces each) of red snapper, haddock, or other firm whitefish
Lettuce leaves
Olives and parsley or cilantro for garnish

SPICY AVOCADO: COLOMBIA *serves four to six*

Place the diced avocados in a large colander. Rinse them thoroughly with cold water and drain well. This will prevent their turning dark. Set aside.

Purée the garlic, onions, bell peppers, chilies, and tomatoes in a blender or food processor. Cook the purée in hot olive oil for 2 to 3 minutes. Add the vinegar and salt and simmer over low heat for 20 minutes.

Cool the sauce to room temperature, and then gently stir in the diced avocados and bacon. The sauce without the avocados may be frozen.

Serve as an appetizer with crackers or tortilla chips.

3 to 4 large ripe avocados, peeled and diced
2 cloves garlic
2 medium onions
2 red or green bell peppers, seeded
2 to 3 serrano or jalapeño chilies, seeded
2 tomatoes, peeled and seeded
1/4 cup olive oil
1/4 cup white wine vinegar
Salt to taste
1/2 pound bacon, diced, fried crisp, and drained well (optional)

PUMPKIN SOUP: ARGENTINA *serves four to six*

1/4 pound bacon, chopped
2 onions, chopped
4 pounds fresh pumpkin, peeled, seeded, and cut into small pieces, or a 29-ounce can of unseasoned pumpkin meat
2 to 3 serrano or other medium-hot chilies, seeded and minced
2 teaspoon cumin seeds, ground
8 to10 cups chicken stock
1½ cups grated Muenster cheese
3 tablespoons chopped parsley

In a large pan, cook the bacon until it is almost crisp. Add the onions and sauté until they are very soft. Combine with the pumpkin meat. Stir in the chilies and cumin and add the stock. Bring to a boil, then reduce heat and simmer for 20 minutes.

When ready to serve, add the cheese and heat through, but do not boil. Garnish with chopped parlsey.

MARINATED TURKEY: CHILE *serves four*

To make the marinade, combine the garlic, salt, pepper, wine, and orange juice in a shallow dish. Add the turkey, cover, and refrigerate for 6 hours, or overnight. Turn the turkey in the marinade several times.

Remove the turkey and reserve the marinade. In a heavy casserole, sauté the turkey in the butter and oil until it is nicely browned on all sides. Add the onions, tomatoes, bay leaf, jalapeños, and reserved marinade. Cover and bake at 350° F for 30 minutes. Stir in cashews and continue to bake for an additional 30 minutes, or until meat is tender. Correct the seasoning. If a thicker sauce is desired, remove the turkey and reduce the liquid over high heat. Slice the turkey on a platter and serve the sauce separately.

3 cloves garlic, minced
1 teaspoon salt
Freshly ground pepper to taste
1½ cups dry white wine
1½ cups orange juice
Half a turkey breast, 2½ to 3 pounds, or other turkey parts
1 tablespoon butter
1 tablespoon safflower oil
2 medium onions, thickly sliced
4 tomatoes, peeled, seeded, and coarsely chopped
1 bay leaf
2 to 3 jalapeño peppers, seeded and thinly sliced
2/3 cup toasted cashew nuts, ground or finely chopped

KALE GREENS: BRAZIL *serves four to six*

Wash the kale, trim off the stems, and blanch the leaves in boiling, salted water for 2 minutes. Remove them to a colander and refresh with cold water. Drain well and squeeze by hand to remove as much water as possible. Cut the kale into thin slices.

Heat the bacon fat in a large skillet and toss the shredded greens in it to coat. Sauté gently until the greens are tender, about 10 minutes.

2½ pounds kale greens
1/3 cup bacon fat

CORN-TOMATO PUDDING: ECUADOR
serves four to six

2 cups corn kernels
1 cup Muenster or
  Monterey Jack cheese,
  cut up
4 tablespoons butter,
  cut up
Salt and pepper to taste
6 eggs
3 tomatoes, peeled,
  seeded, and finely
  chopped
3 tablespoons minced
  cilantro

Purée the corn, cheese, and butter in a
blender or food processor. Add salt and pepper to taste, then add the eggs, one at a time.
Process until smooth. By hand, stir in the
tomatoes and cilantro, and pour the mixture
into a buttered 6-cup casserole. Bake at 350° F
for about 1 hour, or until set and nicely
browned on top.

For a lighter pudding, more like a soufflé,
separate the eggs. Follow the above recipe,
but add only the egg yolks. Beat the whites
until they form soft peaks and gently fold
them into the corn mixture. Pour into a deep
casserole dish and bake at 325° F for 35 to 40
minutes, or until the pudding is puffed,
golden, and set in the center.

POTATOES WITH CHILIES AND CHEESE: PERU *serves six*

3 pounds red or white new
  potatoes
2 tablespoons safflower oil
3 cloves garlic, minced
1 onion, finely chopped
2 to 3 serrano or jalapeño
  chilies, seeded and
  finely chopped
Salt and pepper to taste
1 cup evaporated milk or
  half-and-half
1/4 pound queso fresco
  (available in Mexican
  markets) or feta cheese,
  cubed or crumbled
3 hard-boiled eggs,
  coarsely chopped

Peel the potatoes, if desired, and boil them in
lightly salted water until done. Drain well
and cut into cubes.

Sauté the garlic, onion, and chilies in the oil
until the onion is golden. Add the milk and
potatoes and salt and pepper to taste, and stir
carefully with a wooden spoon, taking care
not to mash the potatoes. Add the cheese and
eggs and mix just enough to combine.

CORN BREAD: PARAGUAY *serves four to six*

Sauté the onion in butter until it is soft. Purée the corn kernels in a blender or food processor and combine with the cornmeal, sautéed onion, cottage cheese, Muenster, buttermilk, and salt. Mix thoroughly.

Beat the egg yolks until they are thick. Beat the egg whites until they form soft peaks. Fold the yolks carefully into the whites. Add 1/3 of egg mixture to the corn mixture and combine well. Then carefully fold in the remaining egg mixture.

Pour the batter into a buttered 8-by-8-by-2-inch baking pan and place in a 400° F oven for 30 minutes, or until corn bread is nicely browned and tests done. Serve warm with butter.

1/2 cup finely chopped onion
2 tablespoons butter
3/4 cup corn kernels
3/4 cup yellow cornmeal
3/4 cup small-curd cottage cheese
3/4 cup grated Muenster cheese
1/2 cup buttermilk
1/2 teaspoon salt
3 eggs, separated

GRAPEFRUIT AND CUCUMBER SALAD CARIOCA *serves six*

Cut the grapefruit in half and remove the meat. Separate into sections, removing the membranes.

Peel the cucumbers and cut them into quarters lengthwise. Remove the seeds by scraping them out with a spoon. Cut the cucumber quarters into slices.

Combine the grapefruit sections, cucumber slices, and sugar in a bowl and refrigerate for at least 2 hours. Serve the salad in small lettuce-lined dishes, garnished with mint and lightly dusted with paprika or ground chilies.

3 large grapefruit
2 medium cucumbers or 1 English cucumber
2 to 3 tablespoons sugar
Lettuce leaves
Fresh mint
Paprika or finely ground dried red chilies

FRUIT CAKE: BRAZIL *serves ten to twelve*

1 cup raisins
1 cup candied or dried
   fruit, cut up
1/2 cup Madeira
2 tablespoons soft butter
1/2 cup finely ground dry
   bread crumbs
1/2 cup finely ground
   Brazil nuts
1 cup sugar
5 eggs, separated
3 tablespoons ground
   unsweetened chocolate
1/2 teaspoon ground
   cloves
1 tablespoon lemon juice
1½ teaspoons baking
   powder
Red currant or other tart
   jelly
Powdered sugar

Butter two 9-inch cake pans and line the bottoms with parchment paper. Butter the paper.

Soak the raisins and candied or dried fruit in the Madeira. Cream together the butter, bread crumbs, ground nuts, and sugar. Add the egg yolks one at a time and combine well. Add the chocolate, cloves, lemon juice, and baking powder and mix well.

Beat the egg whites until they form soft peaks, and fold into the cake batter. Pour the batter into the prepared pans, making sure the fruit is evenly distributed.

Bake at 350° F for 25 minutes, or until the cakes pull away from sides of pans and appear quite dry. Loosen the edges and cool in the pans for 10 minutes. Turn onto racks and cool completely. Put the layers together with jelly and dust the top with sifted powdered sugar.

Robert Reynolds

IT FELT LIKE THANKSGIVING

*Golden Zucchini Soup with Saffron
and Basil*

*Steamed Whitefish on a Bed of
Bitter Greens*

Fruit Soup with Mint

serves six

Robert Reynolds is the chef-owner of *Le
Trou* in San Francisco. He specializes in regional French cuisine and also offers classes
and apprenticeships, both in San Francisco
and in France. He coauthored *From a Breton
Garden* with Josephine Araldo (Addison-
Wesley, 1990).

*A dear friend told me she had developed a very restricting number of allergies
and needed to know where she might go to learn how food is made, so that she
could understand what and how to order in a restaurant and also learn how to cook.
I designed a series of classes, and the recipes that follow developed from them.*

*It was wonderful to go to the market and make selections from what was
available and then develop techniques for preparing recipes. Our class time would
be spent preparing the dishes, and finally, there was the pleasure of the table. The
participants, the food, and the spirit and effort itself could always be measured by
the satisfying "Mmmmm" that followed the food. It felt like Thanksgiving.*

GOLDEN ZUCCHINI SOUP WITH SAFFRON AND BASIL *serves six to eight*

2 to 4 tablespoons olive oil
1 large onion, thinly
  sliced (1/16 inch)
1 leek, white part only,
  cleaned and thinly
  sliced
4 medium golden
  zucchini, shredded
Generous pinch of Quatre
  Epices, or a pinch each
  of ground cinnamon,
  nutmeg, and cloves
1 tablespoon chopped
  fresh marjoram
1 tablespoon chopped
  fresh tarragon
1 quart chicken stock
Small pinch of saffron
  threads
Salt and freshly ground
  pepper

For garnish:
1/4 cup chopped parsley
1 to 2 cloves garlic, finely
  minced
12 large basil leaves, torn
  into small pieces
1 medium tomato, peeled,
  seeded, and diced

Add enough olive oil to lightly coat the bottom of a large pan. Bring oil to sautéing temperature over medium heat. Add the onions and leeks, season lightly with salt, toss well to coat with oil, and sauté 2 to 3 minutes, until translucent.

Add the zucchini, lightly salt, and toss. Turn the heat to low and cover the pan with a tight-fitting lid. Allow the vegetables to cook slowly. Watch the pot to ensure that the vegetables don't scorch. When they have given up their water, add the spices and fresh marjoram and tarragon. Simmer for 15 minutes.

To prepare the garnish, combine the parsley, garlic, and basil and add to the diced tomato. Set aside.

When the zucchini is cooked, pour in the chicken stock and bring to a boil. Remove from the heat and cool somewhat. Puree in a blender to a smooth liquid. Correct the seasoning with salt and pepper. Return the pureed soup to the pot and add the saffron threads. Allow the soup to steep for 10 to 15 minutes, covered but not necessarily over heat.

When ready to serve, rewarm soup and ladle into bowls. Garnish with tomato and herbs. The soup is also delicious served cold.

STEAMED WHITEFISH ON A BED OF BITTER GREENS *serves six*

Place the spinach and bitter greens in a skillet that has a tight-fitting lid. Don't use aluminum or cast iron, as the spinach will discolor. Season with salt, cover, and cook with no added fat over high heat for a full minute. Shake the pan, but leave the lid in place, allowing steam to build up. After a minute, remove the lid to see if the greens have started to wilt. If they have, toss with olive oil and sprinkle with orange rind. Season with salt and pepper. Remove to a platter and keep warm in a very low oven.

With a mortar and pestle, grind the coriander, fennel, and cumin seeds to a fine powder. Set aside.

To prepare the fish, select a skillet large enough to hold all the pieces without crowding. The skillet should have a tight-fitting lid. Pour in the fish stock or court bouillon and bring to a boil. Set the pieces of fish in the skillet and cover. Over medium heat, cook the fish by steaming until the fish flakes. Cooking time will depend on thickness of the fish. It should take 5 to 7 minutes.

Divide the cooked greens evenly on 6 plates. Place a piece of cooked fish on each bed of greens and season lightly with salt and pepper. Top with 1 or 2 slices of orange and a pinch of the ground spices. Serve at once.

3 bunches spinach, cleaned, with stems removed
Small handful of bitter greens: chicory, radicchio, frisée, curly endive, or dandelion
2 to 3 tablespoons olive oil
Grated rind and thinly sliced flesh of 1 orange
Salt and freshly ground pepper
1/4 teaspoon each coriander, fennel, and cumin seeds
1 cup fish stock, or a court bouillon made from 1 cup cold water, 2 to 3 tablespoons white vinegar, 3 parsley stems, 1 bay leaf, and a pinch of thyme, simmered for 15 minutes
6 portions, 5 ounces each, of fresh, sweet whitefish, such as cod, sea bass, or snapper

FRUIT SOUP WITH MINT *serves six*

1 pint strawberries,
   cleaned and stems
   removed
1/2 ripe melon, cut into
   balls
Grated zest and juice
   of 1 lemon
Juice of 1 to 2 oranges
5 to 6 fresh mint leaves,
   finely shredded

Place the whole strawberries in a bowl with the melon balls. Toss in the lemon zest, lemon and orange juices, and shredded mint leaves. Refrigerate for an hour before serving.

As an alternative, you can toss the fruit with honey, add the lemon zest, and, just before serving, pour in some red wine in place of the fruit juice. Or you can add the juice of a grapefruit to the strawberries and melon, and, shortly before serving, add a chilled glass of white dessert wine such as a Sauternes, Loupiac Gaudiet, Monbazillac, or a California pear brandy made by St. George.

Julian Serrano

A GRAND DINNER
FOR A GOOD CAUSE

*Grilled Spot Prawns with Fried
Vegetables, Tomato Confit, and
Provençal Vinaigrette*

*Rack of Lamb Gratinée with
Potato-Onion Basket and
Cumin Caraway Sauce*

Chocolate Raspberry Gâteau

serves four

A native of Madrid, Julian Serrano trained as a chef in hotel restaurants on the Costa del Sol and in the Canary Islands. He left Spain to work in restaurants in France and Switzerland. In 1984, he came to San Francisco and was hired as sous-chef to the celebrated Masataka Kobayashi, chef-owner of *Masa's*. Masa's death led to Serrano's promotion in 1986 to executive chef. Under his leadership, *Masa's* continues to be a world-class restaurant devoted to nouvelle French cuisine.

Special dinners are a challenge and a nice change of pace. Every year, I devote an evening to benefit the Bay Area Hearing Society. Here's a menu I prepared for them. I enjoy doing this dinner because the cause is important and many people benefit from the society's good work. If the dishes take a lot of preparation, it's because our guests expect this of us, and I think you'll feel, as I do, that the effort is worth it.

GRILLED SPOT PRAWNS WITH FRIED VEGETABLES, TOMATO CONFIT, AND PROVENÇAL VINAIGRETTE *serves four*

For tomato confit:
16 cherry tomatoes, lightly blanched, then peeled
1½ cups extra virgin olive oil
1 teaspoon chopped fresh thyme
1/2 teaspoon coarse sea salt
2 teaspoons sugar (if tomatoes are very sweet, reduce sugar by 1/2 teaspoon)

For vinaigrette:
1 roasted, peeled red pepper, diced small
2 sun-dried tomatoes, diced small
1 cooked artichoke heart, diced small
4 pitted Niçoise olives, diced small
2 leaves basil, julienned
3 chives, finely chopped
3 tablespoons sherry vinegar
3/4 cup extra virgin olive oil
1/2 teaspoon balsamic vinegar
Salt and pepper
Juice of 1 lemon

To prepare tomato confit, line a 9-inch cake pan with aluminum foil and place the peeled tomatoes in it.

In a bowl, mix together the olive oil, chopped thyme, salt, and sugar until the sugar floats in the oil (the salt will not float, as it is too heavy). Spoon all the oil in the mixture over the tomatoes, trying not to get any salt crystals stuck to them. When there is no more oil, spoon the rest of the mixture into the pan with tomatoes. Oil mixture should be 1/8 inch deep in the pan.

Place pan in 175° F oven and bake for 2 to 3 hours. The tomatoes are done when they have become fairly shriveled and slightly pointed on top. They should taste pleasantly sweet and slightly salty. The cooking time depends on the size and ripeness of the tomatoes.

To prepare the vinaigrette, put all the chopped ingredients (they should be 1/4-inch dice) in a mixing bowl. Place the sherry vinegar in a separate bowl, then add the olive oil and whisk together. Add the balsamic vinegar and salt and pepper to taste, and whisk until incorporated. Finally, pour the vinaigrette over the diced ingredients, add the lemon juice, and mix together.

To prepare the fried vegetables, use only the skin of the zucchini. Scoop out the zucchini, and finely julienne 3-inch sections of the zucchini skin. Then, finely julienne 3-inch sections of the leek. Mix them together and, in a deep sauté pan, deep-fry them in vegetable oil over medium-high heat for approximately 10 minutes, until they are crispy. Drain them on paper towels. Sprinkle with salt and remove from towels gently, so as not to break the vegetables. They may be served at room temperature.

To prepare the prawns, peel them but leave the heads on (to retain moisture). Rub the prawns with olive oil and grill (or sauté) them over high heat for 3 minutes each side. If you wish, remove the heads before serving.

Presentation: Place 4 prawns on each plate in a clockwise circle. One cherry tomato confit should be placed between each prawn. A bunch of crispy vegetables should be placed in the center of the prawns. The vinaigrette should be lightly sprinkled over the entire plate, making sure the diced vegetables get sprinkled around the plate as well.

For fried vegetables:
2 yellow zucchini
2 green zucchini
1 leek
Vegetable oil for deep-frying
Salt to taste

16 spot prawns
Olive oil

RACK OF LAMB GRATINÉE WITH POTATO-ONION BASKET AND CUMIN CARAWAY SAUCE *serves four*

2 racks of lamb, about
   3 pounds each

For lamb stock:
Mirepoix of 1 onion, 1
   carrot, and 2 celery ribs,
   cut up
2 to 3 sprigs thyme,
   chopped
1 clove garlic
1 tablespoon tomato paste
4 to 6 black peppercorns
Salt and pepper

For onion-potato baskets:
20 pearl onions
1½ teaspoons sugar
3 teaspoons sherry vinegar
3/4 cup chicken stock
3 tablespoons butter
Salt and white pepper
2 russet potatoes
Vegetable oil for
   deep-frying
1/2 cup heavy cream
1 egg yolk

To prepare lamb stock, clean lamb racks of all fat and meat from around the bones, except for medallions, which should be removed whole and set aside. In a large sauté pan or soup pot, sauté bones and excess meat until completely brown. Drain off fat, add the mirepoix, chopped thyme, garlic, tomato paste, and peppercorns. Cover the ingredients with cold water, bring to a boil, then cook over medium heat for 30 minutes. Strain the stock, reduce to 1 cup, and season with salt and pepper to taste.

To prepare onion-potato baskets, clean, peel, and boil pearl onions in water for 3 minutes to remove acidity. Drain and set aside.

Place sugar in a saucepan over medium heat and allow to caramelize. Remove from heat and stir in sherry vinegar. Add onions, chicken stock, butter, a pinch of salt, and white pepper to taste. Cook for 20 minutes, or until the onions are cooked and sauce is reduced to a couple of teaspoons.

Peel potatoes and cut into 3-inch-long sections. Scoop out insides of potato sections to make a basket. Scoop close to edges so basket deep-fries quickly. In a deep, heavy skillet, heat oil to medium hot and drop in baskets. Remove when crisp and golden.

Whip 1/2 cup cream until very firm and fold in egg yolk. Place some onions into each potato basket, blanket with egg-cream mixture, and place under a broiler to glaze.

To prepare the lamb, salt and pepper the cleaned racks. In a large skillet, heat some olive oil and sauté the racks over medium-high heat until evenly browned. Place skillet in a 400° F oven until the lamb is medium rare, about 5 minutes.

In a saucepan, bring the butter to a boil and mix in the bread crumbs and chopped pecans. The mixture will bubble and rise. Coat the lamb with the mixture. Place the lamb under the broiler to brown the crumb–nut mixture.

To prepare the lamb sauce, place the reduced lamb stock in a saucepan, bring to a boil, and add 1/4 cup cream and the chopped caraway seeds and cumin.

Presentation: Each plate should have half a rack, gently circled with sauce, and an onion-potato basket at the top of the plate. A small packet of green beans tied with chives and 2 baby carrots should be placed on opposite sides of the basket.

For lamb racks:
Salt and pepper
Olive oil
1 cup butter
1 cup fine bread crumbs
1/2 cup pecans, finely
  chopped

For lamb sauce:
1 cup reduced lamb stock
1/4 cup heavy cream
3/4 teaspoon caraway
  seeds, finely chopped
1/4 teaspoon cumin seeds,
  finely chopped

CHOCOLATE RASPBERRY GÂTEAU *serves six*

For chocolate almond cake:
4 ounces almond paste
3/4 cup sugar
3/4 cup butter, softened
2 eggs
1½ tablespoons cocoa
   powder

For chocolate ganache:
1 pound semisweet
   chocolate, chopped
2 cups heavy cream

1 pint raspberries

Preheat oven to 350° F. In an electric mixer, combine almond paste and sugar. When mixture is crumbly, add butter. Mix on high speed until the mixture is light and fluffy.

Add eggs one at a time. Scrape bowl to be sure all ingredients are incorporated. Add cocoa powder, mixing just enough to incorporate.

Spread evenly in a greased, parchment-lined 9-inch-square cake pan. Bake for 35 to 40 minutes. Test for doneness by inserting a toothpick. It should come out clean. Place the cake in refrigerator to cool and set.

To make the ganache (frosting or glaze), place the chopped chocolate in a double boiler over medium-low heat until completely melted. Meanwhile, bring the cream to a boil in a saucepan. Stir cream into the chocolate with a rubber spatula until the mixture is smooth and completely combined. Let cool until set and spreadable.

Cut the cooled cake into 3 layers. Spread a thin layer of ganache on the bottom layer. Arrange raspberries on top. Spread a layer of ganache on top of raspberries and place second layer of cake on top. Repeat process with the second and third layers. Spread a thin layer of ganache on top and sides of the cake. Refrigerate.

Place chilled cake on a wire rack. Melt remaining ganache in double boiler until pourable. Pour glaze over the cake, using a palette knife to coat the cake completely and evenly.

Loni Kuhn

A 49ERS-WATCHING PARTY

Salsa Cheesecake

Beer and Lime Ribs

Black Bean and Corn Salad

Yucatán Salsa

Kahlua Sundae

serves eight

Loni Kuhn is a fourth-generation Californian who operates a cooking school, *Cook's Tours,* in San Francisco. She offers classes by herself and other prominent chefs of the Bay Area. She is also an ardent gardener and 49ers fan.

This menu is for one of my favorite treats — a fall lunch and 49ers-watching party. Almost everything is done ahead, and the flavors are forthright without bludgeoning your taste buds. The seasonings seem appropriate for the fall, and the recipes are easily doubled. Since no knives are required, the food is suitable for your lap. Be relaxed about making substitutions. After all, these are peasant foods.

SALSA CHEESECAKE *serves eight to ten*

6 corn tortillas
3 tablespoons melted
  butter
12 ounces plain goat
  cheese
12 ounces cream cheese
  or Neufchâtel
1¼ cups sour cream, or
  low-fat substitute
2 cloves garlic, minced
2 jalapeño or serrano
  chilies, finely minced
1 cup tomato salsa,
  drained, plus a little
  extra for garnish
3 tablespoons tomato
  paste
1½ teaspoons salt
1 teaspoon freshly ground
  pepper
4 extra-large eggs
1/2 cup chopped cilantro,
  plus some sprigs for
  garnish
2 stiffly beaten egg whites
Watercress for garnish
Sliced avocado for garnish

Oven dry the tortillas at 200° F directly on an oven rack for 45 minutes, until very crackly crisp. When the tortillas are cool, grind very fine in a food processor. Place in an airtight bag until ready to use. May be done several days ahead.

The cheesecake is best not refrigerated, so ideally, it should come out of the oven about 2 hours before serving time.

Preheat oven to 350° F. Brush the inside of a 9-inch springform pan with melted butter and carefully coat with tortilla crumbs. Tap out excess and reserve for topping.

In the bowl of an electric mixer or food processor, beat together the cheeses, sour cream, garlic, jalapeños, salsa, tomato paste, salt, pepper, and eggs. Beat until smooth. Fold in the cilantro and beaten egg whites.

Pour into prepared pan and sprinkle top evenly with remaining tortilla crumbs. Wrap bottom of pan in heavy aluminum foil to prevent leaking. Place pan inside a larger pan with 1 inch hot water. Bake for 60 to 70 minutes. Test center with a knife, which should come out clean. Cool in oven with door ajar. Remove sides from pan, but leave cake on the pan bottom. Place on platter. Surround with watercress. Place a bouquet of watercress on center of the cake. Garnish with crescents of avocado. Cut into wedges to serve with tomato salsa on the side.

BEER AND LIME RIBS *serves eight*

Place ribs in a plastic bag. Combine rest of ingredients for marinade and pour into the bag. Seal the bag and massage the marinade into the ribs.

Refrigerate several hours, or overnight, turning the bag occasionally. Remove ribs from bag when cooking time approaches. Wipe dry with paper towels. Cook on barbecue over hot fire, about 1½ to 2 minutes per side.

4½ pounds beef short ribs cut crosswise, flanken style
6 cloves garlic, minced
1 tablespoon ground cumin
2 tablespoons ground ancho or New Mexico chili powder
1 tablespoon crumbled oregano
12-ounce bottle Mexican beer
1/2 cup lime juice

BLACK BEAN AND CORN SALAD
serves eight to ten

This salad needs to mellow 24 hours in the refrigerator before serving.

Place black beans in a pot, cover generously with water, bring to a full boil, turn off heat, cover pot, and allow to sit for 2 hours. (Never salt beans until after cooking.) Drain the beans, cover with fresh water, bring to a boil, and simmer until just tender. Drain well and place in a large bowl.

Place corn in boiling water and cook for 1 minute. Drain and cut the kernels from the cobs.

Toss all ingredients together in a bowl and cover with plastic wrap. Refrigerate until an hour before serving. Taste for seasoning. Serve with a garnish of tortilla chips.

1½ pounds black beans
6 large ears corn
1 large red onion, chopped
1 to 1½-pound jicama, diced
4 to 6 cloves garlic, chopped
1 cup olive oil
2 to 3 jalapeño peppers, minced
3/4 cup fresh lime juice
2 tablespoons crumbled oregano
1 cup cilantro sprigs (or to taste)
Salt and pepper to taste
Tortilla chips for garnish

YUCATÁN SALSA *serves eight to ten*

1 ripe pineapple, peeled,
   cored, and diced
1 firm but almost ripe
   mango, peeled and
   diced (papaya may be
   substituted)
1 cup chopped onion
1 cup chopped red bell
   pepper
2 to 3 jalapeño peppers,
   minced
2 cloves garlic, minced
   (optional)
Salt to taste

Mix ingredients together well, and allow to mellow for 1 to 2 hours in the refrigerator. This salsa is a delicious counterpoint to salads and most grilled meats.

KAHLUA SUNDAE *serves one*

2 tablespoons Kahlua
1 or 2 scoops vanilla
   ice cream
Powdered chocolate,
   or cocoa
Roasted pecans

Talk about simplicity! Pour the Kahlua over ice cream, dust with chocolate, and top with freshly roasted pecans.

w i n t e r

Madeleine Kamman

PERFECT AFTER-SKI FOOD

Cream of Turnip Soup with Caraway

Fillet of Whitefish Marinated in Chervil and Hazelnuts

Farcement: Potato Pudding with Prunes

Old-Fashioned Walnut Tart

serves six

Madeleine Kamman was born in Paris, spent a good deal of her childhood in the French Alps, and was introduced to the world of food at the age of ten in her aunt's restaurant in the Loire Valley. In 1960, she married an American, Alan Kamman, and moved to Philadelphia, where she started teaching French cooking. On moving to Boston, she opened a professional chef's school, *Modern Gourmet,* and restaurant, *Chez la Mère Madeleine*. In 1980, she returned to the French Alps to run a cooking school in Annecy. She currently spends most of the year in California, as director of Beringer Vineyards' *Napa Valley School for American Chefs* in St. Helena. She is the author of several cookbooks, including *Madeleine Cooks* (Morrow, 1986) and *Madeleine Kamman's Savoie* (Atheneum, 1989).

The sun in the Napa Valley has dimmed my longing for the Alps. I almost have to think about my French mountains to recall the wild days of my youth when, skis fitted with sealskin, we left at the crack of dawn for a first climb up mountain slopes toward the edge of the glaciers. We repeated our climb perhaps

four times during the day for the craziness of sliding down that steep hill at break-
neck speed in a matter of minutes. There were still very few lifts in those days and,
for the real skiers, it was just not "in" to stand in line at the bottom of the hill.

No wonder our appetites were ravenous when we reached Chamonix or
Courchevel again in late afternoon. I have always been lucky enough to have as
good friends some of the best local cooks, and the recipes that you will find here
came from their stoves to our tables after we warmed up with a masterful grog of
the best Martinique rum. My alpine food is certainly not fare to make the modern
doctor smile, but it's perfect food after a day of great skiing. And as long as you
have exercised the whole day, you are more than entitled to its opulence.

CREAM OF TURNIP SOUP WITH CARAWAY
serves six to eight

1/2 cup butter
2 onions, finely chopped
2 pounds small, purple-
  topped turnips, peeled
  and sliced
Salt and freshly ground
  pepper
Pinch of sugar
1/2 teaspoon crushed
  caraway seeds
2 quarts chicken stock
1/4 cup sour cream
3/4 cup heavy cream

For garnish:
3 tablespoons butter
3 tablespoons semidry
  goat cheese
1 clove garlic, finely
  chopped
2 tablespoons chopped
  dill
Salt and coarsely cracked
  pepper

Heat the butter in a large saucepan or soup
pot, and cook the onions over moderate heat
until translucent. Add the turnips and toss
well. Season with salt and pepper. Cook,
covered, until the juices have come out of the
vegetables. Add pinch of sugar and continue
to cook, uncovered, until the juices evaporate
and the turnips have caramelized. Toss every
5 minutes or so. When the turnips are
browned and candied, add the caraway seeds
and the stock. Season with salt and pepper
again and bring to a boil. Turn down heat to
a simmer and cook until turnips fall apart.
Purée in the blender. Add the creams mixed
together and reheat to just below the boiling
point.

To prepare the garnish, cream the butter,
then add the goat cheese, garlic, and dill.
Season with salt and coarsely cracked pepper.

Serve the soup in hot bowls, dropping a dollop of the garnish butter in the center of each
bowl.

FILLET OF WHITEFISH MARINATED IN CHERVIL AND HAZELNUTS *serves six*

Prepare the dressing by mixing the shallots, hazelnuts, salt, pepper, cider vinegar, the larger amount of both oils, and the chervil. Emulsify well and pour half this dressing into the bottom of a large baking dish.

Rub a tablespoon each of the smaller amount of oils on the bottom of two skillets. Add the fish fillets, seasoned well with salt and pepper on both sides. Over very low heat, steam the fillets, covered, for just a few minutes, or until the fish turns translucent.

Transfer the fillets to the prepared baking dish and spoon the remaining dressing over them. Cover with plastic wrap and chill for 24 hours before serving.

2 shallots, very finely chopped
1/4 cup hazelnuts, peeled, toasted, and very finely chopped
Salt and freshly ground pepper
3 tablespoons cider vinegar
1/3 cup plus 2 tablespoons each hazelnut and corn oil
1/3 cup chopped fresh chervil
6 large whitefish fillets (you can also use catfish or pike)

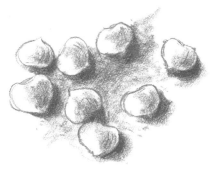

FARCEMENT: POTATO PUDDING WITH PRUNES *serves six to eight*

1 tube pan, 9⅝ by 3¼
  inches
Heavy-duty aluminum
  foil
12 potatoes (yellow Finn,
  Maine, Long Island, or
  California new), peeled
  and washed
4 rashers thick-sliced
  bacon, preferably
  Virginia or Vermont
  smoked
3 eggs
2/3 cup milk, or more
  if needed
1/2 cup cornmeal
1/4 cup currants
2 dried pear halves
  (without sulfur dioxide),
  diced into 1/4-inch
  cubes
Salt and freshly ground
  pepper
2 pounds thin-sliced
  bacon
12 soft pitted prunes

Farcement, or potato pudding, is a strikingly attractive dish, cooked in a tall tube pan, or *rabolire,* which, if you are in the Haute Savoie, can be purchased in all hardware stores. But a great *farcement* can be made in any American tube pan, tightly covered with heavy foil.

Hand-grate the potatoes on the coarse blade of a grater (positively no food processor). Let the potatoes stand in a bowl so the water oozes out. Cover with plastic wrap and do not worry about browning. After 1 hour, rinse the potatoes under cold running water until the water runs perfectly clear. Dry the potatoes completely in tea towels.

Meanwhile, render the thick-sliced bacon and cook it until golden, not crisp. Cut into 1/3-inch-square pieces.

In a large bowl, beat the eggs and milk. Add the cornmeal, cooked bacon, currants, and diced pears and blend well. Add the potatoes. Salt and pepper well. Keep covered while you line the tube pan entirely with the thin-sliced bacon, letting the ends hang over the edges of the pan.

Spoon half the potato mixture into the pan. Pack down by tapping the bottom of the pan on the counter. Top with the soft prunes and add the remainder of the potato mixture. Tap again to pack down.

Flip the bacon hanging out of the pan over the top of the filling. Cover the pan tightly with heavy-duty aluminum foil, dull side out. Put the pan in a 1½- to 2-gallon soup

pot and slowly pour enough water into the
pot to reach 1 inch below the rim of the tube
pan.

Bring to a boil on top of the stove and immediately bake in a 325° F oven for 7 hours. Yes,
you are reading correctly. It takes 7 full hours
to steam the farcement. Make sure you have
the full 7 hours or the taste simply will not be
there.

When done, cool the farcement slightly before unmolding onto a platter. Serve on hot
plates.

OLD-FASHIONED WALNUT TART *serves ten*

For the pastry:
1/2 cup unsalted butter
3 tablespoons brown sugar
Pinch of salt
1 tablespoon dark rum
1 egg
1 egg yolk
1 to 1¼ cups sifted
   all-purpose flour

For the filling:
1/2 cup unsalted butter at
   room temperature
1⅓ cups chopped walnuts
3/4 cup brown sugar
2 eggs
2 tablespoons espresso-
   strength coffee
1 tablespoon dark rum

For the icing:
1/2 teaspoon walnut oil
3½ ounces bittersweet
   chocolate

This old-fashioned tart is common to the Savoie and Dauphiné parts of France. The recipe is my version of one served at the charming *Hôtel du Col du Cucheron*.

Prepare the pastry by creaming all but 1 tablespoon of the butter in a food processor and adding the sugar, salt, rum, and eggs. Pour in the flour through opening of processor until the dough forms a ball. Flatten the dough into a 1/2-inch cake and store between 2 layers of plastic wrap.

With the remaining tablespoon of butter, grease a 10-inch springform pan very well. Roll out the pastry 1/6 inch thick between 2 sheets of plastic wrap. Fit it into the pan and build a small edge.

In the food processor, mix all the ingredients for the filling and process until homogeneous. Pour into the prepared shell. Bake on the lowest shelf of a preheated 350° F oven for 20 minutes, and another 35 minutes on the top shelf. Remove from the oven and cool completely.

To ice, mix the walnut oil and chocolate and melt in a double boiler, cool slightly, and brush evenly on the top of tart. Serve in 1-inch portions since it is very rich, with an excellent cup of double-strength café au lait.

Paul Bertolli

MENU FOR A COLD WINTER DAY

Dungeness Crab Chowder with Artichokes and Leeks

Twice-Cooked Duck

Root Vegetables Baked in Parchment

Lettuces Vinaigrette

Warm Pear Upside-Down Cake

serves four

The head chef of *Chez Panisse* in Berkeley, Paul Bertolli has held the position for ten years and is responsible for creating the restaurant's changing-nightly menu. He is the author of *Chez Panisse Cooking* (Random House, 1988).

Thinking back, I must admit that the happiest moments I have spent at the table haven't always been connected with festive occasions, or even holidays. I usually associate those with a certain forced expectation of conviviality and the usual torpor that accompanies having visited the buffet table too many times.

In fact, my fondest recollections of moments around the table have occurred informally and spontaneously on what might be considered rather ordinary days of the year. I remember unusually hot summer days when friends gathered together on rooftops or in backyards, and the heat of the day held fast into the late hours of the evening. No one would want to go near a stove, so dinner consisted primarily of whatever the host for the evening could pull from the refrigerator that didn't need to be cooked. Or I think of those beautifully dreary days in winter when, housebound and keeping company with the fireplace and smells of the braising pot, it seemed so right to call friends and share what had been simmering for hours on the stove.

Such hot summer days have been my festive occasions; those chilly, foggy Sundays, a wonderful kind of holiday.

DUNGENESS CRAB CHOWDER WITH ARTICHOKES AND LEEKS *serves four*

1 freshly cooked
  Dungeness crab,
  two pounds, or an
  equivalent quantity of
  smaller blue crabs
6 cups whole milk
1 large bay leaf
Small pinch of saffron
  threads
2 tablespoons unsalted
  butter
2 small leeks, white part
  only, finely diced to
  yield 1½ cups
1 small rib of celery,
  finely diced to yield
  1/3 cup
2 small red potatoes,
  peeled and diced
2 large artichokes, pared
  to the bottoms (leaves
  and chokes removed)
  and diced
1 cup water
Juice of 1/2 lemon
Salt and freshly ground
  pepper
1/8 teaspoon ground
  cayenne
1 heaping tablespoon
  chervil

The elements of this soup have been chosen for their understated character, to give the soup body and interest without competing with the central flavor of the crab. There are several options for making the soup, depending upon your time and the availability of fresh crab. Under the best of circumstances, begin with whole, live crab. A Dungeness crab takes 12 minutes of boiling in the pot. Smaller blue crabs should be allowed 6 to 8 minutes. If you cannot locate whole, live crabs, or if time doesn't permit, you may simply substitute fresh picked crabmeat, although the finished flavor of the soup will be much milder by comparison.

It is possible to enrich the soup by using half-and-half or cream. However, I have found that the flavor of crab is most clear if milk is used as the primary liquid. Furthermore, milk gives the soup an appealing lightness.

Pull away the top shell from the boiled crab and set it aside, cavity side up. Separate the legs and claws from the body of the crab. Use a nutcracker, kitchen shears, or meat mallet to crack or cut the shells of the crab, and pick out the meat. You should end up with about 1¾ cups (12 ounces) crabmeat. Drain any liquid from the top shell of the crab, but don't let any of the solids escape. Spoon out the crab butter — the white and orange solids inside the shell — which will add considerable flavor and richness to the soup. You should have 1/3 cup. Set it aside. Discard the top shell. Combine the picked shells with the milk, bay leaf, and saffron in a heavy-bottomed pot (about 4-quart capacity). Set the pot over me-

dium heat and warm the milk to the scalding
point. Turn off the heat and let stand to infuse
for 45 minutes.

Melt the butter in a saucepan and add the
diced leeks, celery, potatoes, artichokes, and
water. Season with the lemon juice, salt, and
a few turns of the pepper mill. Stir the vegetables and seasonings together. Bring to a
boil, reduce the heat to medium, and cover
the pan. Let the vegetables cook for 10 minutes. Remove the cover, raise the heat, and
allow any moisture in the pan to evaporate.

Strain the infused milk over the vegetables
and add the cayenne. Add the crabmeat and
crab butter. Warm the soup gently and season
with salt and pepper. Just before serving, stir
in the chervil, and ladle the soup into warm
bowls.

TWICE-COOKED DUCK *serves four*

4 duck legs, about 2
  pounds altogether
1 tablespoon kosher salt
3/4 teaspoon freshly
  ground pepper
2 medium yellow onions,
  diced
2 medium carrots, diced
1 stalk celery, diced
1 bay leaf
Fresh thyme sprigs
2 cups full-bodied
  poultry broth

Trim the fat in the pockets under the skin of the duck legs. With the flat end of the knife blade, scrape the fat to the side, or cut it free. Trim the excess skin so it extends slightly beyond the flesh of the leg.

Mix together the salt and pepper, and sprinkle both sides of the legs with the mixture. Set the legs on a plate at room temperature for 1½ hours to absorb the salt.

Preheat the oven to 350° F. Place the onions, carrots, celery, bay leaf, and thyme in a baking dish and place the duck legs on top. Pour the broth over the legs. Cover the dish tightly and place it in the oven for 1½ hours. When done, the legs should be tender throughout and yield easily to a toothpick.

Remove the duck legs from the baking dish and pour the braising liquid through a sieve into a saucepan. Skim off any surface fat. It works best if you set the pan with the braising liquid slightly off the burner and turn the heat as high as it will go. The fat will rise to one side of the pan. Reduce the liquid until it is slightly thick and about 1 cup remains. Set aside.

There are two options for finishing the duck: it may be slowly browned in a cast-iron pan, or on a charcoal grill. In either case, set the legs to brown over a low fire until the skin is crisp and develops an even mahogany color. Rewarm the sauce and pour over each serving. Serve with root vegetables baked in parchment.

ROOT VEGETABLES BAKED IN PARCHMENT
serves four

Preheat oven to 350° F.

Peel and dice the vegetables 1/2 inch thick and put them in a bowl. Cut up the butter into small pieces and add it to the bowl. Salt and pepper the vegetables, add the chopped parsley, and pour the lemon juice over them.

Cut two large pieces of wax paper, or baking parchment, and two pieces of foil. Set the wax paper on top of the foil and place two thyme sprigs in the middle. Arrange half the seasoned vegetables on top of the thyme. Add half the water. Fold the paper around the vegetables. Do the same with the foil, and crimp the edges of the foil tightly. Repeat with the second piece of paper and remaining vegetables.

Set the packages on a baking sheet and bake for 35 minutes. Remove the foil, transfer the packages to a warm platter, and open at the table. Serve with the twice-cooked duck.

1/2 pound carrots
1/2 pound parsnips
1/2 pound celery root
1/2 pound turnips
2 tablespoons butter
Salt and freshly ground
  pepper
1 tablespoon chopped
  parsley
Juice of 1/2 lemon
4 fresh thyme sprigs
1/4 cup water

WARM PEAR UPSIDE-DOWN CAKE *serves eight*

3/4 cup unsalted butter
3/4 cup brown sugar
4 to 6 ripe pears (Winter
  Nellis)
1 cup granulated sugar
2 large eggs, separated
1 teaspoon vanilla extract
1½ cups all-purpose flour
2 teaspoons baking
  powder
1/2 cup milk
Pinch of salt
Whipping cream

Because of its basis of melted brown sugar, this cake accommodates fruits that are tart or slightly astringent. Blood oranges, cranberries, gooseberries, red currants, fresh pineapple, even rhubarb may be substituted successfully.

Preheat oven to 350° F.

Place 4 tablespoons butter and the brown sugar in a 9-inch cake pan and melt over low heat, mixing with a fork to combine well. Remove from heat. Peel the pears and cut them into segments about 1 inch thick. Arrange the pears on top of the melted sugar and butter in a close, circular pattern.

Using a whisk or an electric mixer, cream the remaining 1/2 cup butter with the granulated sugar. Beat in the egg yolks and vanilla.

Mix in half the flour and baking powder, then the milk. Add the other half of the flour mixture and continue to mix until very smooth.

Beat the egg whites and pinch of salt to firm peaks and fold them into the batter. Work quickly and keep the mixture light. Spread the batter evenly over the pears. Bake for about 45 minutes, or until the cake is golden brown on top and set in the center. Transfer the cake to a rack and cool for 10 minutes. Invert while still warm and serve with lightly whipped cream.

AN EXCEPTIONAL DINNER FOR THE HOLIDAYS

Smoked Trout Salad

Chicken Pie with Morels

Wolfgang's Fruitcake

serves four

Austrian-born chef Wolfgang Puck has built an immensely successful restaurant empire in California, first with *Spago* and *Chinois on Main* in Los Angeles, then with *Postrio* in San Francisco, and more recently with *Eureka Brewery & Restaurant* in West Los Angeles and *Granita* in Malibu. He is the author of *The Wolfgang Puck Cookbook* (Random House, 1986).

For me, the Christmas holidays are a celebration of love and all the good things in life. When I plan a holiday dinner party, I make sure I have time to enjoy the company of my friends. These recipes are simple yet exceptional, and can be prepared in advance, so that you don't have to spend the entire evening in the kitchen.

SMOKED TROUT SALAD *serves four*

For the vinaigrette:
2 large shallots, minced
    (1 heaping tablespoon)
1 tablespoon Dijon
    mustard
2 tablespoons Zinfandel
    vinegar
2 tablespoons sherry
    vinegar
1/2 cup olive oil
1/2 cup vegetable oil
Salt and freshly ground
    white pepper

2 cups escarole or frisée
1 bunch watercress
1 baguette of French
    bread
1 cup sour cream
1 tablespoon grated
    horseradish
Juice of 1/2 lemon
Salt and pepper
2 small smoked trout
3 ounces salmon roe

Prepare the vinaigrette in a small bowl.
Whisk together the shallots and mustard.
Whisk in the vinegars and then the olive and
vegetable oils. Season with salt and pepper
to taste. Transfer to a covered container and
refrigerate until needed.

Wash the greens and pick the stems from the
watercress. Tear lettuce into bite-size pieces.

Cut the baguette into 12 slices, about 1/2
inch thick. Toast the slices on one side and set
aside.

Mix sour cream, horseradish, lemon juice,
and salt and pepper to taste until well
combined.

Remove skin and bones from smoked trout.
Let trout fall into pieces.

Spread sour-cream mixture on untoasted side
of bread slices. Spread some smoked trout
evenly on each crouton, and spoon some
salmon roe on top.

In a large bowl, toss greens with vinaigrette.
Divide evenly and place in center of 4 salad
plates. Place 3 croutons on each plate around
the greens. Serve immediately.

CHICKEN PIE WITH MORELS *serves four to six*

Soak the morels overnight in enough water to cover. Drain and cut in half lengthwise, and wash carefully to remove all the sand.

Season chicken pieces with salt and pepper to taste, and dust lightly with flour. In a large sauté pan, sauté the chicken in 1 tablespoon each of butter and oil, and cook until golden brown on all sides.

Remove the chicken from the pan and pour off the fat. Add the shallots and morels and deglaze the pan with port wine. Add the cream and stock and bring to a boil. Return the chicken to the pan and simmer, covered, for 10 minutes. The sauce should thicken slightly. Whisk in the remaining 3 tablespoons butter, one small piece at a time. Season to taste with salt, pepper, and lemon juice.

Divide the chicken and sauce equally among 4 or 6 individual casseroles. Set aside to cool.

Roll out the puff pastry, keeping it at least 1/4 inch thick. Cut rounds of pastry 2 inches larger than the casseroles. When the chicken has cooled, brush sides of casseroles with egg wash and cover with the pastry rounds, pressing the edges down gently against sides of casseroles. Do not make any holes in the pastry. Refrigerate for 1 hour or longer. It's important to chill the pastry thoroughly before baking, otherwise the crust will collapse into the casseroles.

Preheat oven to 400° F. Brush pastry with egg wash and bake for 35 minutes, or until crust is a rich golden brown. Serve immediately.

24 dried morel mushrooms
2 whole chickens (2½ pounds each), cut into 8 pieces
Salt and freshly ground white pepper
1 tablespoon all-purpose flour
4 tablespoons unsalted butter
2 tablespoons peanut oil
2 shallots, minced
1 cup port wine
1 cup heavy cream
1 cup chicken stock
Juice of 1/2 lemon
1 pound puff pastry
1 egg, lightly beaten, for egg wash

WOLFGANG'S FRUITCAKE *serves six or more*

1 cup Marsala or
   Sauternes
1 cup water
1 cup raisins
1 cup dried apricots
1 cup walnuts
1/2 cup dried pears
1/2 cup dried figs
1/2 cup pecans
4 ounces unsalted butter
1/2 cup sugar
1 teaspoon ground
   cinnamon
1/4 teaspoon ground
   cloves
2 cups all-purpose flour
2 teaspoons baking soda
1/2 teaspoon salt

You can use any dried fruit that is available and to your taste. At Spago, we use only un-sulfured fruit, which can be purchased at organic or health-food stores. We do not use candied fruit. The cake is better when made 1 or 2 days before serving. And the recipe can be increased easily to make 2 or more cakes.

Preheat oven to 350° F. Butter a loaf pan (8½ by 4 by 3½ inches) and dust with flour, shaking out any excess.

In a medium saucepan, combine the Marsala, water, raisins, apricots, walnuts, pears, figs, and pecans. Bring to a boil and then simmer until the fruits are tender, about 5 minutes. Let cool. Drain, reserving the liquid, and coarsely chop the fruits and nuts. Transfer to a large bowl with the reserved liquid. In a small saucepan, melt the butter with the sugar, cinnamon, and cloves, stirring occasionally, until the sugar is completely dissolved. Let cool.

Meanwhile, in a bowl, sift together the flour, baking soda, and salt. Stir in the melted butter mixture and then pour the batter into the fruits and nuts, combining thoroughly. Don't be afraid to mix with your hands. This is a very thick batter. Scrape into the prepared pan, patting down as necessary to level.

Bake for 60 to 70 minutes, until the cake is firm to the touch and nicely browned. Invert onto a parchment-lined wire rack and let cool. Wrap well and use as needed. To serve, cut into thin slices.

Hubert Keller

A GOURMET MENU
FOR CHRISTMAS EVE

*Gratin of Oysters with a Chive
Zinfandel Cream Sauce*

*Norwegian Salmon in a Corn
Pancake with Golden Caviar*

*Lamb Chops Baked in a Julienned
Potato Crust au Jus*

*Warm Bosc Pear and Pecan Cream
Tart*

Marrons Glacés

serves four

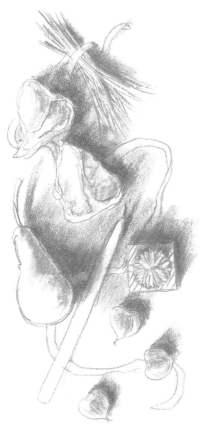

Hubert Keller was born into a family of
pastry chefs in the Alsatian wine village of
Ribeauville and trained under such renowned
French chefs as Paul Bocuse, Gaston Lenôtre,
and Roger Vergé. He is currently executive
chef and managing partner of San Francisco's
Fleur de Lys restaurant. His notable career
also took him to São Paulo, Brazil, where he
worked for two years as chef at Roger Vergé's
Cuisine du Soleil restaurant. He recalls a
Christmas in Brazil with this menu.

*My most memorable candlelight meal took place at Christmas in Brazil. My
wife and I were invited by a Swiss family to celebrate Christmas Eve at their farm
in Buzios, north of Rio de Janeiro. I remember Brazil having the hottest Christmas next to Bastille Day in the south of France.*

*Nevertheless, an arara palm tree with its decorations transformed itself into a
one-of-a-kind Christmas tree. The large table had been set very elegantly with a
lace tablecloth, marvelous china, and antique silverware. However, what really
took effect on the whole room, creating a special ambience, were four English*

candelabra with off-white candles. Since the candles provided the only light in the dining room, they created a Christmas atmosphere which carried us away from the tropical heat of Brazil.

Close to midnight, my wife and I probably thought of home simultaneously on hearing "Silent Night" sung by the guests and taken up by the servants of the farm. It was a wonderful and unforgettable Christmas Eve.

GRATIN OF OYSTERS WITH A CHIVE ZINFANDEL CREAM SAUCE *serves four*

24 oysters, shucked
  (reserve deeper half of
  the shell plus the oyster
  liquor)
2 bunches spinach
6 tablespoons butter
1 teaspoon chopped
  shallots
3 tablespoons Zinfandel
1 cup cream
2 egg yolks
Salt and freshly ground
  pepper
2 tablespoons finely
  cut chives
Rock or coarse salt
1/8 teaspoon nutmeg
2 tablespoons tomato
  concassé (1 medium-
  sized tomato, peeled,
  seeded, and chopped)

This oyster course is served on the half shell on a bed of spinach leaves with a light chive and Zinfandel cream sauce.

Preheat the grill or broiler to hot. Remove spinach stems completely, and thoroughly wash the leaves. Place the leaves in a heated sauté pan with 2 tablespoons of butter, stirring occasionally until the leaves are wilted but still bright green, about 3 to 4 minutes. Drain in a colander, let cool, then squeeze all the moisture from the spinach.

Heat 2 tablespoons of butter in a small saucepan. Add the chopped shallots and sauté to a light golden color. Deglaze with the Zinfandel and add the strained oyster juice. Reduce the mixture by half and pour in 2/3 cup cream. Bring to a boil and lower the heat to a simmer for 10 minutes.

In a small bowl, whisk remaining cream until smooth and fold in the egg yolks. Slowly whisk this mixture into the cream sauce over low heat and cook gently. Do not allow the sauce to boil or the yolks will curdle. Taste and adjust seasoning with salt and pepper. Pour the sauce through a sieve and add the chives. Fill a large shallow baking dish to a depth of 1/4 inch with rock or coarse salt.

Heat the spinach leaves in remaining 2 tablespoons butter, adding salt, freshly ground pepper, and nutmeg. Divide the spinach equally into each oyster shell. Top with an oyster, sprinkle with the chopped tomato, and blanket with a tablespoon of the cream sauce. Arrange the filled shells side by side in the salt-lined baking dish. Broil for 1½ minutes, until the sauce is browned. Serve at once.

NORWEGIAN SALMON IN A CORN PANCAKE WITH GOLDEN CAVIAR *serves six*

This dish of thinly sliced Norwegian salmon is cooked in a tender corn pancake, topped with golden caviar and accented with a watercress cream sauce. It has a pretty contrast of colors and a delightful taste that comes from the richness of the salmon and caviar blended with the corn pancake and watercress sauce.

Peel off corn husks and silk. Bring 4 quarts of salted water to a boil. Add the corn and boil 5 minutes, then quickly dip in cold water. Cut the kernels from the corn. In a food processor fitted with a chopping blade, place the corn, 3 eggs, 2 tablespoons flour, salt, and pepper. Blend well. Adjust the seasoning, and transfer batter to a small mixing bowl.

To prepare sauce, wash the watercress and trim off the leaves. Discard the stems. Cook the leaves in boiling salted water just until tender, about 3 minutes. Drain in a strainer.

For pancake batter:
3 to 4 ears young, tender corn
3 eggs
2 tablespoons flour
Salt and pepper

For watercress sauce:
1 bunch watercress
1/2 tablespoon butter
1 tablespoon chopped shallots
2 tablespoons dry white wine
2 tablespoons veal glaze (or 1 tablespoon powdered chicken base)
3/4 cup heavy cream

(continued next page)

6 ounces fillet of fresh
  Norwegian salmon
3 ounces golden caviar
  (or sturgeon caviar)
2 tablespoons cooking oil
18 cooked asparagus tips
2 tablespoons sour cream
1 tablespoon finely cut
  chives

Refresh the leaves under cold running water, then squeeze out all the moisture.

In a small saucepan, heat 1/2 tablespoon butter. Add the chopped shallots and sauté to a light golden color. Deglaze with white wine and reduce almost to dry. Add the veal glaze (or chicken base) and cream. Bring to a boil and lower the heat to a simmer for about 5 minutes. Add the watercress leaves. Check seasoning. Transfer the mixture to an electric blender and blend for one minute. You will obtain a light, very tasty watercress cream sauce.

Slice evenly and thinly 6 scallopinis of salmon. Spread them out on a plate and top each one with a teaspoon of caviar. Fold the scallopinis so that the caviar is sealed in between layers of salmon. Season the salmon on both sides with salt and pepper.

Grease a crêpe or sauté pan with oil, and heat. Add about 1½ teaspoons of the pancake mixture. Top with a salmon scallopini and barely cover with another thin layer of corn mixture. You can cook 4 to 6 pancakes at a time. Cook until golden brown on one side, then turn and cook on the other side.

When the pancakes are done, cover the centers of warm plates with the watercress sauce. Place a pancake on each plate and garnish them attractively with the cooked asparagus tips. Top the pancakes with a teaspoon of sour cream and a teaspoon of caviar. Sprinkle with chives.

LAMB CHOPS BAKED IN A JULIENNED POTATO CRUST AU JUS *serves four*

Preheat oven to 375° F.

To prepare shallot-thyme jus, heat 1 tablespoon olive oil in a saucepan, add chopped shallots, and sauté to a golden color. Pour in red wine and reduce almost to dry. Add the lamb stock (or beef broth) and thyme. Bring to a boil. Check the seasoning.

Peel the garlic cloves. Drop them into a small saucepan half filled with water and bring to a boil. Pour off the water. Add more water to the saucepan with garlic and bring to a boil again. Drain the garlic.

Note: Don't worry about the odor of the garlic disturbing your guests, since the two cookings will dissipate the heavy aroma of the garlic. In any case, don't forget that garlic is a remedy for many illnesses.

Heat the remaining olive oil in a small sauté pan and sauté the garlic to a light brown color. Season the lamb chops with salt and pepper on both sides. With a small pointed knife, make an incision in each chop just large enough to stuff with a single clove of garlic.

Slice the potatoes into thin julienne-style strips. Do not mash or put the potatoes in water. It would remove the starch, which is needed to keep the julienned potatoes together. Squeeze out all the moisture and season the potatoes with salt. In the center of a plate, lay out a thin layer of potato the size of a lamb chop. Lay one chop on the potato. Cover the chop with another layer of potato, making sure that the chop is completely enclosed, except for the bone.

2 tablespoons virgin olive oil
2 tablespoons finely chopped shallots
1/3 cup red wine
3/4 cup lamb stock or beef broth
2 sprigs fresh thyme
8 cloves garlic
8 loin lamb chops, about 3 ounces each, trimmed of any fat
Salt and pepper
3 to 4 peeled Idaho potatoes
2/3 cup vegetable oil

(continued next page)

Heat the vegetable oil in a large skillet over medium-high heat. Place the wrapped lamb chops in the pan and let the julienned potato turn into a golden crust on one side. Turn the chops over carefully and place the pan in the preheated oven for about 8 or 9 minutes. Transfer the lamb chops to a cutting board and slice them on the bias with a serrated knife.

Arrange the chops on 4 dinner plates so that the slices overlap. You will observe that the lamb chops stay perfectly pink after being cooked 8 to 9 minutes. Serve the jus on the side.

WARM BOSC PEAR AND PECAN CREAM TART *serves four*

7 ounces puff pastry
  dough
6 tablespoons unsalted
  butter
3 tablespoons sugar
4 tablespoons ground
  pecans
1 large egg
2 to 3 Bosc pears
2 tablespoons honey

Preheat oven to 375° F. On a lightly floured surface, roll out dough to 1/8 inch thick. Cut out four circles 5½ inches in diameter, and place on a parchment-lined baking sheet. Refrigerate while preparing filling.

Place 3 tablespoons butter in the bowl of an electric mixer fitted with a paddle. Mix until butter is white and smooth. Add sugar and mix for another 20 seconds. Add ground pecans and blend well. Incorporate egg and continue blending until mixture is homogeneous.

Peel and core pears and slice into thin wedges. Spread the creamy pecan mixture on top of the pastry circles to within 1/2 inch of edge. Arrange the pear slices on top in overlapping concentric circles. Dot with remaining butter and drizzle with honey. Bake for 20 to 25 minutes. Serve immediately with crème fraîche, passion-fruit sorbet, apricot coulis, or caramel sauce.

MARRONS GLACÉS *serves four*

Marrons glacés are chestnuts covered with candied sugar, as if frosted. They take three days to make but are wonderful served with coffee.

2½ cups chestnuts
1 tablespoon vegetable oil
Juice of 1 lemon
3 cups sugar

To shell chestnuts, make two crescent-shaped gashes in their flat side with a sharp-pointed knife. Place the nuts in a skillet over high heat with a tablespoon of oil. Shake them until coated, then place in a moderate oven until the shells and inner brown skin can be easily removed. Soak the peeled chestnuts for about 8 hours in cold water and lemon juice.

Drain the chestnuts. Bring a pot of water to a boil. Add the chestnuts and simmer until tender but crisp. Drain the chestnuts.

Prepare the syrup by cooking to the soft-ball stage (234° F) 3 cups of sugar in 2 cups of water. Slowly place the nuts in the boiling syrup and simmer gently about 10 minutes. Set aside and cover the pot, letting the nuts cool overnight.

(continued next page)

Preheat oven to 250° F. Drain the chestnuts, reserving the syrup. Put the nuts on a baking sheet and dry in the oven for 1½ hours.

Meanwhile, reduce the syrup until very thick. Transfer nuts to a jar and fill up with the heavy syrup. Let sit for 8 hours. Repeat the process of drying and dipping 3 times until you reach the final point of glazed chestnuts. Store in a tightly covered tin.

Let's finish with some festive words from Roger Vergé: "Perfect, so there you are, the fire is burning, your attire is comfortable, the armchair is deep. . . . Without further delay, let the celebration begin. First a marron glacé, in the mouth, then a generous glassful of Armagnac. Let's close our eyes and chew slowly, slowly, slowly."

How sad life would be without marrons glacés.

René Verdon

A FRENCH CHRISTMAS DINNER

Oysters with Sweet Garlic Butter

Consommé en Croûte

Fillet of Salmon, Sauce Vierge

Roast Leg of Lamb with Juniper Berries

Stuffed Potatoes

Watercress Salad

Chocolate Soufflé Cake with Crème Anglaise

serves eight

René Verdon's illustrious career includes a year as chef aboard the S.S. *Liberté*. In the sixties, he was the White House chef under presidents Kennedy and Johnson. He subsequently settled in San Francisco, where he operated *Le Trianon* restaurant from 1972 to 1986. He has written four cookbooks: *The White House Chef* (Doubleday, 1967), *French Cooking for the American Table* (Doubleday, 1974), *The Enlightened Cuisine* (Macmillan, 1985), and *Convection Cuisine* (William Morrow, 1988).

Christmas dinner in France is very much a family affair. Usually the father and other relatives accompany the children to Christmas mass while the mother stays at home to put the finishing touches on a very special menu.

Traditionally, most French families have a turkey on Christmas Day. But since in America turkey is identified with Thanksgiving, I propose something different — a marinated leg of lamb prepared in the manner of boar or venison. Moreover, a leg of lamb can accommodate a family of eight people.

A French Christmas dinner nearly always starts with oysters, which are at their best this time of year. Next comes a clear soup and a fish course. The main course is served with a vegetable garnish and is followed by a salad. This serves to refresh the palate and aid the digestion. And it makes for a break before dessert. Naturally, the portions are small. This meal is supposed to delight the palate, not put the diners to sleep.

The inevitable French dessert is a Bûche de Noël, a sponge log filled and frosted with chocolate buttercream. But I find it too heavy after so many courses. Instead, I propose small portions of a dark, not-too-sweet chocolate soufflé cake with a light, delicate custard sauce.

The Christmas menu I have put together contains many of the classic elements, but lightened and updated, and so designed that nearly all the preparation can be done the day before. In fact, the cook spends only five minutes in the kitchen between courses, so the whole family can be together and enjoy themselves.

OYSTERS WITH SWEET GARLIC BUTTER
serves eight

1 cup butter, softened
4 cloves garlic, finely
  chopped
2 tablespoons chopped
  parsley
2 tablespoons chopped
  watercress
Freshly ground black
  pepper
24 fresh oysters in
  the shell
Seaweed or coarse salt
  (optional)
Bread crumbs made from
  6 slices home-style
  white bread

Mix together the butter, garlic, parsley, watercress, and pepper (about 2 turns of the mill). Place on a piece of plastic wrap and form into a roll the diameter of a silver dollar. Refrigerate until firm. This can be done a day ahead.

Open oysters and discard the top shell. If possible, arrange in a shallow pan on a bed of damp seaweed or a thick layer of coarse salt, to keep the shells steady. Sprinkle each oyster with bread crumbs. Cut the roll of seasoned butter into 1/8-inch slices, and put one slice on top of each oyster.

Place under preheated broiler for 2 minutes and serve immediately, setting the shells on seaweed or small paper doilies. Serve 3 per portion.

CONSOMMÉ EN CROÛTE *serves eight*

This presentation is most impressive, but very simple to achieve. You will need 8 small porcelain soup bowls — inexpensive Chinese porcelain rice bowls, about 4½ inches in diameter, will do very well. The bowls are filled with cold soup, covered with puff pastry, and refrigerated. They are transferred to a hot oven until the pastry rises into a golden dome. Surprisingly, this does not damage the bowls. But be sure not to use your best china. When served, each diner breaks open the pastry with a spoon and breaks it into the soup. You can make your own puff pastry, or buy the frozen variety. Packages of frozen puff-pastry patty shells come 6 to a box.

Fill each bowl with consommé to within 1 inch of the top. Roll out puff pastry on a lightly floured surface to 1/8 inch thick, and cut out 8 circles 1 inch larger than your bowls. If using frozen dough, let thaw in refrigerator before using.

Brush surface of circles with beaten egg and fit over bowls, egg side down. Secure dough with your cupped hand around edges of bowls. The pastry should stick to the sides of the bowls, and there must be no holes, or it will not rise. Place bowls on a baking tray and refrigerate until required. Reserve remaining beaten egg.

Preheat oven to 400° F. Brush top of pastry with beaten egg, and place the tray with bowls in the oven. Bake 10 to 15 minutes, until puffed and golden brown.

6 to 8 cups rich chicken consommé, homemade or canned
1 pound puff pastry
1 egg, beaten

FILLET OF SALMON, SAUCE VIERGE *serves eight*

1 pound salmon fillet
  (bass, snapper, or cod
  will also do)

For sauce vierge:
1 cup extra virgin olive oil
2 ripe tomatoes, peeled,
  seeded, and diced
2 sprigs parsley, without
  stems, chopped
2 sprigs chervil, chopped
Pinch chopped fresh
  tarragon
2 cloves garlic
1 teaspoon coriander
  seeds, finely crushed
Juice of 1 lemon
Salt and freshly ground
  pepper to taste

This is a steamed salmon dish with a wonderful sauce that's put together in a food processor.

About 1 hour before needed, combine sauce ingredients in a food processor or blender. Mix until amalgamated. Sauce will form into a salmon pink emulsion. Taste and adjust seasoning. Pour into warmed bowl and set this in a saucepan half filled with hot water. Place at side of stove to keep warm; the flavors will develop on standing. Sauce should be served lukewarm, not hot. Heat will cause it to separate. Makes 2 cups.

Cut the salmon into 2-ounce portions. It's best to buy a little extra fish so pieces can be trimmed to the same size for even cooking. When ready to serve, place fish on the rack of a steamer. Steam for 2 minutes over simmering water, covered. Pour half a cup of sauce vierge onto each plate and top with a slice of fish.

ROAST LEG OF LAMB WITH JUNIPER BERRIES *serves eight*

6-pound leg of lamb
1/4 cup vinegar
2 tablespoons olive oil
2 slices onion
1 bay leaf
1 sprig parsley
1 clove garlic, crushed
Pinch of thyme
5 juniper berries

If you have the butcher remove the upper bone from the lamb, it will be easier to carve, but it's not absolutely necessary. I was taught to judge the doneness of the meat by quickly putting a finger inside the bone cavity. If the meat feels lukewarm, it is cooked rare and ready to come out of the oven. Like roast beef, lamb should be served medium rare to be at its succulent best. You can find dried juniper berries in the spice section of most supermarkets.

Remove the skin and all but an extremely thin layer of fat from the lamb. Combine vinegar, oil, onion, bay leaf, parsley, garlic, thyme, juniper berries, salt, and pepper in a large, deep dish. Place the lamb in the marinade, cover, and let stand in a cool place for 24 hours. Turn meat occasionally.

Preheat oven to 375° F. Drain meat and reserve marinade. Rub with butter and sprinkle lightly with salt and pepper. Place on a rack in a roasting pan. Roast for 75 to 90 minutes, basting frequently, until the interior temperature reaches 140° F (for well done, 165° F). Remove meat, leaving it on the rack, and keep warm. If you don't have a warming oven, set the lamb on top of the range under an aluminum-foil tent. Let stand for 20 minutes so the juices can be redistributed throughout the meat. The oven heat will drive them to the surface.

Pour the pan drippings into a skillet. Drain the marinade, reserving the liquid, and sauté the onion and herbs for a few minutes. Spoon off the surface fat. Add marinade liquid and beef broth. Cook over medium heat until reduced by one-third. Degrease again. Strain into a clean saucepan.

Just before serving, return to boiling point. Dissolve cornstarch in one tablespoon cold water. Stir into sauce with currant jelly and mustard and let cook for 2 minutes, until clear and slightly thickened. Taste for seasoning and adjust if necessary. Pour into a warmed sauceboat. Serve hot with the meat.

Salt and pepper to taste
3 tablespoons butter
3 cups beef broth
2 teaspoons cornstarch
1 tablespoon red currant jelly
Pinch of dry mustard powder

STUFFED POTATOES *serves eight*

4 baking potatoes, about
   8 ounces each, or
   8 small ones
1 tablespoon butter
8 to 10 ounces sour cream
2 egg yolks
1/2 cup grated Gruyère
   cheese
2 tablespoons chopped
   chives
Dash of nutmeg
Salt and pepper to taste

Preheat oven to 350° F. Wash and dry potatoes. Prick with a fork to prevent bursting and place on rack of oven. Bake for about 1 hour, or until done. Cut in half and scoop out the pulp into a bowl. Reserve the shell. Mash the potato with a fork (or in an electric mixer) until smooth. Beat in the remaining ingredients. Add another 2 ounces sour cream if necessary to make the mixture light and fluffy. Using a pastry bag with a large open-star tip, fill the skins with the mixture.

WATERCRESS SALAD *serves eight*

2 quarts watercress leaves,
   very lightly packed
1/2 cup walnut meats,
   coarsely chopped
1 Granny Smith apple,
   peeled, cored, and diced
Juice of half a lemon
1/2 teaspoon salt
1/2 teaspoon vinegar
1/4 cup olive oil
Freshly ground black
   pepper

If you wish, you may add other greens to the salad, such as dandelion leaves or small, young spinach leaves.

Wash, dry, and remove coarse stems from the watercress. Place in salad bowl and add walnuts. Mix apple cubes with lemon juice to prevent discoloring, and add to greens.

The order of making the dressing is important. In a small bowl, dissolve the salt in the vinegar. Whisk in the olive oil and add black pepper to taste. Toss with greens just before serving.

CHOCOLATE SOUFFLÉ CAKE WITH CRÈME ANGLAISE *serves eight to ten*

You can make this cake the day before. But do not sprinkle with confectioner's sugar until shortly before serving.

Preheat oven to 275° F. Butter and flour a 10-by-2-inch round cake pan and line with a circle of parchment paper.

Put chocolate, butter, orange zest, vanilla, and almonds in top of double boiler. Melt over hot water, stirring occasionally. Remove from heat as soon as chocolate is melted.

Beat egg yolks with half the sugar (in electric mixer, if desired) until mixture is thick and a slowly dissolving ribbon drops from a lifted beater. Fold lukewarm chocolate mixture into egg-sugar mixture with a large rubber spatula. Whip egg whites until foamy, then gradually add remaining sugar. Continue beating until stiff peaks form. Using rubber spatula, blend lightly but thoroughly into chocolate-egg mixture. Pour batter into prepared pan and bake for 1 hour and 20 minutes.

Remove cake from oven and loosen sides with a sharp knife. Unmold onto a wire rack, then quickly and carefully reverse onto a second rack so the cake is right side up. Cake will have a crisp sugar bloom on the outside and will sink slightly. Let cool.

To make crème anglaise, whisk egg yolks and sugar together, or beat in an electric mixer, until thick and lemon colored. Mix cornstarch with a little cold milk and add to rest of milk. Scald milk and pour over yolk mixture, whisking constantly. Pour custard into

7 ounces semisweet
   chocolate, cut up
7 tablespoons unsalted
   butter
Grated zest of 1 orange
2 teaspoons vanilla extract
1 tablespoon finely
   ground almonds
5 eggs, separated
1/2 cup plus 1 tablespoon
   sugar
Powdered sugar for
   dusting

For crème anglaise:
8 egg yolks
1/2 cup sugar
1 teaspoon cornstarch
1 quart milk
1 teaspoon vanilla extract

(continued next page)

a heavy pan, preferably of tin-lined copper. Avoid using a plain aluminum pan, which discolors sauce.

Stir with a wooden spoon over low to medium heat until custard starts to coat spoon and reaches 165° F on a candy thermometer. Do not cook over too high a heat, or the eggs will curdle.

Strain into a clean, dry bowl and stir in vanilla. Let cool, stirring occasionally to prevent skin from forming. Cover with plastic wrap and refrigerate. Makes 6 cups.

Before serving, sprinkle cake with sifted powdered sugar. If you wish, cut a large Christmas star of light cardboard and lay on top of the cake before dusting with sugar. Carefully remove the star, and the pattern will remain. Serve wedges of cake on dessert plates on a pool of crème anglaise.

Marion Cunningham

SUPPER MENUS FOR
THE HOLIDAYS

Oyster Stew with Hot Buttered Toast

Cranberry Cake Roll

or

Goldenrod Eggs with Salmon Roe and Smoked Salmon

Fresh Lemon Juice Ice and Cookies

or

Cold Roast Beef, Boiled Small Red Potatoes, Green Sauce, and Sweet Gherkins

Cinnamon Cream Pie

serves six

Marion Cunningham writes a weekly column, "Home Cooking," for the *San Francisco Chronicle*. She revised *The Fannie Farmer Cookbook* (Knopf, 1979) and is the author of *The Fannie Farmer Baking Book* (Knopf, 1984) and *The Breakfast Book* (Knopf, 1987).

The best way to achieve the spirit of Christmas is to stop serving dinners and start serving suppers. Most of us do more entertaining during the holidays than at any other time, and producing a festive dinner of four courses is the quickest way I know to run out of spirit and smiles.

My definition of supper is a two-course meal — a savory and a dessert. The savory or main dish is rounded out sometimes with the addition of preserves such as chutneys, relishes, pickles, olives, jellies, any of these, and/or a plain plate of watercress and butter lettuce, carrots, cucumbers, slices of papaya, avocado, what-

ever agrees with the main dish. Preserves or side dishes can be what jewelry is to an understated dress, the complement or the completion.

One rule to remember about suppers: there must be enough of each dish so appetites are replete. Allowing guests to leave a table hungry is inhospitable and unfriendly. Merry Christmas.

OYSTER STEW WITH HOT BUTTERED TOAST *makes six cups*

2 cups milk
2 cups cream
2 cups oysters with
    their liquor
Salt and pepper
3 tablespoons butter

Oyster stew seems quite complete with nothing more than lots of hot buttered toast. One could add cold chopped celery dressed in a light sharp mustard vinaigrette as a small side dish, but this is an afterthought. I have to wonder why we have not seen a bowl of oyster stew for years on any restaurant menu. How could such a splendid classic be forgotten?

Heat the milk and cream in a pan, but do not boil. Add the oysters and liquor and simmer just until the edges of the oysters curl a little. Season with salt and pepper to taste. Add the butter and serve very hot.

CRANBERRY CAKE ROLL *serves six to eight*

The cranberry cake roll is tart and sweet, with a light, delicate cake. It is especially right for the holidays.

Preheat the oven to 350° F. Grease a 15½-by-10½-by-1-inch jelly-roll pan, and line with parchment or waxed paper. Grease and lightly flour the paper.

Put the eggs and sugar in a mixing bowl and beat for 4 minutes (an electric mixer is almost a must), until pale, light, and fluffy.

Mix the flour, baking powder, and salt in a bowl, stirring with a fork to blend well. Turn the mixer to the lowest speed and sprinkle the flour mixture and vanilla over the egg mixture. Mix for just a few seconds. Remove the bowl from the mixer, and, using a spatula, gently finish folding the flour into the egg mixture until no white streaks show.

Spread the batter evenly in the pan. Bake for about 12 minutes, until the top of the cake is golden.

Spread a tea towel on the counter and sift a little powdered sugar evenly over the towel. Invert the cake onto the towel. Remove the paper and roll the cake, wide side up, in the towel. Leave rolled up until you're ready to fill it. Unroll, spread the cranberry jelly evenly over the cake, reroll, and place on a serving plate. Dust the top with powdered sugar. Slice and serve.

5 eggs
1/2 cup granulated sugar
1/2 cup cake flour
1/2 teaspoon baking powder
1/4 teaspoon salt
1 teaspoon vanilla extract
Powdered sugar
1½ cups cranberry jelly

GOLDENROD EGGS WITH SALMON ROE AND SMOKED SALMON *serves two*

4 hard-boiled eggs,
   shelled
2 tablespoons butter
2 tablespoons flour
1¼ cups milk
Salt and pepper
1 raw egg yolk
2 tablespoons lemon juice
2 slices buttered toast
4 tablespoons salmon roe
1/4 pound smoked salmon
Butter-lettuce leaves
   and lemon wedges
   for garnish

Increase this recipe for more servings.

I learned to do goldenrod eggs in my first cooking lesson in junior high school, and it is just as good today as it was then. Creamy, satisfying, and very attractive, it is a perfect foil for the salmon roe and smoked salmon.

Separate the whites and yolks of the hard-boiled eggs. Dice the whites and set aside. Reserve the yolks.

Put the butter in a small saucepan and melt over medium-low heat. Stir in the flour and cook, stirring constantly, until the butter and flour are well blended. Then cook over low heat, stirring, at least 2 minutes more.

Slowly add the milk, stirring constantly, and cook 5 minutes, stirring until the sauce has thickened. Add salt and pepper to taste.

In a small mixing bowl, combine the raw yolk and lemon juice. Stir several tablespoons of the hot sauce into the yolk mixture, then add the mixture to the sauce. Cook another minute or two, until smooth and hot. Add the diced egg whites to the sauce.

Assemble by spooning the sauce over the toast. Using a sieve, or the fine side of a grater, rub a cooked yolk or two over each portion. Divide the salmon roe and sprinkle over the top. Place the smoked salmon on leaves of butter lettuce and put next to the eggs. Garnish with lemon wedges. Serve hot. Capers or finely chopped onions bring out the best in this dish.

FRESH LEMON JUICE ICE AND COOKIES
serves six

Put the sugar in a bowl and pour the boiling water over it. Stir until the sugar dissolves. Let cool and add the lemon juice and zest. Pour into ice trays or a bowl and freeze. Remember to remove from the freezer a few minutes before serving so it isn't too hard. It helps to spoon it into dishes or glasses and return it to the freezer until serving time. Serve with appropriate cookies of your choice.

1½ cups sugar
4 cups boiling water
3/4 cup freshly squeezed
  lemon juice
1 tablespoon grated
  lemon zest

COLD ROAST BEEF, BOILED SMALL RED POTATOES, GREEN SAUCE, AND SWEET GHERKINS *serves six*

Many people serve hot roast beef during December; if you do, think of inviting friends for cold, thinly sliced leftover beef. It is really as, or more, delicious than the hot version. The green sauce also sauces the boiled potatoes. If you don't plan to roast a cut of beef, the delicatessens all carry cold sliced beef. It's expensive, but on the other hand, you may feel too frazzled even to turn on the oven. Garnish with a good brand of sweet gherkins.

For 1 cup green sauce:
1/2 cup olive oil
2 tablespoons water
1½ tablespoons cider
  vinegar
1/2 teaspoon kosher salt
Pepper to taste
1 teaspoon Dijon mustard
2 teaspoons cream-style
  horseradish
2 large cloves garlic
1/3 cup parsley, chopped
2 scallions, sliced

To make the green sauce, combine the olive oil, water, vinegar, salt, and pepper in a food processor and process until well blended. Add the mustard, horseradish, garlic, parsley, and scallions and blend well. Store in an airtight jar in the refrigerator until needed.

CINNAMON CREAM PIE *serves six to eight*

1 baked 8-inch pie shell
1/2 cup sugar
3 tablespoons flour
1 tablespoon cornstarch
1/4 teaspoon salt
1¼ teaspoons ground
   cinnamon
1¼ cups milk
3 egg yolks, lightly beaten
1 tablespoon butter
1/2 cup heavy cream,
   whipped with 1/2
   teaspoon ground
   cinnamon and 2
   tablespoons sugar

Combine the sugar, flour, cornstarch, salt, and cinnamon in a heavy-bottomed saucepan. Mix well over medium–low heat. Gradually add the milk, stirring constantly. Cook, stirring, until the mixture is smooth and thickened. Remove from the heat and add several spoonfuls of the hot mixture to the egg yolks. Stir briskly to blend. Add the yolk mixture and butter to the pan, return to medium–low heat and continue to stir. Cook another 2 to 3 minutes, until the yolks and butter are smoothly blended into the milk mixture. Remove from the heat. Cool, stirring occasionally. Fill the baked pie shell. Spread the whipped cinnamon cream in a smooth layer on top just before serving. Refrigerate if not serving for more than a few hours.

You can substitute bourbon for cinnamon in this recipe. If you do so, omit the cinnamon and add 3 tablespoons bourbon when you remove the custard from the heat. Also omit cinnamon from whipped cream.

Julie Ann Ring

A MEXICAN CHRISTMAS FEAST

Shrimp Ceviche Tostados with
Salsa and Fresh Cheese

Cesarea Gonzales's Chicken
Mole Poblano

Roast Potatoes with Garlic
and Thyme

Salad of Avocado, Papaya, Jicama,
and Tomato in a Fresh Lime
Dressing

Vanilla Custard and Churros

serves six

Julie Ann Ring is a Chicago–born chef who established her reputation in San Francisco with the restaurant *Rings*. She has since moved on to *Julie's Supper Club*, where she is the chef and part owner.

> For many years, my family spent Christmas in Manzanillo, Colima, Mexico. Traditionally, a feast of Mexican specialties was prepared, and the meal was served on the patio of our casita overlooking the Pacific Ocean.
> Some years were more daring than others. For instance, there was the year I ordered a whole suckling pig to be pit roasted on the beach. Overly excited, I headed for the butcher on Christmas Eve and, to my horror, was handed a plastic sack containing a complete pig's hide. No meat! Thank God for the Super Pollo.
> As the years went by, my Spanish improved, and I learned to rely on more familiar ingredients. What follows is a menu that is simple and combines the local foods of the area. The recipe for the mole poblano is from a dear friend and talented cook, Cesarea Gonzales. If it were not for her dedication and knowledge, my love for Mexican cuisine would be at a great loss.

SHRIMP CEVICHE TOSTADAS WITH SALSA AND FRESH CHEESE *serves six*

3 pounds fresh shrimp

For marinade:
1 quart fresh lime juice
1 Bermuda onion,
   finely chopped
4 jalapeño peppers,
   finely chopped
1 bunch cilantro,
   finely chopped
Kosher salt and freshly
   ground pepper

For salsa:
4 large tomatoes, chopped
1 Bermuda onion,
   finely chopped
2 red jalapeño peppers,
   chopped
4 tablespoons cilantro,
   chopped
1/2 cup lime juice
Kosher salt

For garnish:
12 crispy corn tostadas
6 ounces grated queso
   fresco (fresh Mexican
   cheese, available in
   Latin markets)

Peel and devein the shrimp. Mix marinade ingredients in a large bowl. Place shrimp in marinade for 20 minutes.

Combine salsa ingredients, and place around the outside of a large serving dish. Remove the shrimp ceviche from marinade with a slotted spoon and pile in the middle of the plate. Serve the tostadas in a basket and the cheese in a serving bowl. Ice-cold Bohemia beer is best to drink with this dish.

CESAREA GONZALES'S CHICKEN MOLE POBLANO *serves six*

Sauté mole ingredients, except chocolate and stock, in lard or rendered pork-back fat. After each item is browned, drop into a stock pot. Add chocolate. Pour in chicken stock and puree with a hand or wand blender. Or use a Waring-style blender and puree ingredients in batches. The sauce should be very smooth. Bring the mixture in the stock pot to a boil. Reduce heat and simmer for 40 minutes.

Season the chicken with salt, pepper, and oregano. Roast over a mesquite grill. Or roast in a 400° F oven for 35 minutes. Serve chicken with plenty of sauce.

3 frying chickens,
  2½ pounds each,
  cut into fourths
Salt and pepper
Fresh oregano

For mole sauce:
6 dried pasilla chilies
4 New Mexico chilies
10 sweet butter cookies
10 saltine crackers
3 ripe bananas
4 corn tortillas
1½ cups raw peanuts
1 cup pumpkin seeds
1/2 cup sesame seeds
1 large yellow onion,
  quartered
2 large tomatoes, chopped
4 tomatillos
1 tablespoon ground
  cinnamon
1 teaspoon freshly ground
  pepper
1 teaspoon ground cumin
4 to 5 cloves garlic,
  chopped
6 ounces Ibarra Mexican
  chocolate (available in
  Latin markets)
1/2 cup lard or rendered
  pork-back fat
2 quarts warm chicken
  stock

ROAST POTATOES WITH
GARLIC AND THYME *serves six*

6 baking potatoes
Salt and pepper
3 cloves garlic, chopped
3 tablespoons fresh thyme

Wash and quarter potatoes. Season with salt, pepper, garlic, and thyme. Wrap in foil and roast 20 minutes over mesquite, or 25 minutes in 400° F oven.

SALAD OF AVOCADO, PAPAYA, JICAMA, AND
TOMATO IN A FRESH LIME DRESSING *serves six*

2 to 3 avocados
2 papayas
1 jicama
2 to 3 tomatoes
1/2 cup fresh lime juice
Salt and pepper

Cut up julienne pieces of avocado, tomato, jicama, and papaya. Marinate the ingredients a few minutes in lime juice, salt, and pepper. Toss and serve.

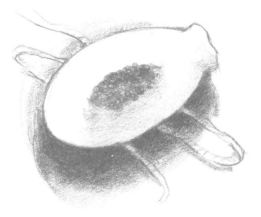

VANILLA CUSTARD AND CHURROS *serves six*

To make custard, put milk, vanilla bean, and extract in a heavy saucepan. Bring to a boil, and remove from heat.

In a large bowl (or electric mixer), beat the egg yolks and sugar until thick. Add cornstarch and stir. Strain hot milk mixture and slowly add to egg mixture. Mix well.

Pour into a saucepan and cook over low heat, stirring constantly, until mixture coats a metal spoon. Add butter. Remove from heat and stir. Cool until a skin forms. Skim off skin. Pour into large serving glasses and refrigerate for 3 hours.

To make churros, bring water and salt to a boil, and remove from heat. Combine flour and baking powder and add to water all at once. Stir with a wooden spoon until batter is smooth. Return to heat and stir in egg yolks one at a time. Continue to beat until the batter becomes smooth. Cool.

Put batter in a pastry bag fitted with fluted tip. Heat oil in a large skillet. Press out 4-inch strips into oil. Brown on all sides. Drain on paper towels. Before serving, squirt a little lime juice on each churro, and roll in sugar.

For vanilla custard:
1½ quarts milk
1 vanilla bean
2 tablespoons vanilla
  extract
8 egg yolks
1½ cups sugar
1/4 cup cornstarch
2 tablespoons melted
  butter

For churros:
1 quart water
1½ to 2 teaspoons salt
3 cups flour
1 teaspoon baking powder
4 egg yolks
3 cups vegetable oil

2 limes
Sugar to taste

Regina Charboneau

A NATCHEZ CHRISTMAS

Oyster Stew with Sweet Corn

Cheddar and Chive Biscuits

Carriage House Tomato Aspic

Roast Turkey with Creole Gravy

Andouille and Cornbread Stuffing

Cranberry-Orange Relish

Yellow Squash Casserole

Bourbon-Glazed Baby Carrots

Pecan-Cinnamon Ice Cream and Drunken Apples

serves eight

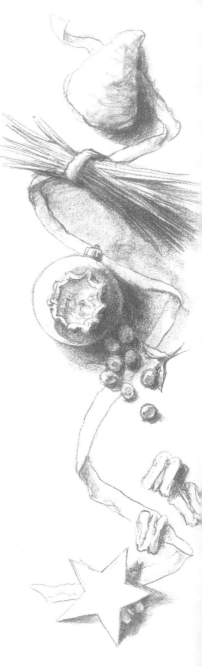

Regina Charboneau was born in Natchez, Mississippi, up the river from New Orleans. Her father, Joseph Phillip Trosclair, was a restaurateur and chef who was a master of Louisiana cuisine. It was from him that Regina learned the old family recipes and techniques of French Creole cooking. After attending Louisiana State University, Regina moved to Alaska and cooked at a bush camp on Chignik Lake. Her aim was to save enough money to study at La Varenne Cooking School in Paris. After Paris, she returned to Alaska and became the chef-owner of a Creole restaurant, *Regina's*, in Anchorage. She sold it three years later and moved to San Francisco to open her present restaurant, also called *Regina's*, in the downtown theater district.

My fondest memories are of my first twenty-four Christmases at my mother's family home, Liberty Hill, in Natchez, Mississippi, when family and friends gathered together for a great dinner. The group easily exceeded fifty, and I miss that yearly event dearly.

Now, I find it difficult during the busy holiday season to get away from the restaurant to join my family in Natchez. But I have enough friends, customers, and staff who can't get home for Christmas either to create a touch of Natchez for them in San Francisco. So here is a typical Christmas buffet that I prepare for my extended family.

OYSTER STEW WITH SWEET CORN *serves eight*

In a 6-quart heavy soup or sauce pot, sauté the vegetables and seasonings in butter until soft. Add the flour and cook over low heat for less than 5 minutes. Add oyster liquid and cream and let reduce for 15 minutes. On low heat, add corn and half-and-half, and let simmer (never boil) for 5 minutes. Add oysters 5 to 10 minutes before serving. Adjust seasoning to taste.

1 onion, finely diced
1 cup finely diced celery
1/2 cup finely diced
  green bell pepper
4 cloves garlic, minced
1 jalapeño pepper,
  seeded and minced
1/2 cup finely diced
  scallions
1/4 teaspoon salt
1/4 teaspoon crushed
  red pepper
1/2 cup butter
4 tablespoons flour
Liquid from 2 pints
  oysters
1 pint heavy cream
2 cups sweet corn
1 quart half-and-half
2 pints oysters (preferably
  Gulf or East Coast)

CHEDDAR AND CHIVE
BISCUITS *makes eighteen biscuits*

1½ pounds (5 cups) flour
1/4 cup baking powder
1/4 cup sugar
1/2 teaspoon salt
1/2 cup butter
1½ cups margarine
1½ cups grated cheddar
  cheese
1/2 cup chopped chives
1½ cups buttermilk

In a large metal or glass bowl, mix together the flour, baking powder, sugar, and salt. Cut butter and margarine into large cubes and, with your hands, work into the flour mixture until the pieces are the size of peas. Mix in the cheese, chives, and buttermilk to make a soft dough.

On a well-floured surface, roll dough out 3/4 inch thick, and cut with a 2-inch biscuit cutter. Arrange 1 inch apart on a sheet pan. Place in the refrigerator (will last up to 24 hours before baking). Bake in a 350° F oven for about 10 minutes, until golden brown.

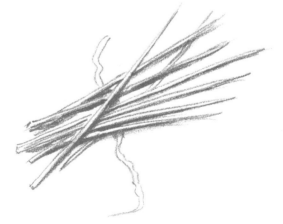

CARRIAGE HOUSE TOMATO
ASPIC *serves eight to ten*

A famous Natchez recipe, this tomato aspic is a signature dish of the *Carriage House* restaurant, situated behind the historic antebellum home Stanton Hall.

Heat the tomato juice almost to boiling. Add the gelatin and stir well to make certain it is completely dissolved. Add all other ingredients.

Lightly brush with vegetable oil (or spray with Pam) 2 molds, 1 quart each. Fill them halfway with the aspic mixture. Chill in refrigerator for 1 hour. Leave out rest of aspic at room temperature.

Spread filling on top of chilled aspic, then spoon on remaining aspic. Chill overnight.

When ready to serve, set molds in a bowl of warm water for a few minutes, then turn out onto a tray. Garnish with watercress or chiffonade of lettuce. Top with mayonnaise, or more of the mayonnaise-cream cheese mixture.

For a nice variation, especially as a lunch dish, add 2 cups of cooked shrimp to the aspic mixture.

3 cups tomato juice
3 tablespoons gelatin, dissolved in 1/2 cup cold water
1 teaspoon salt
1 teaspoon sugar
2 tablespoons Worcestershire sauce
1 teaspoon horseradish
1 teaspoon Tabasco
1/2 cup minced scallion
1/2 cup minced green bell pepper
1/2 cup minced celery
Juice of 1 lemon

For filling and topping:
1 cup mayonnaise blended with 8 ounces cream cheese

ROAST TURKEY WITH CREOLE GRAVY
serves twelve to sixteen

1 turkey, 16 to 18 pounds
1/2 cup butter
6 cloves garlic, minced
2 tablespoons chopped
  fresh basil
1 tablespoon chopped
  fresh thyme
2 tablespoons chopped
  fresh sage
2 tablespoons cracked
  black pepper
1 tablespoon salt
1/4 cup Worcestershire
  sauce

For turkey cavity:
4 cloves garlic
2 onions, peeled and
  quartered
4 ribs celery, cut up

2 small cans flat anchovies
  (though this sounds
  strange, I promise there
  is no anchovy taste in
  the turkey or in the
  gravy)
1 cup red wine

For Creole gravy:
1/4 cup vegetable oil
6 tablespoons flour
Turkey drippings
2 cups water

Remove neck and giblets from turkey. Rinse turkey and pat dry.

Mix together the butter, garlic, herbs, salt and pepper, and Worcestershire sauce, and rub all over the turkey. Stuff the cavity with the garlic, onion, and celery. Lay the anchovies in a design over top of the turkey.

Place turkey in a deep roasting pan. Place giblets around it, as they will enhance gravy flavor. Put aluminum foil on both sides of the roaster, leaving 1/4-inch opening down the center. Pour 1 cup of red wine and 1 cup of water in the bottom of the roaster.

Bake in a 225° F oven for 7 hours, or at 350° F for 4 hours. If you bake it at 350° F, you need to baste it every hour. Pierce the thigh with a skewer to test doneness. Skewer should go in easily and juices should run clear, not pink.

To prepare Creole gravy, combine oil and flour in a cast-iron skillet over medium heat to make a dark roux. Stir constantly with a wooden spoon until chocolate brown.

Remove turkey from roaster and add 2 cups water to the drippings. Bring to a boil and skim off fat. Add 1/4 cup dark roux and cook slowly for 20 minutes, until the gravy thickens. Add more roux, if needed for desired consistency. Adjust seasoning with salt and pepper. Strain the gravy. Serve with turkey and andouille and corn bread stuffing.

ANDOUILLE AND CORN BREAD STUFFING
serves twelve

Boil the vegetables, sausage, and seasoning in stock for 20 minutes. Crumble in the stale corn muffins. Add the cream and eggs.

Place the mixture in a large greased baking dish. Bake in 350° F oven for 70 minutes, until the dressing is firm. Serve with the turkey.

6 ribs celery, diced
2 onions, diced
1 green or red bell pepper, diced
1 pound andouille sausage, diced
1 tablespoon minced garlic
1 tablespoon chopped fresh sage
1 teaspoon black pepper
1 quart chicken or turkey stock
12 stale corn muffins
1 pint heavy cream
4 eggs, beaten

CRANBERRY-ORANGE RELISH *serves eight*

In a food processor, purée oranges with sugar, then turn off processor and let stand for 10 minutes so sugar will dissolve. Add the cranberries and pecans, then pulse processor until cranberries and pecans are coarsely chopped. Refrigerate for at least 4 hours before serving.

2 seedless oranges, unpeeled and quartered
2 cups sugar
12-ounce package fresh cranberries
1 cup pecans

YELLOW SQUASH CASSEROLE *serves eight*

1 pound bacon, diced
2 onions, julienned
1 quart sliced yellow
    squash
2 tablespoons minced
    basil
Juice of 1 lemon
Salt and pepper to taste

For béchamel sauce:
1½ tablespoons butter
2 tablespoons flour
1 cup milk, heated
Pinch of salt

1 cup grated Parmesan
    cheese
3/4 cup plain or Italian-
    style bread crumbs
1/2 cup butter

In a large sauté pan, cook bacon until crisp. Drain off grease. Add onions to pan and cook until soft. Add squash, basil, lemon juice, and seasoning to taste. Cook until squash is slightly soft, about 5 minutes.

Make a béchamel sauce by melting butter in a sauté pan over low heat. Whisk in flour, and cook while stirring until you have a smooth white roux. Pour in the hot milk and salt, and cook, whisking constantly, for 5 minutes, until the sauce thickens.

Add the béchamel and 1/2 cup Parmesan to the vegetables and mix well. Place in a buttered casserole and cover with remaining Parmesan mixed with the bread crumbs. Dot the top with butter. Bake in a 350° F oven for 40 to 50 minutes.

BOURBON-GLAZED BABY CARROTS *serves eight*

2 pounds baby carrots,
    peeled
1 cup brown sugar
1/2 cup butter
1/4 cup bourbon

Drop carrots into boiling water and cook for about 5 minutes, until they are cooked through but still firm. Drain well.

In a sauté pan, melt the butter with the brown sugar and bourbon. Add the carrots and coat with the sauce. Cook over high heat until the carrots are slightly browned.

PECAN-CINNAMON ICE CREAM AND DRUNKEN APPLES *serves eight*

In a mixing bowl, beat the egg yolks and brown sugar until well blended. In a heavy stainless-steel saucepan, bring milk and vanilla to a simmer. Remove from heat and slowly whisk in egg-yolk mixture. Place mixture in a double boiler over medium heat and whisk continuously until custard begins to bubble in the center. Remove from heat and cool to room temperature. Whisk in cream and cinnamon. Chill in refrigerator.

To prepare glazed pecans, heat sugar and water in a heavy skillet. Take hold of handle and swirl and tilt skillet as sugar begins to caramelize. Add the chopped pecans and coat with the caramelized sugar. Pour onto a greased cookie sheet, and separate coated pecans, or chop like brittle.

Finish ice cream by placing custard in an ice-cream maker, and process according to manu-facturer's instructions. Add pecans when ice cream is almost set. Store in freezer.

To make drunken apples, peel, core, quarter, and slice apples. Sauté the slices in butter, brown sugar, and rum for 10 minutes. Serve warm over ice cream.

8 egg yolks
1 cup brown sugar
2 cups milk
1 tablespoon vanilla
  extract
1 cup heavy cream
1 teaspoon cinnamon

For glazed pecans:
1 cup sugar
1 teaspoon water
1 cup chopped pecans

For drunken apples:
4 Granny Smith apples
2 tablespoons butter
4 tablespoons brown sugar
4 tablespoons dark rum

Judy Rodgers

WHEN ALL YOU WANT
IS TRUFFLED EGGS

Truffled Eggs

serves two

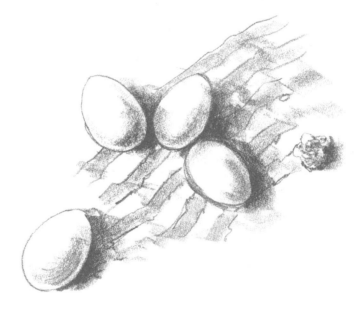

Judy Rodgers stumbled into cooking as an
exchange student in 1973 when she was
placed with the Troisgros brothers at their
restaurant in Roanne, France. She was the
original chef at the restored *Union Hotel* in
Benicia, California, and has been the chef at
the *Zuni Cafe* in San Francisco since 1987.

*The Christmas holidays are actually a quiet time for me. It may be the only
time all year that I'm not planning meals for four hundred people. In reaction, I
hardly plan at all and usually end up eating truffled eggs for supper. The meal is
perhaps more a celebration of truffles at their best than it is of Christmas, but then,
this is how most holiday menu traditions evolved.*

TRUFFLED EGGS *serves two*

Store the whole truffle in a sealed container with the whole eggs until the day you plan to eat it. A few hours before the meal, break the eggs into a bowl. Trim and mince the truffle into the lightly beaten eggs and leave covered in a cool spot.

Cook the eggs in a sauté pan (I use an enamel Le Creuset pan). Gently melt a tablespoon of butter and then add the eggs. Rub a wooden spoon with the cut garlic clove, and use this to stir the eggs constantly over a very low flame. Season the eggs and incorporate the remaining butter in tiny parcels over the next 10 minutes. If it doesn't take that long, you are cooking the eggs too quickly. The finished brouillade should be only slightly curded, like creamy cottage cheese. The character should be suave, harmonious, and comforting. The only sensible thing to have with truffled eggs is toast. I have never found a perfect wine to drink with this meal, but a knowledgeable friend suggests a white Jura.

1 pungent black truffle, approximately 1/2 ounce
4 to 5 eggs
5 tablespoons unsalted butter
1 clove garlic, peeled and cut in half
Salt

Anne and David Gingrass

A NEW YEAR'S DAY DINNER

*Crispy Sautéed Scallops with
Soy-Ginger Vinaigrette*

Main Lobster with Curry Risotto

*Roasted Rack of Lamb with Black
Olive Sauce and Garlic Mashed
Potatoes*

Lemon Espresso Mousse Cake

serves four

Anne and David Gingrass met will studying at the Culinary Institute of America in
Hyde Park, New York. Their teamwork in
the kitchen began in 1986 at Wolfgang Puck's
Spago in Los Angeles and presently continues
at Puck's San Francisco restaurant, *Postrio,*
where they are the executive chefs.

*When asked how we manage to make our marriage and professional relation-
ship work, we like to say that it's because Anne is the chef de cuisine and David is
the chef de paperwork. At home, Anne does most of the cooking and David does
most of the dishwashing. On New Year's Day, we prefer a quiet dinner, like this
one for four people, selected from our favorite* Postrio *recipes.*

CRISPY SAUTÉED SCALLOPS WITH SOY-GINGER VINAIGRETTE *serves four*

To prepare vinaigrette, mix all ingredients in a small bowl and whisk. Set aside. The flavors will come out and improve with time.

Lay all the scallops flat on a plate, not overlapping, and season well with salt and pepper.

In a large, deep pan or deep fryer, heat the peanut oil to 350° F and fry the potato slices until crisp and brown. Salt lightly. Drain on paper towels.

Mix baby lettuces and julienned vegetables, and toss with enough vinaigrette to cover lightly. Separate the endive leaves and arrange them around 4 plates. Place the dressed greens in the center of each plate.

Heat a large sauté pan until very hot, adding enough olive oil to coat the bottom of the pan. Place the scallops in the pan, seasoned side down, without any overlapping. Cook until golden brown on one side but still rare on the other side. Remove scallops from pan and place on the greens with crispy side up. Garnish with potato chips. Serve immediately.

For soy-ginger vinaigrette:
1/2 cup peanut oil
1/4 cup lime juice
1/4 cup soy sauce
3 shallots, peeled and
  chopped
1 tablespoon finely
  chopped fresh ginger
1/4 cup cilantro leaves,
  coarsely chopped

1 pound sea scallops,
  sliced 1/4 inch thick
  across grain
Salt and pepper
4 cups peanut oil
2 medium new potatoes,
  sliced thin
4 cups mixed baby
  lettuces
1/2 cup julienne of carrot,
  daikon, and red onion
1 head Belgian endive
2 tablespoons olive oil,
  approximately

MAINE LOBSTER WITH CURRY RISOTTO
serves four

2 Maine lobsters,
   1½ pounds each

For curry sauce:
4 tablespoons olive oil
1 cup chopped scallions
5 large cloves garlic, sliced
1 cup sliced fresh ginger
1/4 cup curry powder
1 teaspoon red chili flakes
1 cup plum wine
1 cup port wine
2 cups chicken stock
1 cup heavy cream
Salt and black pepper

For risotto:
2 tablespoons olive oil
1 small carrot, diced fine
1 stalk celery, diced fine
1 small onion, diced fine
Pinch of saffron
1/2 cup white wine
2 cups Arborio rice
4 cups chicken stock
2 tablespoons butter
1/4 cup grated Parmesan
   cheese

To finish the dish:
2 tablespoons olive oil
2 tablespoons butter

In a large pot, bring enough water to a boil to hold the two lobsters. Cook lobsters for 5 minutes. Remove and let cool. Separate the claws and the tail from the body and set aside. Remove outer shell of body and discard. Chop body and small legs into quarters.

To prepare lobster-curry sauce, heat 4 tablespoons olive oil in a 2-quart saucepan. Sauté the chopped lobster bodies and small legs for 4 minutes, or until lightly browned on all sides. Add scallions, garlic, and ginger, and sauté for 1 minute. Add curry powder and chili flakes, then deglaze with plum wine and port wine. Reduce wine by half. Add chicken stock and reduce by half again. Add cream and reduce until mixture coats the back of a spoon.

Press sauce through a strainer, getting all the juices from the lobster and vegetables. Season with salt and pepper. Keep warm while you make the risotto.

To prepare risotto, heat 2 tablespoons olive oil in a 2-quart saucepan. Add vegetables and sauté until slightly softened. Add saffron and wine and bring to a boil. Reduce by half. Add rice and 1/4 cup chicken stock. Stir constantly until liquid is absorbed. Repeat procedure until all the chicken stock is used. Rice should be al dente. Finish by stirring in 2 tablespoons butter and the Parmesan cheese. If you prefer the rice cooked more, add additional chicken stock.

Using a heavy knife, cut through the shells of the lobster tails at the separation. Leave meat in the shells. Remove end of the claw shells.

Heat a pan large enough to sauté all the lobster pieces. Add 2 tablespoons olive oil and then the lobster. Cook only long enough to reheat lobster. Add the sauce and finish with 2 tablespoons butter. Remove from heat.

Divide risotto among 4 serving plates and arrange lobster around risotto. Pour sauce over to coat.

Garnish, if you wish, with deep-fried spinach.

ROASTED RACK OF LAMB WITH BLACK OLIVE SAUCE AND GARLIC MASHED POTATOES *serves four*

To prepare the sauce, use a saucepan to sauté the garlic, shallots, and peppercorns in 1 tablespoon butter until lightly browned. Add the Madeira and red wine, rosemary and tomato. Simmer until reduced by two-thirds, leaving about 1 cup total.

Add the demiglace and return to a boil. Whisk in remaining butter slowly until all is incorporated. Strain sauce through a fine strainer, then transfer to a blender. Add half the olives and purée the sauce until almost smooth. Roughly chop the remaining olives and add to the sauce. Season with salt and black pepper to taste. Set aside in a warm place until serving time.

Allow 30 minutes to prepare the potatoes. (You can start them while letting the lamb racks come to room temperature.) Peel the potatoes and cut them into 4 or 5 pieces. Place the potatoes and garlic in a medium-

(continued next page)

For the sauce:
4 garlic cloves, peeled and crushed
4 shallots, peeled and chopped
1 tablespoon black peppercorns
1 cup unsalted butter
2 cups Madeira
2 cups red wine
1 small rosemary sprig
1 medium tomato, diced
1 cup demiglace
1/2 cup pitted Niçoise olives
Salt and black pepper

For the garlic mashed potatoes:
4 large baking potatoes
1 cup garlic cloves, peeled
3/4 teaspoon salt

1 cup heavy cream
1/4 cup sour cream
1/4 teaspoon ground
   white pepper
2 tablespoons unsalted
   butter

2 lamb racks, 8 chops
   each, chine bones and
   fat removed
4 tablespoons virgin
   olive oil
Salt and black pepper
1 rosemary sprig, leaves
   only, chopped

sized pot with water to cover and 1/4 teaspoon salt. Bring to a boil and simmer until
potatoes and garlic become tender, about
10 to 15 minutes. Drain well.

Add the heavy cream to the pot that the potatoes were cooked in and bring to a boil. Return the potatoes and garlic to the pot, along
with the sour cream, 1/2 teaspoon salt, white
pepper, and butter. Stir well and heat through.

Purée the potato mixture through a food
mill. Adjust the consistency with warm
cream, and correct seasoning with salt and
white pepper to taste. Keep warm.

To prepare the lamb racks, make sure all the
fat and bone fragments are removed. Rub
well with olive oil and season with salt, pepper, and rosemary. Allow to come to room
temperature.

Heat a roasting pan or large sauté pan until
very hot. Add a few drops of oil and sear the
lamb racks on all sides until brown. Place the
racks bone side down in the hot pan and
transfer the pan to a 400° F oven. Roast to
medium rare, or to desired doneness, 10 to
20 minutes.

To complete the dish, allow the lamb to rest
for 15 minutes, then slice into 8 chops per rack.

Spoon the mashed potatoes onto the centers
of four plates. Ladle the sauce around the potatoes. Place the lamb chops, 4 to a plate,
around the potatoes. Garnish with lightly
cooked vegetables of your choice.

LEMON ESPRESSO MOUSSE CAKE
serves four to six

The recipe for this extraordinary cake was contributed by Barbara Hazen, *Postrio's* pastry chef.

To prepare the sponge cake, whisk 4 tablespoons sugar into the 4 egg yolks. Place the bowl over a small saucepan of boiling water and continue whipping until yolks are slightly warm. Remove from heat and whip yolk mixture until it is cool and forms a thick ribbon. Stir in the liquid espresso. Set aside.

In a separate bowl, whip the 4 egg whites and 4 tablespoons sugar to medium-stiff peaks. Fold whites into the yolks. Sift the flour and 2 tablespoons ground espresso over the batter and fold in.

Cut a circle of parchment or wax paper to fit the bottom of a 9-inch springform pan. Do not butter or flour the pan. Pour the batter over the paper and spread it evenly in the pan. Bake in a 350° F oven for approximately 15 to 20 minutes. Cake should spring back in the center when done. Cool completely in the pan.

Run a knife around the edge of the pan to loosen cake. Turn out onto a work surface. Remove paper from bottom and reinvert. Trim top of the cake evenly. Divide the cake into three equal layers. Place one cake layer on a flat plate or on the bottom of the springform pan. Place springform ring around the cake. Brush cake with liquid espresso and let it soak in.

Prepare the filling by whisking the sugar into the egg yolks. Place bowl over a saucepan of

For sponge cake:
1/2 cup sugar
4 eggs, separated
1/4 cup liquid espresso,
   plus 3/4 cup for soaking
5 tablespoons all-purpose
   flour
2 tablespoons dry ground
   espresso

For filling:
5 tablespoons sugar
3 egg yolks
1 tablespoon plain gelatin
1 tablespoon warm water
1/2 pound mascarpone
1/2 vanilla bean, seeds
   only
2 tablespoons finely
   grated lemon zest
2 tablespoons lemon juice
1/2 cup heavy cream

For glaze:
2 tablespoons corn syrup
1/2 cup liquid espresso
3/4 cup heavy cream
1 pound white chocolate
4 ounces milk chocolate

1/2 cup dry ground
   espresso

(continued next page)

25 The Open Hand Celebration Cookbook

boiling water and continue whipping until eggs are slightly warm. Dissolve the gelatin in warm water and add to the eggs. Whip egg mixture until it is cool and forms a thick ribbon. Place mascarpone, vanilla, and lemon zest and juice in a large bowl. Fold the yolk mixture into the mascarpone in thirds. Whip the cream to soft peaks and fold into mascarpone mixture in thirds.

Pour half the filling over bottom sponge layer. Top with second cake layer. Brush cake with liquid espresso. Pour remaining filling over second layer. Top with last sponge layer and brush with espresso. Chill for 2 hours.

Prepare the glaze by bringing corn syrup, liquid espresso, and cream to a boil in a saucepan. Add the two chocolates and stir to dissolve. Cool for 15 minutes.

Unmold the cake. Trim off any excess filling so cake is flush on the sides. Turn cake over onto a wire rack. Place rack on a sheet pan to catch the glaze. Pour glaze over the cake. Let it run off the sides for 5 minutes. Transfer cake to a serving plate. Chill well. Press ground espresso into sides of the cake. Use remaining glaze as sauce for the cake, adding a little ground espresso to thin it out.

Martin Yan

JOYOUS FOOD FOR
A CHINESE BANQUET

*Rainbow Chicken Salad with
Glazed Pecans*

*Fish of Abundance with Red
Envelope Sauce*

Seafood Harvest Lettuce Cups

Creamy Walnut Soup

serves eight

Martin Yan is a popular television host and
chef who has 650 half-hour cooking shows to
his credit. Raised in Guangzhou, China, he
trained to cook in Hong Kong and came to
this country to attend the University of California, Davis, where he received a master's
degree in food science in 1975. His PBS
show, *Yan Can Cook,* started in 1983 and
emanates from San Francisco. He has written
five cookbooks, including *The Joy of Wokking*
(Doubleday, 1982), *Martin Yan, the Chinese
Chef* (Doubleday, 1985), *A Wok for All
Seasons* (Doubleday, 1988), and *Everybody's
Wokking* (Harlow & Ratner, 1991).

*To me, cooking is a labor of love. It presents itself as my opportunity to reach
out to people and teach them to have fun with an everyday task.*

*Growing up in China, I found that my friends and family would make all
kinds of excuses to get together and have a banquet dinner. Eating was a way of
life, a form of socializing, celebrating joy and happiness, surrounded by an abundance of food and tea.*

*I always knew the Chinese were crazy about food. Typical dinnertime
conversation included what they were going to eat, what they were eating, and,
finally, what they would eat next. As far as a Chinese meal is concerned, eating
and love are a daily celebration.*

RAINBOW CHICKEN SALAD WITH GLAZED PECANS *serves six to eight*

For dressing:
1/4 cup Chinkiang or
   Japanese rice vinegar
3 tablespoons sesame seed
   paste or peanut butter
3 tablespoons vegetable oil
2 tablespoons sesame oil
2 tablespoons soy sauce
1 teaspoon hot pepper
   sauce
2 tablespoons sugar
1/4 teaspoon black pepper

For salad:
4 cups mixed salad greens
   or shredded iceberg
   lettuce
1/4 cup cilantro leaves
1 cup shredded cooked
   chicken
1 small carrot, cut into
   matchstick pieces
1/2 cucumber, peeled,
   seeded, and cut into
   matchstick pieces
1/2 red bell pepper, cut
   into matchstick pieces
2 tablespoons finely
   shredded fresh Thai or
   regular basil

For glazed pecans:
1/2 cup vegetable oil
1/4 cup sugar
1/2 cup pecans
Vegetable oil for deep-
   frying
4 wonton wrappers, cut
   into 1/4-inch strips, for
   garnish

There are as many variations of Chinese chicken salad as there are moves in a game of mah-jongg. This is a colorful, light salad with a festive touch.

Combine dressing ingredients in a small bowl. Whisk until smooth. Set aside. Combine salad ingredients in a large bowl. Cover and refrigerate until ready to serve.

To make glazed pecans, place a wide frying pan over medium heat. Add oil, swirling to coat the pan's surface. Add sugar and stir until dissolved. Add pecans and stir until they are coated with caramelized sugar. Immediately transfer to a foil-covered plate. Separate nuts with two forks.

Set wok in a ring stand and add vegetable oil to a depth of 2 inches. Place over medium-high heat until oil reaches 360° F. Add wonton strips. Cook for 15 seconds, or until golden brown. Lift out strips and drain on paper towels.

Pour dressing over salad and toss until evenly coated. Place salad in a wide, shallow bowl. Sprinkle glazed pecans over the top, and surround with wonton strips.

FISH OF ABUNDANCE WITH RED ENVELOPE SAUCE *serves four*

Increase this recipe for additional servings.

Red is a lucky color to the Chinese. In a special celebration, like New Year, we exchange gifts of red envelopes to ensure good fortune. In this dish, a spicy sweet-and-sour sauce is the "red envelope" bearing a gift of succulent deep-fried fish. Fish is also symbolic of good fortune and abundance.

Combine sauce ingredients in a small saucepan. Place over medium-high heat and cook, stirring, until sauce boils and thickens slightly. Keep warm while preparing fish.

Score fillets by cutting 1/4 inch deep into fish lengthwise at 1-inch intervals. Then score crosswise at 1-inch intervals. Lightly sprinkle fish with salt and pepper. Place egg and flour in separate shallow bowls. Dip fish in egg, drain briefly, then dredge with flour, shaking off excess. Set aside.

Set wok in a ring stand and add oil to a depth of about 2 inches. Over high heat, bring oil to 375° F. Slowly dip fish fillets into hot oil and cook, turning occasionally, for 3 minutes, or until golden brown. Lift out and drain on paper towels. Transfer to a platter. Pour warm sauce over fish. Garnish with tomato slices around platter.

Note: You can also make this dish by frying the fish in one whole piece.

For red envelope sauce:
1/2 cup drained sliced Chinese sweet mixed pickles or sweet gherkins
1/4 cup brown sugar
1/4 cup red wine vinegar
1/4 cup ketchup
3 tablespoons water
1 tablespoon soy sauce
1 teaspoon hot pepper sauce
1/8 teaspoon red food coloring (optional)
1 tablespoon cornstarch mixed with 2 tablespoons water

1¾ pounds mild-flavored, firm whitefish fillets such as red snapper, halibut, or sea bass, each about 3/4 inch thick
Salt and pepper
1 egg, lightly beaten
Flour for dry coating
Vegetable oil for deep-frying
Tomato slices for garnish

SEAFOOD HARVEST LETTUCE CUPS
serves eight

For marinade:
1 tablespoon Shao Hsing
  wine or dry sherry
1 teaspoon cornstarch
1/4 teaspoon salt

1/2 pound medium raw
  shrimp, peeled,
  deveined, and diced
1/2 pound bay scallops
6 dried black mushrooms
2 tablespoons vegetable
  oil
1 teaspoon minced fresh
  ginger
1 small carrot, diced
1/2 cup chicken broth
1 stalk celery, cut into
  1/2-inch squares
1/2 cup diced water
  chestnuts
2 scallions, including tops,
  thinly sliced
2½ tablespoons soy sauce
1/8 teaspoon white pepper
1/2 teaspoon cornstarch
  mixed with 1 teaspoon
  water
1/2 cup toasted pine nuts
  or coarsely chopped
  peanuts
1/4 cup hoisin sauce
8 to 12 iceberg lettuce
  leaves

Not all Chinese food is meant to be eaten with chopsticks. In this light and refreshing dish, spoonfuls of diced shrimp, scallops, and vegetables are rolled inside lettuce leaves and eaten with the fingers. Lettuce is often used in festivities to symbolize the offerings of prosperity and good fortune.

Combine Shao Hsing wine (or dry sherry), cornstarch, and salt for marinade in a medium bowl. Add shrimp and scallops, stir to coat, and set aside for 30 minutes.

Soak mushrooms in warm water to cover for 30 minutes. Drain. Cut off and discard stems. Dice the caps.

Place a wok or wide frying pan over high heat. Add oil, swirling to coat sides. Add ginger and cook, stirring, until fragrant, about 5 seconds. Add shrimp and scallops, and stir-fry for 1½ minutes, or until shrimp turn pink. Remove shrimp and scallops from wok.

Add mushrooms, carrot, and broth, and cook for 1 minute. Add celery, water chestnuts, and scallions. Cook for 1½ minutes, or until celery is crisp-tender.

Return shrimp and scallops to wok and add soy sauce and pepper. Add cornstarch solution and cook, stirring, until sauce boils and thickens. Stir in pine nuts (or peanuts). Transfer to a serving platter.

To eat, spread a little hoisin sauce on a lettuce leaf, spoon in some seafood mixture, wrap lettuce around filling, and eat with your fingers.

CREAMY WALNUT SOUP *serves eight*

Because of the lack of refrigeration, Chinese cooks developed hot desserts like this sweet soup. Traditionally, it's served in small porcelain bowls with delicate porcelain spoons. You can use a variety of nuts. Peanuts, almonds, and black sesame seeds are commonly used.

Spread walnuts in a shallow baking pan. Bake, stirring occasionally, in a 350° F oven for 10 to 12 minutes, until toasty brown. Remove pan from oven and let nuts cool. Combine nuts (reserving a few for garnish), 2 cups of the water, and peanut butter in a blender. Process until smooth. Set aside. Combine brown sugar and remaining water in a medium pan. Place over high heat and cook until sugar dissolves. Add walnut mixture, half-and-half (or evaporated milk), and coconut milk. Reduce heat to medium low. Cook, stirring, just until mixture simmers. Add cornstarch solution. Cook, stirring, until soup boils and thickens slightly. To serve, ladle hot or warm soup into small bowls. Sprinkle with the reserved toasted walnuts, chopped.

1¾ cups walnut halves
4¼ cups water
2 tablespoons peanut butter
1/3 cup packed brown sugar
1/2 cup half-and-half or evaporated milk
1/3 cup coconut milk
1/4 cup cornstarch mixed with 1/2 cup water

Carol Field

A MIDWINTER LATE-NIGHT BIRTHDAY SUPPER

Torta Fritta with Prosciutto

Two Pastas:
Rigatoni with Basil
Tagliatelle with Mushrooms and
Black Olives

Winter Salad

Persimmon Sorbet

serves twenty

Although a resident of San Francisco, Carol Field has spent a good part of her life exploring Italy and its food. She has written three books on the subject, *The Hill Towns of Italy* (Dutton, 1983), about the towns between Florence and Rome, *The Italian Baker* (Harper & Row, 1985), a collection of diverse regional breads and desserts, and *Celebrating Italy* (Morrow, 1990), about the festivals of Italy and its food.

Great friends, a pianist playing Cole Porter and Gershwin, champagne, and a late-evening Italian supper made a very special birthday celebration for my husband one year.

The recipes come from traveling in Italy over the years, but the one with the most sentimental meaning is the rigatoni with basil, which we discovered years ago when we were living in a little Ligurian village. We fell in love with the place, the dish, and the trattoria where it was made, and have gone back to eat there as often as we are in the area.

The cooks make it with penne, but I have substituted rigatoni, which is such a sturdy pasta that it can be cooked ahead and reheated.

TORTA FRITTA WITH PROSCIUTTO *serves twenty*

To prepare the torta dough, stir the yeast into the warm water and leave until creamy, about 10 minutes. Stir in the lard or butter and vinegar, then add the flour and salt, mixing until the dough comes together. Knead on a lightly floured work surface until the dough is smooth and tender, about 8 to 10 minutes by hand, 3 minutes by mixer. Set the dough in a lightly oiled container, cover it well with plastic wrap, and let rise until doubled, about 3 hours.

For shaping dough and second rise: turn the dough onto a floured work surface, punch down, knead briefly, and roll out 1/8 inch thick. Use a pizza cutter to cut diamond shapes out of the dough. Set them on parchment-lined cookie sheets, cover with a towel, and let them rest for 15 minutes, so the dough can relax.

Pour vegetable or olive oil to a depth of 3 inches in a deep, heavy pot and bring to a slow boil. Slide a few pieces of dough at a time right into it. Cook until they are puffed up, golden, and crisp at the edges. Drain on paper towels and eat immediately. Serve with slices of prosciutto.

For torta dough:
1 tablespoon plus
   1 teaspoon active
   dry yeast
2 cups less 2 tablespoons
   warm water (105° to
   115° F)
1/4 cup best-quality lard
   or butter
2 tablespoons white wine
   vinegar
5 cups unbleached
   all-purpose flour
2 teaspoons salt

Vegetable or olive oil for
   deep-frying
1/3 pound thinly sliced
   prosciutto

RIGATONI WITH BASIL *serves twelve to twenty*

3/4 cup unsalted butter
3 pounds, 8 ounces
   canned plum tomatoes,
   drained and chopped
2 pounds rigatoni
24 basil leaves
1/2 to 3/4 cup heavy
   cream
Salt and freshly ground
   pepper
2 cups freshly grated
   pecorino cheese

Melt the butter in a large saucepan and add the chopped tomatoes. Cook for 10 minutes over low to medium heat.

At the same time, bring a large pot of abundantly salted water to a boil. Add the rigatoni and cook until it is about 4 minutes from being done. Drain.

Add the rigatoni immediately to the tomato mixture and cook for about 3 minutes, then add the basil, cream, salt, pepper, and cheese. If the sauce seems too thick, add some milk.

Serve immediately with additional grated cheese. You may also transfer the mixture to an oiled or buttered 9-by-12-inch Pyrex dish and reheat later in a 325° F oven for about 30 minutes. You may need to add slightly more cream.

TAGLIATELLE WITH MUSHROOMS AND BLACK OLIVES *serves twelve to twenty*

About 30 minutes before you are ready to cook, soak the dried porcini mushrooms in warm water. Drain, and save the water for soup or some other use. Put a large pot of well-salted water on to boil.

Wipe the fresh mushrooms with a damp cloth. Slice very fine, using a knife or food processor. In a 10- or 12-inch skillet, heat the butter and half of the oil. Add the fresh mushrooms and cook over medium heat until they have released their juices and are soft, about 5 minutes. Add the drained porcini mushrooms and cook another 3 to 4 minutes.

Meanwhile, cook the tagliatelle until done, about 1½ minutes. Remove pasta sauce from the heat and stir in the olives and parsley. Drain the pasta and toss with the sauce and the remaining olive oil.

1½ ounces dried porcini mushrooms
1⅓ pounds fresh mushrooms, preferably cremini
6 tablespoons butter
1¼ cups olive oil
3 pounds fresh tagliatelle
10 ounces black olives, preferably oil–cured and herbed, pitted and finely chopped
6 to 8 tablespoons chopped Italian parsley

WINTER SALAD *serves twenty*

1½ cups walnuts
1/2 pound aged Parmesan
   cheese
20 handfuls arugula
4 medium heads radicchio,
   trimmed and leaves
   separated

For vinaigrette:
1 cup mild olive oil
1 cup fruity olive oil,
   preferably extra virgin
1/2 cup lemon juice
1 tablespoon balsamic
   vinegar
Salt and freshly ground
   pepper

Toast the walnuts in a preheated 350° F oven for 10 to 15 minutes, until they begin to brown. Set aside to cool. Use a potato peeler or truffle cutter to slice the Parmesan into fine, curly slivers.

Rinse the arugula and radicchio leaves and dry well. Combine the vinaigrette ingredients and whisk until emulsified. In a large bowl, toss the salad leaves gently with the vinaigrette. Arrange them on a large platter and garnish with the walnuts and fine slivers of Parmesan cheese.

PERSIMMON SORBET *makes five cups*

To make enough for 20 servings, you will
need 2 recipes of sorbet.

Be sure you have very mature, completely
soft persimmons. Cut them in half, strain
out skin and seeds, and puree the pulp in a
blender or food processor. Heat about 2 cups
of the puree in a small, noncorroding saucepan with the sugar, stirring until the sugar
has dissolved. Add this to rest of the puree,
flavor with the lemon juice and optional
liqueur. Taste for sweetness.

You can freeze in an ice-cream maker or in
a shallow pan. If you use the pan, set in the
freezer until the mixture is firm around the
edge, then remove and briefly beat the sorbet
in a food processor or electric mixer until
smooth. Return to the freezer and freeze until
firm. If you use an ice-cream maker, follow
manufacturer's instructions.

**About 8 pounds large,
very ripe persimmons
to make 4 cups pureed
pulp**
**2/3 to 1 cup granulated
sugar, depending on
the sweetness of the
persimmons**
2 teaspoons lemon juice
**1 tablespoon and
1 teaspoon Grand
Marnier or Curaçao
(optional)**

Lindsey Shere

A CASSOULET FOR GROUNDHOG DAY

Oysters on the Half Shell

*Cassoulet of Goose or Duck Confit
and Pork*

Green Salad

Tangerines

serves twenty-five

Lindsey Shere has been the pastry chef at
Chez Panisse in Berkeley since the restaurant
opened in 1971. She is the author of *Chez
Panisse Desserts* (Random House, 1985) and is
the co-owner with her daughter, Therese,
and Kathleen Stewart of the *Downtown Bakery
and Creamery* in Healdsburg, California.

*For nearly fifteen years, my husband, Charles, and I have been making a
cassoulet once a year or so, which is shared with the same group of cassoulet afi-
cionados each time. It has become a ritual for us that starts with making the goose
stock from the holiday goose and continues until Groundhog Day, with the week
before being an intense time of making goose or duck confit, sometimes making the
sausages, making more stock, soaking the beans, and gathering all the bits and
pieces that are needed.*

*We always assemble and bake the cassoulet the day before we serve it and
reheat it the day of our dinner, because it tastes better the second day, and we can
catch our breath and clean up after the assembly process.*

*For the dinner itself, we usually start with champagne and oysters on the half
shell, then the cassoulet with good bread, a few pickled sour cherries, and a bottle
or two of Bandol. A green salad comes afterward, and we usually have some
perfect tangerines for dessert.*

*Like bouillabaisse, cassoulet is one of those dishes that you can make year
after year, always trying to find the perfect version. We have consulted many
sources. We end up always making something a little different and very good, but
always leaving room for even greater perfection the next time. And it's always fun
for everyone involved.*

CASSOULET OF GOOSE OR DUCK CONFIT AND PORK *serves twenty-five*

Prepare the goose or duck confit at least a week ahead.

Remove the backbones from goose or ducks, and cut each into 10 pieces: wings, legs, thighs, and 4 breast quarters. Reserve backbones for stock. Mix together the salt, bay leaves, garlic, juniper berries, peppercorns, and thyme. Rub the goose or duck pieces with the mixture, and put them in a crock. Cover and weight down, and refrigerate for 1 to 2 days.

Remove the goose or duck pieces and wipe clean. Melt the fat in a casserole big enough to hold the pieces in one layer. When the fat is hot, add the goose or duck pieces. There should be enough fat to cover the pieces. Cook at a gentle simmer for 1 hour, covered, and then another 30 minutes, partially covered, or until the thigh reaches an internal temperature of 200° F.

Let cool briefly, then remove goose or duck pieces from fat, reserving the fat. Let the fat cool and pour it through a strainer, making sure you don't get the juices from bottom of the pan. (Reserve these juices for your stock.) Place the goose or duck pieces in an earthenware crock. Pour the cooled fat over them to cover completely and refrigerate for a week, or longer.

The goose stock should be made several days ahead.

Place ingredients in a large pot with cold water to cover. Bring to a boil, skim the stock, then simmer gently for 1½ hours. When cool, pour through a strainer into a

(continued next page)

For goose or duck confit, from Victoria Wise's American Charcuterie *(make at least a week ahead):*
1 goose, 9½ to 10 pounds, or 2 ducks, 4½ to 5 pounds
4 tablespoons kosher salt
5 bay leaves, crumbled
3 large cloves garlic, sliced
15 juniper berries, bruised
1 tablespoon black peppercorns, cracked
2 teaspoons dried thyme
6 cups goose or duck fat

For goose stock (make several days ahead):
Carcass and neck of a holiday goose, combined with backs, necks, and feet of goose or ducks that have been cut up for confit. A few chicken backs, necks, and wings may be used if you haven't enough goose. Pigeon or quail bones, heads, and feet are especially good.
1 to 2 onions, cut up
2 bay leaves
Pinch of dried thyme, or 3 sprigs of fresh thyme
6 to 10 peppercorns
8 parsley stems

For pork ragoût (three days ahead):

3-pound pork loin, cubed
4 pig's feet, split
3 pounds pork skin, rolled and tied
Salt and pepper
1 pound unsalted or blanched pork belly, or pancetta, diced
2 to 3 tablespoons goose fat
1 onion, chopped
12 ounces ham, diced
2 tablespoons tomato purée
1 quart goose stock
2/3 cup white wine
Bouquet garni of parsley, thyme, bay leaf, and celery
6 whole cloves
2 cloves garlic
2½ pounds sausages: andouille, garlic, Toulouse, saucisson de campagne, or, best of all, homemade

8 pounds small white, or Great Northern beans
8 ounces pork fat plus 12 cloves garlic, pureed in a processor
4½ additional pounds sausage
3 cups bread crumbs
Walnut oil for serving

container. Skim off all but a thin layer of fat (and reserve the excess fat). The stock can be frozen, or will hold for a couple of weeks in the refrigerator if protected by the layer of goose fat at the top. You need 8 quarts of stock for this recipe. Other poultry stock can be used to extend the goose stock.

Start preparing the pork ragoût three days before serving.

Season the pork loin, pig's feet, and pork skin with salt and pepper, and refrigerate overnight in a covered dish.

Brown the pork loin, pig's feet, pork belly, and pork skin in goose fat in a large casserole. Add the onion and ham and cook until soft. Add the tomato purée, goose stock, wine, bouquet garni, whole cloves, and garlic.

Cook 2½ pounds sausages in simmering water for 1/2 hour. Slice them into pieces, and add to the ragoût.

Let the ragoût simmer for 1½ hours, until the meat is tender and the flavors are well combined. Cool, then cover and refrigerate.

Start the white beans two days ahead by soaking in water to cover for at least 4 hours. Drain the beans and cook in lightly salted goose stock at a simmer until done. Cool and refrigerate.

Assemble the cassoulet a day before serving.

Bring the goose or duck confit to room temperature and remove the pieces from the fat.

Return the pork ragoût to a simmer, and stir in the puréed pork fat and garlic. This touch, recommended by Paula Wolfert, is inspired, since it thickens, binds, and tenderizes the ragoût.

Use a deep casserole for the cassoulet. If you don't have one big enough, use 2 or more casseroles. The choice of pot is important. It may be the significant variable in the entire operation. Shallow pots won't work at all, and those too deep don't allow proper cooking or serving. We prefer traditional Provençal earthenware casseroles measuring 2 to 3 quarts.

Remove the pork skin from the ragoût, flatten it, and cut it to line bottoms of casseroles, fat side down. Remove the pig's feet and pull off the meat. Start layering in the ingredients, first the beans, then the meat from the pig's feet, the pork loin, the sausage pieces, and the confit. Start the process again with more beans and any remaining meat. The top layer should be beans. Finally, simmer the remaining 4½ pounds of sausages in water for 10 or 15 minutes, until stiffened. Then broil them on one side only and add them, uncooked side up, to the casseroles.

Add goose stock to each casserole to fill it almost to the top. Then sprinkle with a layer of bread crumbs. Dribble a bit of warm goose or duck fat over the bread crumbs.

Bake the cassoulets, uncovered, in a slow oven (250° to 300° F) for 2 hours or so, until the flavors are well combined and the sausages are done. Add more stock if necessary to keep the liquid level just under the bread crumbs. We usually punch the crumbs down into the cassoulets once during the baking, sprinkling a few more crumbs over to replace them, and dribbling on a little more fat. Refrigerate the casseroles, covered, until needed.

The day of the dinner, reheat the cassoulet in a 300° F oven until it bubbles, about 1 hour. (Add stock again if there is not enough liquid below the crumbs.) Serve with a sprinkling of walnut oil.

Todd Muir

SLOW-BOAT-TO-CHINA DINNER

*Crab Wontons with
Buckwheat Noodles*

Prawns Asian-Style

*Salmon Stuffed with Eggplant and
Scallops with Szechuan Sauce*

Maureen's Coconut Flan

serves four

Todd Muir is a graduate of the California Culinary Academy in San Francisco. He worked at *Chez Panisse* before branching out on his own as chef–owner of *Madrona Manor*, a country inn and restaurant, in Healdsburg, California. He currently hosts an international chefs' exchange program at *Madrona Manor* during the winter months.

My menu is for a fun dinner party with an Asian theme, maybe for Chinese New Year, which is why I call it my Slow-Boat-to-China Dinner. Hence, the dishes, except for dessert, are made with fish and have an Asian influence. They're playful, easy, and different — like making your own pancakes and cooking salmon in plastic wrap.

CRAB WONTONS WITH BUCKWHEAT NOODLES *serves four*

To prepare the plum sauce, cook plums with a bit of water in a saucepan over moderate heat for 10 minutes, or until tender. Season to taste with ginger, vinegar, and sugar. Cool and set aside.

Combine crabmeat, half the sliced scallion, and half the sesame seeds. Place small amount in center of each wonton skin. Brush edge with egg wash. Fold to make a triangle, pressing edges together.

Deep-fry in hot peanut oil (about 365° F) until golden brown. Place on bed of buckwheat noodles tossed with sesame oil and remaining sliced scallion and sesame seeds. Serve with sauce.

1/2 cup crabmeat
2 scallions, stalks only, thinly sliced
2 teaspoons black sesame seeds
1 package wonton skins
1 egg, beaten, for egg wash
3 cups peanut oil for deep-frying
1 pound buckwheat noodles, cooked
1 tablespoon Chinese sesame oil

For plum sauce:
12 Santa Rosa plums, pitted and roughly chopped
1 tablespoon grated ginger
Rice wine vinegar to taste
Sugar to taste

PRAWNS ASIAN-STYLE *serves four*

8 scallions
8 ounces prawns
1 plantain cut into
   1/4-by-4-inch sticks
2 tablespoons peanut oil

4 ounces Chinese
   cellophane noodles,
   cooked and cooled
1 tablespoon diced red
   bell pepper
1/2 cucumber, seeded
   and sliced
1/2 cup thinly sliced
   Napa cabbage
1/2 cup peanuts, chopped
4 to 6 mint leaves,
   chopped
1 cup hoisin sauce

For Chinese pancakes:
2 cups flour
1 cup boiling water
1/4 cup Chinese sesame oil

Trim scallions, and cut 2-inch lengths from white root end. Make lengthwise slits for scallion brushes. Soak in ice water until they curl. Set aside for garnish. Thinly slice green part of 2 scallions, and set aside. Remove shells from prawns and devein. In a food processor, puree prawns to a thick paste. Wrap some prawn paste around each plantain stick. Dampening hands will keep paste from sticking. Steam prawn plantains in simmering water in a covered pan until paste has set.

Remove from pan and brush with peanut oil; then grill or broil until lightly colored. Serve with Asian salad.

To make Asian salad, combine noodles, red pepper, cucumber, cabbage, peanuts, sliced scallion greens, and mint. Dress with a little peanut oil and sesame oil.

To make pancakes, combine boiling water and flour. Mix thoroughly. Knead for 5 minutes. Roll out in 1-inch logs and cut into 1/2-inch "corks." Flatten the corks and brush with sesame oil. Stack them in twos and roll out pancakes as thinly as possible.

In a heavy skillet over medium heat (without oil), cook pancakes on both sides for a few minutes. While still warm, peel apart, and cover to prevent them from drying out. Serve with prawn plantains, Asian salad, onion brushes, and hoisin sauce.

SALMON STUFFED WITH EGGPLANT AND SCALLOPS WITH SZECHUAN SAUCE *serves four*

Whisk together Szechuan sauce ingredients. Set aside.

Slice salmon into 8 slices, 2 ounces each. Place between sheets of plastic wrap and pound lightly.

In a skillet, toss eggplant in hot peanut oil. Transfer to 350° F oven for 15 minutes. Remove to a mixing bowl. Add scallops, scallion, ginger, sesame oil, and salt.

Stuff salmon by placing small amount of eggplant-scallop mixture on slices. Roll salmon around filling, and wrap in plastic, twisting and tying ends together.

Poach stuffed salmon in a pan of simmering water for 8 to 10 minutes. Remove from plastic and place 2 pieces on each plate. The dish may be served with a ring of rice and garnish of blanched snow peas and cooked carrots sliced on a bias. Spoon Szechuan sauce over top.

1 pound salmon fillet
1/4 pound eggplant, diced small
3 tablespoons peanut oil
4 ounces scallops, chopped and lightly sautéed
1 tablespoon thinly sliced scallion
1 teaspoon grated ginger
1/2 teaspoon Chinese sesame oil
Salt to taste

For Szechuan sauce:
1/4 cup peanut oil
1 tablespoon soy sauce
1 tablespoon Szechuan pepper oil

MAUREEN'S COCONUT FLAN *serves nine*

4 cups unsweetened
   coconut milk (found
   in Asian markets, or
   Oriental section of
   supermarkets)
2 cups whole milk
9 egg yolks
9 eggs
1½ cups sugar

For caramel:
1½ cups sugar
1/2 cup water
1 lemon

This recipe is from Maureen Morehouse,
pastry chef of *Madrona Manor*.

Preheat oven to 350° F. To prepare caramel,
combine sugar and water with a few drops of
lemon juice in a heavy saucepan. Cook over
low heat until sugar is dissolved. Raise to
high heat and cook to a light amber. Remove
from heat and divide the caramel evenly
among 9 ramekins or soufflé dishes (5-ounce
size), entirely covering the bottoms. Chill.

To prepare the custard, bring coconut milk
and whole milk to a simmer in another saucepan. Meanwhile, combine the egg yolks,
eggs, and sugar, mixing well. While constantly stirring, pour hot milk mixture over
egg mixture until combined. Divide this
mixture among the caramel-lined ramekins.

Place ramekins in a pan of water, with water
coming halfway up sides of dishes. Heat
water bath on stove to boiling.

Transfer pan to oven. Cook for about 30 minutes, or until a knife inserted in flan comes
out clean. Allow to come to room temperature, then chill for 4 to 5 hours. Invert onto
serving plates. May be served with fresh fruit
such as pineapple, mango, papaya, melon,
and/or strawberries.

Joel S. Guillon

A VALENTINE'S DAY DINNER

Smoked Scallops

Artichoke and Herb Frittata

*Grilled Tuna with Scallions,
Ginger, and Sesame Oil*

Blood-Orange and Almond Tart

serves two

J oel S. Guillon received his formal training as a chef in France, working with such celebrated chefs as Alain Chapel, Marc Meneau, and Antoine Westermann. He joined the Meridien hotel chain in 1975 as executive sous-chef at the *Guadeloupe Meridien* in the French West Indies. From there, he went to Meridien hotels in Morocco, Reunion Island, Kuwait, and Saudi Arabia. In 1983, he assumed his present post as executive chef of the *San Francisco Meridien.*

I have chosen this menu to blend the different culinary influences that California has inherited from various ethnic groups, making it such a dynamic culinary center. The result is a light, well-balanced dinner highlighting the traditional flavors of each cooking style. The smoked scallops represent California, the frittata is Italian, the grilled tuna is Oriental, and the almond tart is French.

SMOKED SCALLOPS *serves two*

1/2 pound very fresh
   medium sea scallops
Salt and pepper

Smoking mixture:
1 ounce each oak, hickory,
   apple, cherry, and olive
   sawdust
2 whole black
   peppercorns
2 whole juniper berries
1 whole cardamom pod
Pinch each of paprika,
   thyme, sage, and
   rosemary
1 tablespoon olive oil

Salad dressing:
1 tablespoon olive oil
1 teaspoon lemon juice
1 tablespoon scallop juice
   from smoking process
1 teaspoon chopped
   chervil
Salt and pepper to taste
Mixed baby lettuces

Soak scallops in salted water for 15 minutes. Wash scallops in cold water and dry. Season with salt and pepper to taste. Place them on the grill of a smoker or barbecue fed with sawdust, spices, and herbs. Close the lid and then start flame to smoke scallops for 30 minutes. When done, brush scallops with olive oil.

Whisk together salad-dressing ingredients. Toss baby lettuces in dressing. Serve with scallops.

ARTICHOKE AND HERB FRITTATA *serves four*

Cook the artichoke bottoms in a saucepan of water, lemon juice, and salt for approximately 10 minutes. Cool and slice very thinly. Mix the artichoke slices with the herbs, cheeses, and beaten eggs. Season with salt and pepper to taste. Butter 4 small ramekins and fill with mixture. Cover ramekins with aluminum foil. Bake in a 300° F oven for 30 minutes. Remove frittatas from ramekins before serving.

Cook the tomatoes concassé with shallot, garlic, and olive oil in a sauté pan over low heat for 5 minutes. Serve with frittatas.

2 fresh-artichoke bottoms
Juice of 1 lemon
1 tablespoon chopped
  fresh basil, oregano,
  and thyme
1/3 cup each ricotta,
  grated mozzarella, and
  grated Emmentaler
  cheeses
4 eggs, beaten
Salt and pepper

For tomatoes concassé:
2 tomatoes, peeled,
  seeded, and diced
1 medium shallot,
  chopped
1 clove garlic, chopped
1 tablespoon olive oil

GRILLED TUNA WITH SCALLIONS, GINGER AND SESAME OIL *serves two*

Marinate tuna with half the soy sauce and sesame oil, and all the lemon juice, for 30 minutes. Mix the scallions and ginger with other half of soy sauce and sesame oil.

Broil or grill the tuna at a very high temperature for approximately 2 minutes on each side, until medium rare. Be careful not to overcook the fish. Cover with sauce containing ginger and scallions.

1 pound fresh tuna
1/4 cup soy sauce
1/4 cup sesame oil
Juice of 1 lemon
4 scallions, sliced at an
  angle
2 ounces fresh ginger,
  peeled and julienned

BLOOD–ORANGE AND ALMOND TART
serves ten

5 blood oranges, peeled
  and sliced

For syrup:
1/2 cup sugar
1/2 cup water

For sugar pastry:
1/2 cup butter
4 tablespoons sugar
3 egg yolks
2 cups all-purpose flour

For almond cream:
2 cups sugar
1¼ cups finely ground
  blanched almonds or
  almond powder
  (available in specialty
  stores)
4 eggs
1 tablespoon flour
2 tablespoons dark rum

Powdered sugar

Prepare a heavy syrup by placing sugar and water in a saucepan. Cook over moderate heat until sugar dissolves, about 10 minutes. Cook orange slices in the syrup at a gentle simmer until candied, about 30 minutes. Drain candied orange slices and discard syrup.

To prepare sugar pastry, combine butter, sugar, egg yolks, and flour in an electric mixer fitted with a paddle. Be sure not to overmix or add too much flour, as dough will become stiff.

Roll out dough on lightly floured surface to 1/8 inch thick. Handle dough carefully, as it will be delicate. Fit into a 9-inch tart pan with removable bottom. Cover with plastic wrap and chill.

To make almond cream, mix sugar and ground almonds, then eggs, one at a time, and finally, the flour and rum. You may use electric mixer.

To assemble tart, fill chilled tart shell with almond cream. Top with candied orange slices. Bake in a 300° F oven for approximately 30 minutes, or until lightly browned. Remove and sprinkle with sifted powdered sugar. Bake for 2 more minutes. When cool, remove from tart pan.

Heidi Haughy Cusick

A ST. PATRICK'S DAY MENU (FOR THE IRISH IN US ALL)

Devil-May-Kerry Eggs

Emerald Salad

Potatoes Patrick

Corned Beef and Cabbage

Mustard Sauce

Carrots of Orange

Irish Soda Bread

Black Irish Pastry

serves eight

Heidi Haughy Cusick is a free-lance food writer who lives in Mendocino, California. She writes regularly for the *San Francisco Chronicle,* the *Mendocino Beacon,* and the *Fort Bragg Advocate-News.* She is the author of *The Advocate-News Centennial Cookbook* and is currently working on a book about northern California cuisine.

Ever since I was a kid and went to the St. Patrick's Day feasts my grandfather prepared at the American Legion Hall in San Francisco, it's been my favorite holiday. Now, St. Patrick's Day is a family celebration, when my parents, five brothers and sisters, their spouses and twelve offspring come to my house in Mendocino to spend the day with my husband, two children, and me.

It's a raucous twenty-four-hour event centered around our corned-beef dinner. We eat, drink, catch up on news, and sing and dance as only those who love being Irish (if only for a day) know how to do.

DEVIL-MAY-KERRY EGGS *serves eight to ten*

8 hard-boiled eggs
1 to 2 ounces smoked
  salmon, chopped
1/4 cup mayonnaise
2 scallions, finely chopped
1 tablespoon Dijon
  mustard
Salt and pepper

I always stuff a few eggs just for old time's
sake, adding a little smoked salmon to ap-
proximate some I had in Dublin a few years
ago.

Cut the eggs in half and scoop out the yolks.
Mix the yolks with remaining ingredients
and spoon back into the whites. Refrigerate
one or more hours, or overnight, to blend the
flavors.

EMERALD SALAD *serves eight*

1/2 pound asparagus, cut
  into 2-inch lengths
1 bunch broccoli, florets
  only
1/2 pound snow peas
1/2 cup hazelnut or
  walnut oil
3 tablespoons fresh
  lime juice
Salt and pepper
1 head butter lettuce
2 to 3 tablespoons
  chopped fresh basil
  or parsley

Blanch separately in lightly salted water the
asparagus, broccoli florets, and snow peas.
When cool, toss with hazelnut oil and lime
juice seasoned with salt and pepper. To serve,
line serving plate with lettuce leaves. Arrange
vegetables over and sprinkle with chopped
basil or parsley.

POTATOES PATRICK *serves eight*

Preheat oven to 375° F. Wash potatoes, removing eyes and discolored spots. Prick once
with a fork. Place in the middle rack of the
oven. Bake for one hour, or until very soft to
the touch. Remove from oven and let sit until
cool enough to handle.

Slice potatoes in half and scoop pulp into a
mixing bowl. Reserve skins. Mash with a
fork and add, in this order, butter, cheese,
cabbage, chives, parsley, salt, and pepper.
Mix well after each addition. Add enough
milk to soften potatoes, but keep them firm
enough to hold a shape.

Choose the eight best potato-skin shells and
divide three-fourths of the mixture among
them, filling each two-thirds full. Put remaining potato mixture into pastry bag fitted
with a large decorative tip. Pipe rosettes onto
each potato.

Thirty minutes before serving, preheat oven
to 375° F. Place stuffed potatoes in a shallow
pan and bake 25 minutes, until heated
through and rosette ridges are slightly
browned.

8 medium-sized red new
  potatoes
2 tablespoons butter
1/2 cup grated farmer's
  cheese or ricotta
1/2 head cabbage, grated
  and cooked crisp-tender
1/2 cup chopped fresh
  chives
1/2 cup chopped fresh
  parsley
1 teaspoon salt
1/2 teaspoon freshly
  ground pepper
1/2 to 3/4 cup milk,
  warmed

CORNED BEEF AND CABBAGE *serves eight*

5 pounds corned beef
1 sprig thyme
1 sprig parsley
2 cloves garlic, crushed
1 teaspoon cracked pepper
1 head cabbage, cut into
    eight wedges

There's nothing like home-corned beef. My butcher, Alvin Mendosa, in Mendocino, corns some every year. If that's unavailable, I prefer the kind with all the pickling spices and peppercorns in the package.

Wash the corned beef and place in a deep iron kettle, or pot. Cover with cold water. Add herbs, garlic, and pepper, and any spices from the package. Bring to a boil over high heat, skimming foam from top. Cover pot and simmer, turning meat every 45 minutes. Cook until tender, 2½ to 3 hours, until a fork inserts easily.

Remove meat from pot and keep warm. Or if you wish to do ahead, remove meat to a roasting pan and ladle over it a cup or two of the cooking liquid. Cover with foil, and reheat in 350° F oven for 20 minutes before serving.

About 20 minutes before serving, bring cooking liquid to a boil. Add cabbage wedges and cook until crisp-tender, 5 to 7 minutes. Serve both with mustard sauce.

MUSTARD SAUCE *makes one and a half cups*

Melt butter in a heavy saucepan and sauté onions over low heat until very soft and sweet. Sprinkle with flour and mustard. Beat egg yolks with milk and slowly whisk into onion mixture. Place pot over another saucepan containing simmering water. Stir until thickened. Add lemon juice, salt, and pepper. Taste for seasoning and add more lemon juice, if necessary.

4 tablespoons butter
1/2 cup finely chopped onions
3 tablespoons flour
2 to 3 tablespoons dry mustard
2 egg yolks
1½ cups milk
1/2 to 3/4 cup lemon juice
Salt and pepper

CARROTS OF ORANGE *serves eight*

Peel and cut carrots into 2-inch-long sticks. Cook in lightly salted boiling water until just tender, about 8 minutes. Drain.

Melt butter in saucepan. Add carrots. Add sugar and juice. Cook and stir until liquid and sugar are reduced to a glaze. Stir in orange zest. Season with salt and pepper.

1 pound carrots
3 tablespoons butter
1 tablespoon brown sugar
3 tablespoons lemon or orange juice
1 teaspoon grated orange zest
Salt and pepper

IRISH SODA BREAD *makes two loaves*

3 cups unbleached
  all-purpose flour
1 cup whole-wheat flour
1 teaspoon salt
1 teaspoon baking soda
3 tablespoons sugar
4 tablespoons butter
1 egg
1½ cups buttermilk

Sift together dry ingredients. Cut in butter. Beat egg with buttermilk. Pour into the dry ingredients and stir just until moistened. Turn out onto a floured surface and lightly knead until smooth.

Divide dough into two pieces. Shape each into a smooth, round loaf. Place on a buttered baking sheet. Evenly press down each loaf to flatten slightly. Cut a cross 1/2 inch deep in the top with a knife, "to keep the Devil away."

Bake in a 375° F oven for 30 to 40 minutes, or until a skewer inserted in the center comes out clean.

BLACK IRISH PASTRY *makes sixty one-inch pastries*

2⅔ cups all-purpose flour
1 teaspoon salt
1 cup cold unsalted butter
1/2 cup ice water
12 ounces semisweet
  chocolate
1 cup chopped nuts:
  hazelnuts, almonds,
  walnuts

Combine flour with salt. Cut in butter with pastry cutter. Stir in water and form into a ball. Wrap in plastic and refrigerate 30 minutes to an hour. Melt chocolate and stir in nuts.

Take half the dough and roll it out on a floured surface into a rectangle 1/8 inch thick. Spread half the chocolate mixture over the pastry. Roll it up from the long side, jelly-roll style, and place the roll on a lightly buttered baking sheet, seam side down. Repeat with other half of dough. Refrigerate until the chocolate is hard. Cut the rolls into rounds 1/2 to 1 inch thick, and arrange next to each other on the sheet pan. Bake in a 375° F oven for 20 to 25 minutes, until lightly browned.

INDEX